P9-CDP-244

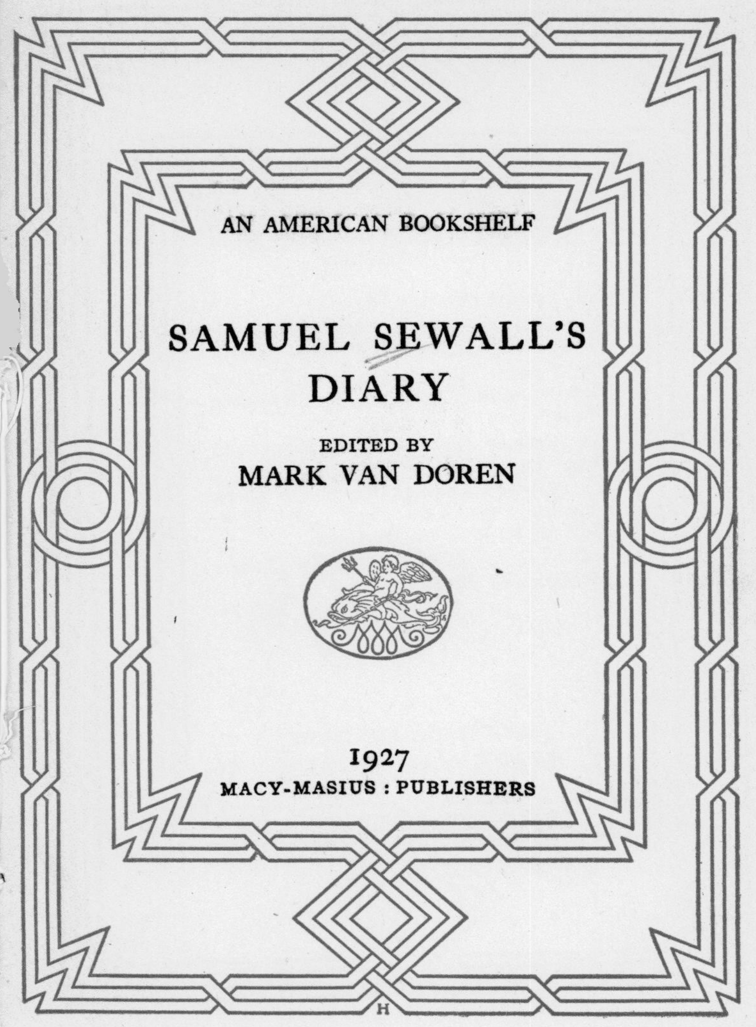

AN AMERICAN BOOKSHELF

SAMUEL SEWALL'S DIARY

EDITED BY
MARK VAN DOREN

1927
MACY-MASIUS : PUBLISHERS

H

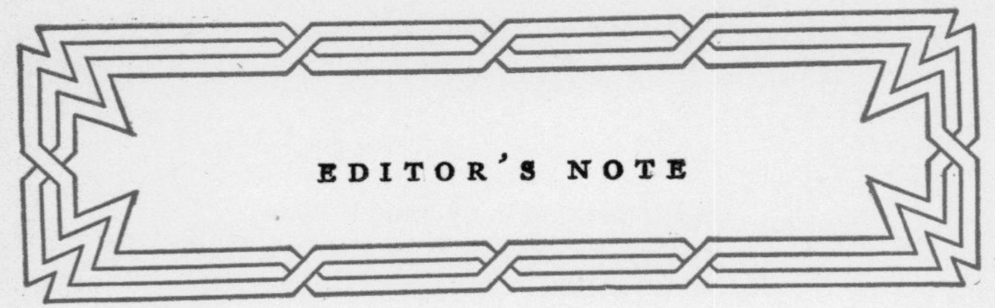

EDITOR'S NOTE

The Diary of Samuel Sewall, of which the present volume is an abridgement, was first published in three volumes by the Massachusetts Historical Society (1878-1882). It is the most intimate record now available of life in New England during the important period which it covers, and the genius of the author for self-revelation has frequently won him the compliment of a comparison with Samuel Pepys, his English contemporary. One difference between the two Diaries, however, is that while that of Pepys was kept for only ten years, that of Sewall covers the major portion of his life. Sewall was born in England in 1652. He came to New England at the age of nine, studied divinity at Harvard, entered the ministry, married, and thereafter devoted himself to public affairs. He held numerous offices in the Massachusetts colony, becoming in 1692 a judge of the Superior Court, and in 1718 its Chief Justice. He died in Boston in 1730. He was involved in the legal machinery which condemned the Salem witches to death, but later published a recantation, standing in church while it was read. The Diary is valuable not only for its picture of public life between 1680 and 1730 but for its picture of the author himself in the privacy of his confessional. His relations with his wife and their fifteen children, his journeys to towns outside of Boston, his business observations, his devotions, and especially his full account towards the close of his famous courtship of Madam Winthrop—these, with innumerable minor details, are the materials of a rich and appealing narrative.

M. V. D.

THE DIARY

April 4, 1675, Sab. day. I holp preach for my Master, [Mr. Parker] in the afternoon. Being afraid to look on the glass, ignorantly and unwillingly I stood two hours and a half.

April 29 Brother John and Sister Hañah Sewall begin to keep house at the Falls.

My Father having found things out of order at the Little Farm, viz, Fences down, ground Eaten and rooted up by Cattle and hogs, and wanting a good Tenant, the Season of the year now spending, resolves and goes to live there, notwithstanding the littleness and unpretines of the home.

July 31, at midnight, Tho. Wood, Carpenter of Rowly, had his house and goods burnt, and, *væ malum,* a daughter of about 10 years of age, who directed her brother so that he got out, was herself consumed to ashes.

This said Saturday night, in a dream, I fancyed myself to have Mrs. Richardson's child in my arms, and herself following me up a pair of stairs going to heaven, all sorrowfull and weeping. I went up innumerable steps and still saw nothing, so that I was discouraged, doubting with myself whether there was such a place as *sedes beatorum.* Yet I strengthened myself as well as I could, considering how apt things only heard of are to be doubted (if difficultly obtained and not of a long time) though they be never so true. Thus thinking, I went on; at last I came to a fair chamber with goodly lodgings. When I saw that was all, I earnestly prayed that God would help us, or else we should never get to our journey's end. Amazed I was, not being able to conceive how furniture should be brought up those stairs so high. Afterward it was a chamber in the N. Building, [at the College], after, part of an old [house] (Goff, as I take it) that joined to it, of the same height. A schollar told me that those things were drawn up by a pully, and so took in at a window which was all ranshacled like that in Goff Colledge over the Fellows' chamber, and all things began to seem more vile.

Nov. 11. Morning proper fair, the wether exceedingly benign, but (to me) metaphoric, dismal, dark and portentous, some prodigie appearing in every corner of the skies. Father went to Attach Ben Goodridge, at which (as all) so especially Mother, troubled and disswaded him.

N. B. Tuesday, Dec. 21, 1675, about the time of the Eclips Sister Sewall was delivered in my chamber of a daughter, Goodwife Brown being Midwife.

Saturday Even. Aug. 12, 1676, just as prayer ended Tim. Dwight sank down in a Swoun, and for a good space was as if he perceived not what was done to him: after, kicked and sprawled, knocking his hands and feet upon the floor like a distracted man. Was carried pickpack to bed by John Alcock, there his cloaths pulled off. In the night it seems he talked of ships, his master, father, and unckle Eliot. The Sabbath following Father went to him, spake to him to know what ailed him, asked if he would be prayed for, and for what he would desire his friends to pray. He answered, for more sight of sin, and God's healing grace. I asked him, being alone with him, whether his troubles were from some outward cause or spiritual. He answered, spiritual. I asked him why then he could not tell it his master, as well as any other, since it is the honour of any man to see sin and be sorry for it. He gave no answer, as I remember. Asked him if he would goe to meeting. He said, 'twas in vain for him; his day was out. I asked, what day: he answered, of Grace. I told him 'twas sin for any one to conclude themselves Reprobate, that this was all one. He said he would speak more, but could not, &c. Notwithstanding all this semblance (and much more than is written) of compunction for Sin, 'tis to be feared that his trouble arose from a maid whom he passionately loved: for that when Mr. Dwight and his master had agreed to let him goe to her, he eftsoons grew well.

Friday, Aug. 25. I spake to Tim of this, asked him whether his convictions were off. He answered, no. I told him how dangerous it was to make the convictions wrought by God's spirit a stalking horse to any other thing. Broke off, he being called away by Sam.

Oct. 10. Last night, H. S.[1] somewhat feverish, slept not so well as formerly, yet indifferently; cheerly notwithstanding, this day. Violent rain and cold.

Oct. 13. Mother and wife had a good night. Mement. Made an Hen Coop. Mr. Clark came and stood by me.

Oct. 14. Last night very comfortable to wife and Mother. Oct. 15, a good night.

16. Good night. Mr. Brackenbury, the 17th. Best night that mother has yet had, slept without so much as dreaming. 18, 19, 20, all Good nights. Mother conversant in the Kitchen and our chamber. My Wife every day since the Sabbath goes to Mothers chamber without hurt. 21 Good night, all Hands.

Oct. 23. Went from Boston about five T. P. to Milton, there accidentally meeting with Moses Collier, Mr. Senderlen and I went on to Hingham, to John Jacobs. Oct. 24, Tuesday, went from thence to Plymouth, about noon; refreshed there. Note, James Percival met us there, and so we went cheerfully together from thence about 2. T. P.; got to Sandwich about a quarter of an hour by sun: lodged at Percivals with Mr. Senderlen. Oct. 25, Wednesday, Breakfasted at Stephen Skiphs. He, Percival and I rode out about 12 miles, within sight of Marthah's Vinyard, to look Horses: at last happily came on 11, whereof five my Fathers, viz, three chess-

---

[1] Hannah Sewall, his wife.

nut coloured Mares, and 2 Colts: put them in Mr. Bourns sheep-pen all night. Note. Supped at Mr. Smiths, good Supper. Oct. 26, Thursday, Took up the young four yeer old Mare, slit the two near ears of the Colts, their colour was a chesnut Sorrel, whiteish Manes and Tails. The Bigger had all his Hoofs white: the Lesser all black. Both Stone-Colts. The Hair of the Tails cut square with a knife. After this Mr. Smith rode with me and shewed me the place which some had thought to cut, for to make a passage from the South Sea to the North: said 'twas about a mile and a half between the utmost flowing of the two Seas in Herring River and Scusset, the land very low and level, Herrin River exceeding Pleasant by reason that it runs pretty broad, shallow, of an equal depth, and upon white sand. Showed me also the 3 Hills on the which 4 towns kept Warders, before which was such an Isthmus of about 3 miles and barren plain, that scarce any thing might pass unseen. Moniment Harbour said to be very good. Note. Had a very good Supper at Mr. Dexter's. Being in trouble how to bring along my Mare, in came one Downing and Benjamin his son, who, being asked, to my gladness promised Assistance. Oct. 27, Got very well to Plymouth, Tailing my Mare, and Ben strapping her on, though we were fain to come over the Clifts the upper way because of the flowing Tide. There saw Acorns upon bushes about a foot high, which they call running Oak; it is content with that Stature. From Plimouth Ben and 's father mounted a Trifle before me, I waved my Hat and Handkerchief to them, but they left me to toil with my tired jade: was fain at last to untail and so drive them before me, at last ride and lead the Mare with great difficulty. When came to Jones his Bridge, (supposing the house had been just by) put the bridle on the Horses neck, drove him on the Bridge, holding the Halter in my Hand. When I came on the other side, could not catch my Horse, but tired myself leading my tired Mare sometimes on the left Hand into the Marsh, sometimes on the right Hand: at last left him, went to the Bridge to ensure myself of the path, so led her to Tracies about ½ mile. He not at Home, could scarce get them to entertain me, though 'twas night. At length his son John put up my Mare, then took up his own Horse, and so helped me to look for mine, but could not find him: after his Father and he went on foot, and met him almost at the House, Saddle Cover lost, which John found in the Morn. Oct. 28, Saturday, Goodman Tracy directed and set me in the way, so I went all alone to the end, almost, of rocky plain, then, by God's good providence, Mr. Senderlen overtook me, so we came along cheerfully together, called at my Aunt's [in Braintree], refreshed, left my tired jade there, set out to Boston ward about half an hour by Sun, and got well home before shutting in, Praised be God. Note. Seeing the wonderfull works of God in the journeye, I was thereby more perswaded of his justice, and inhability to do any wrong: put in mind likewise of Mr. Thachers Sermon, Oct. 22.

Novem. 27, 1676, about 5 M. Boston's greatest Fire brake forth at Mr. Moors, through the default of a Taylour Boy, who rising alone and early to work, fell asleep and let his Light fire the House, which gave fire to the next, so that about fifty Landlords were despoyled of their Housing. N. B. The House of the Man of God, Mr. Mather, and Gods House were burnt with fire. Yet God mingled mercy, and sent a considerable rain, which gave check in great measure to the (otherwise) masterless flames: lasted all the time of the fire, though fair before and after. Mr. Mather saved his Books and other Goods.

Dec. 14, 1676, Seth Shove was brought to our House to dwell, i. e. Father Hull's. N. B. In the evening, seeing a shagged dogg in the Kitchin, I spake to John Alcock, *I am afraid we shall be troubled with the ugly dogg*: whereupon John asked which way he went. I said out at the Street door. He presently went that way, and meeting Seth (who went out a little before) took him for the dogg, and smote him so hard upon the bare head with a pipe staff, or something like it, that it grieved me that he had strook the dogg so hard. There arose a considerable wheal in the childs head, but it seems the weapon smote him plain, for the Rising was almost from the forehead to the Crown, grew well quickly, wearing a Cap that night. 'Twas God's mercy the stick and manner of the blow was not such as to have spilled his Brains on the Ground. The Devil, (I think) seemed to be angry at the childs coming to dwell here. Written, Dec. 18, '76.

Dec. 18, Mr. Rowlandson and Mr. Willard came and visited my Father. While they were here, Mr. Shepard also came in and discoursed of Reformation, especially the disorderly Meetings of Quakers and Anabaptists: thought if all did agree, i. e. Magistrates and Ministers, the former might easily be suprest, and that then, The Magistrates would see reason to Handle the latter. As to what it might injure the country in respect of England, trust God with it. Wished, (speaking of Mr. Dean's) that all the children in the country were baptised, that religion without it come to nothing. Before Mr. Shepards coming in, one might gather by Mr. Willards speech that there was some Animosity in him toward Mr. Mather: for that he said he chose the Afternoon that so he might have a copious auditory: and that when the Town House was offered him to preach to his Church distinct, said he would not preach in a corner.

Jan. 10, 1676. Cloudy, Cold, noren wind. Note, went on foot to Mr. Flints at Dorchester, there to be in the company of Ministers: but none came save Mr. Torry. Mr. Fisk was gone to his sick Father: Mr. Hubbard and Adams hindred (as conjectured) by the wether. So that there was Mr. Flint, Mr. Torry, Elder Humphreys, John Hoar, Mrs. Stoughton, Mrs. Flint, Senior, Junior, Mrs. Pool and her daughter Bethesda, with a Nurse named Clap. Notwithstanding the fewness of persons, the day (thro. Gods grace) was spent to good purpose. Mr. Flint prayed, then preached singularly well from that place,

Cant. 1. 6. But my own Vineyard have I not kept; which he handled well, Pressing every particular person to look to their own Souls. Elder H. prayed. After some pause (because the day much spent and I to goe home) Mr. Torrey prayed onely: which he did divinely, that we might not think strange of fiery Tryal, might be sure not to deceive ourselves as to our union with Christ. Indeed, the exercise was such, preaching and praying, as if God did intend it for me. I prayed earnestly before I went that God would shew me favour at the meeting, and I hope he will set home those things that were by him Carved for me. Mr. Flint sent his Man after the Exercise, so when I had well supped, comfortably rode home.

Jan. 30. Sent a letter to Cousin Quinsey, which enclosed a piece of Gold that cost me 23^{s}. Gave the Letter to Mr. Josson. In it ordered to buy 2 pair of Silk Stockings, pink colored, black, 1 pair Tabby Bodyes, cloath-coloured, ½ wide and long wastied: also Turkish Alcoran, 2^{d} Hand, Map of London. Sent him a copy of verses made on Mr. Reyner. Jan. *ult.*, sent a letter to Mr. Thacher, by the Bagg, in which Salutations, and some newes. Wednesday, 31 Brother John Sewall brought down Sister Jane to live with Mrs. Usher, but the next morn I went to her and she gave me to understand that she thought Jane would not come, and so had supplyed herself. Father Hull kindly invited her to stay here till she should change her condition if she so liked. Note. Just now wanted a Maid very much, courted Goodwife Fellows Daughter: she could not come till spring: hard to find a good one. So that Jane came in a critical time.

Feb. 23, 1676 . Mr. Torrey spake with my Father at Mrs. Norton's, told him that he would fain have me preach, and not leave off my studies to follow Merchandize. Note. The evening before, Feb. 22, I resolved (if I could get an opportunity) to speak with Mr. Torrey, and ask his Counsel as to coming into Church, about my estate, and the temptations that made me to fear. But he went home when I was at the Warehouse about Wood that Tho. Elkins brought.

Satterday, Mar. 3, 167⁶⁄₇. Went to Mr. Norton to discourse with him about coming into the Church. He told me that he waited to see whether his faith were of the operation of God's spirit, and yet often said that he had very good hope of his good Estate, and that one might be of the Church (i. e. Mystical) though not joined to a particular Congregation. I objected that of Ames, he said *vere quærentibus,* the meaning was that such sought not God's kingdom in every thing. I said it was meant of not at all. He said, was unsettled, had thoughts of going out of the country: that in coming into Church there was a covenanting to watch over one another which carried with it a strict obligation. And at last, that he was for that way which was purely Independent. I urged what that was. He said that all of the Church were a royal Priesthood, all of them Prophets, and taught of God's Spirit, and that a few words from the heart were worth a great deal: intimating the Benefit of Brethrens prophesying: for this he cited Mr. Dell. I could not get any more. Dr. Mason (whom I have often seen with him) came in, after him Mr. Alden, so our Discourse was broken off.

March 16. Dr. Alcock dyes about midnight. Note, Mrs. Williams told us presently after Dutyes how dangerously ill he was, and to get John to go for his Grandmother. I was glad of that Information, and resolved to goe and pray earnestly for him; but going into the Kitchen, fell into discourse with Tim about Mettals, and so took up the time. The Lord forgive me and help me not to be so slack for time to come, and so easy to disregard and let dye so good a Resolution. Dr. Alcock was 39 yeers old.

March 19, 1676 Dr. Alcock was buried, at whoes Funeral I was. After it, went to Mr. Thachers. He not within, so walkt with Capt. Scottow on the Change till about 5, then went again, yet he not come. At last came Elder Rainsford, after, Mr. Thacher, who took us up into his Chamber; went to prayer, then told me I had liberty to tell what God had done for my soul. After I had spoken, prayed again. Before I came away told him my Temptations to him alone, and bad him acquaint me if he knew any thing by me that might hinder justly my coming into Church. He said he thought I ought to be encouraged, and that my stirring up to it was of God.

March 22. 23. Plenty of Rain after a great deal of dry and pleasant wether. In the afternoon of the 23[d], Seth and I gather what herbs we could get, as Yarrow, Garglio, &c.

March 30, 1677. I, together with Gilbert Cole, was admitted into Mr. Thacher's Church, making a Solem covenant to take the L. Jehovah for our God, and to walk in Brotherly Love and watchfulness to Edification. Goodm. Cole first spake, then I, then the Relations of the Women were read: as we spake so were we admitted; then alltogether covenanted. Prayed before, and after.

April 1, 1677. About Two of the Clock at night I waked and perceived my wife ill: asked her to call Mother. She said I should goe to prayer, then she would tell me. Then I rose, lighted a Candle at Father's fire, that had been raked up from Saturday night, kindled a Fire in the chamber, and after 5 when our folks up, went and gave Mother warning. She came and bad me call the Midwife, Goodwife Weeden, which I did. But my Wives pains went away in a great measure after she was up; toward night came on again, and about a quarter of an hour after ten at night, April 2, Father and I sitting in the great Hall, heard the child cry, whereas we were afraid 'twould have been 12 before she would have been brought to Bed. Went home with the Midwife about 2 o'clock, carrying her Stool, whoes parts were included in a Bagg. Met with the Watch at Mr. Rocks Brew house, who bad us stand, enquired what we were. I told the Woman's occupation, so they bad God bless our labours, and let us pass. The first Woman the Child sucked was Bridget Davenport.

April 3. Cousin Flint came to us. She said we ought to lay scarlet on the Child's head for that it had received some harm. Nurse Hurd watches. April 4. Clear cold weather. Goodwife Ellis watches. April 7, Saturday, first laboured to cause the child suck his mother, which he scarce did at all. In the afternoon my Wife set up, and he sucked the right Breast bravely, ...

April 8, 1677. Sabbath day, rainy and stormy in the morning, but in the afternoon fair and sunshine, though a blustering Wind. So Eliz. Weeden, the Midwife, brought the Infant to the third Church when Sermon was about half done in the afternoon, Mr. Thacher preaching. After Sermon and Prayer, Mr. Thacher prayed for Capt. Scottow's Cousin and it. Then I named him John, and Mr. Thacher baptized him into the name of the Father, Son, and H. Ghost. The Lord give the Father and Son may be convinced of and washed from Sin in the blood of Christ.

Note. [May] I went out this morning without private prayer and riding on the Comon, thinking to escape the Souldiers (because of my fearfull Horse); notwithstanding there was a Company at a great distance which my Horse was so transported at that I could no way govern him, but was fain to let him go full speed, and hold my Hat under my Arm. The wind was Norwest, so that I suppose I took great cold in my ear thereby, and also by wearing a great thick Coat of my Fathers part of the day, because it rained, and then leaving it off. However it was, I felt my throat ill, the danger of which I thought had been now over with the winter, and so neglected it too much, relapsed, and grew very sick of it from Friday to Monday following, which was the worst day: after that it mended. Mr. Mather visited me and prayed on that day.

June 17. Sabbath day about 7 m, John Sewall had a Convulsion Fit. He was asleep in the Cradle, and suddenly started, trembled, his fingers contracted, his eyes starting and being distorted. I went to Mr. Brackenbury, and thence to Charlestown, and set him to the child.

June the nineteenth he had another about noon.

June 21, 1677. Just at the end of the Sermon (it made Mr. Allen break off the more abruptly) one Torrey, of Roxbury, gave a suddain and amazing cry which disturbed the whole Assembly. It seems he had the falling sickness. Tis to be feared the Quaker disturbance and this are ominous.

July 8, 1677. New Meeting House *Mane:* In Sermon time there came in a female Quaker, in a Canvas Frock, her hair disshevelled and loose like a Periwigg, her face as black as ink, led by two other Quakers, and two other followed. It occasioned the greatest and most amazing uproar that I ever saw. Isaiah I. 12, 14.

Jan. 13, 167 6/7. Giving my chickens meat, it came to my mind that I gave them nothing save Indian corn and water, and yet they eat it and thrived very well, and that that food was necessary for them, how mean soever, which much affected me and convinced what need I stood in of spiritual food, and that I should not nauseat daily duties of Prayer, &c.

Jan. 22. Went to Mr. Thachers, found him at home, mentioned my desire of communion with his Church, rehearsed to him some of my discouragements, as, continuance in Sin, wandering in prayer. He said 'twas thought that was the Sin Paul speaks of, Rom. VII. At my coming away said he thought I ought to be encouraged.

Feb. 15. Having been often in my mind discouraged from joining to the Church by reason of the weakness, or some such undesirableness in many of its members: I was much relieved by the consideration of 1 Cor. 1. 26, 27. which came to my mind as I was at prayer. What is spoken there was set home on me, to take away my pride and be content with God's wisdom: thought it might seem to uncovenanted reason foolishness.

Having often been apt to break out against God himself as

if he had made me a person that might be a fit subject of calamity, and that he led me into difficulties and perplexing miseries; I had my spirit calmed by considering what an absurd thing it was to say to God—"Why hast thou made me thus?," and startled at the daring height of such wickedness. These thoughts had reference to Isaiah XLV. 9, 10. This was at prayer time, Feb. 19. *Mane.* Death never looked so pleasingly on me as Feb. 18 upon the hearing of Mr. Thachers 3 Arguments. Methought it was rather a privilege to dye, and therein be conformed to Christ, than, remaining alive at his coming, to be changed.

March 167$\frac{8}{9}$. Note. I have been of a long time loth to enter into strict Bonds with God, the sinfullness and hypochrisy of which God hath showed me by reading of a Sermon that Mr. Burgess preached before the House of Comons, Nov. 17, 1640, and by the forementioned Sermons and prayers. *Omnia in bonum mihi vertas, O Deus.* I found the Sermon accidentally in Mr. Norton's Study.

Remember, since I had thoughts of joining to the Church, I have been exceedingly tormented in my mind, sometimes lest the Third church [the South] should not be in God's way in breaking off from the old. (I resolved to speak with Mr. Torrey about that, but he passed home when I was called to business at the Warehouse. Another time I got Mr. Japheth Hobart to promise me a Meeting at our House after Lecture, —but she that is now his wife, being in town, prevented him.) Sometimes with my own unfitness and want of Grace: yet through importunity of friends, and hope that God might communicate himself to me in the ordinance, and because of my child (then hoped for) its being baptised, I offered myself, and was not refused. Besides what I had written, when I was speaking [at his admission to the Church] I resolved to confess what a great Siñer I had been, but going on in the method of the Paper, it came not to my mind. And now that Scruple of the Church vanished, and I began to be more afraid of myself. And on Saturday Goodman Walker came in, who used to be very familiar with me. But he said nothing of my coming into the Church, nor wished God to show me grace therein, at which I was almost overwhelmed, as thinking that he deemed me unfit for it. And I could hardly sit down to the Lord's Table. But I feared that if I went away I might be less fit next time, and thought that it would be strange for me who was just then joined to the Church, to withdraw, wherefore I stayed. But I never experienced more unbelief. I feared at least that I did not believe there was such an one as Jesus Xt., and yet was afraid that because I came to the ordinance without belief, that for the abuse of Xt. I should be stricken dead; yet I had some earnest desires that Xt. would, before the ordinance were done, though it were when he was just going away, give me some glimpse of himself; but I perceived none. Yet I seemed then to desire the coming of the next Sacrament day, that I might do better, and was stirred up hereby dreadfully to seek God who many times before had touched my heart by Mr. Thacher's praying and preaching more than now. The Lord pardon my former grieving of his Spirit, and circumcise my heart to love him with all my heart and soul.

Wednesday Febr. 11, 1684—5.—Joshua Moodey and self set out for Ipswich. I lodge at Sparkes's. Next day, Feb. 12, goe to lecture which Mr. Moodey preaches, then I dine with Mr. Cobbet, and so ride to Newbury; visit Mr. Richardson sick of the dry Belly ake. Monday, Febr. 16, Get Mr. Phillips and Payson to Town and so keep a Fastday, Mr. Moodey Preaching Forenoon, Mr. Phillips Afternoon, Mr. Woodbridge and Payson assisting in Prayer; was a pretty full Assembly, Mr. Moodey having given notice the Sabbath-day, on which he preached all day. At Wenham and Ipswich, as we went, we were told of the Earthquake in those parts and at Salem (Feb 8). the Sabbath before about the time of ending Afternoon Exercise; That which most was sensible of was a startling dolefull Sound; but many felt the Shaking also, Peter and Jane

Topan. Mr. Phillips had not finished his Sermon, and was much surprised at the Sound, expecting when the House would have Crackt. In several places Exercise was over.

Tuesday Febr. 17, I and Brother, sister Stephen Sewall Ride to Sparkes's by the Ferry, great part in the Snow; Dined with Ipswich Select-Men. 18th. I Lodged there; the Morn was serene; came to Salem, seeing Mrs. Hale by the way; staid Lecture, came to Boston, found all well. *Laus Deo.*

Apr. 14th 1685. A Ship arrives from New castle and brings News of the death of Charles the 2nd, and Proclamation of James the 2nd, King. Brought a couple of printed Proclamations relating to that affair. News came to us as we were busy opening the Nominations just before Dinner; it much startled the Governour and all of us. In the morn before I went the Governour said that a Ship master had been with him from Nevis, who told him Gov.r Stapleton should say, we should have a new Governour before he got to Boston. Master dined with Magistrates and Commissioners at Capt. Wing's. Carried my wife to George Bairsto's yesterday, April 13th.—Thorsday, April 16th, a Vessel arrives from London. Mr. Lord, commander, brings Orders to the several Colonies to proclaim the King. Mr. Blathwayt writes to Simon Bradstreet, Esq. superscribed For His Majestie's Service, advising that 't would be best for us early to doe it; and our Charter being vacated in Law and no Government settled here, was the reason we were not writt to: Copies and forms sent to us as to the other Colonies, but no mention of Governour and Company. Also another letter was writt to Simon Bradstreet, Wm. Stoughton, Jos. Dudley, Peter Bulkeley, Sam'l. Shrimpton, Richard Wharton, Esquires, to proclaim the King. Suppose this was done lest the Government should have neglected to do it. The Council agreed to proclaim the King before they knew of the Letter. Major Richards counted the Votes for Mr. Dudley, told them twice over, and still found them 666, and so 'twas entered and sent to the Towns.

Monday April 20th. The King is Proclaimed; 8 Companies, the Troop, and several Gentlemen on horseback assisting; three Volleys and then Canon fired. This day a child falls upon a Knife which run through its cheek to the Throat, of which inward Wound it dies, and is buried on Wednesday. 'Tis one Gees child.—Thorsday, April 23, Mother Sewall comes by Water in Stephen Greenleaf to see us.

Friday May 8th—past 6, even, Walk with the honored Governour [Bradstreet] up Hoar's Lane, so to the Alms House; then down the length of the Common to Mr. Dean's Pasture, then through Cowell's Lane to the New Garden, then to our House, then to our Pasture by Engs's, then I waited on his Honour to his Gate and so home. This day our old Red Cow is kill'd, and we have a new black one brought in the room, of about four years old and better, marked with a Cross and slit in the Left Ear, and a Cross off the right Ear, with a little hollowing in. As came with his Honour through Cowell's Lane, Sam. came running and call'd out a pretty way off and cried out the Cow was dead and by the Heels, meaning hang'd up by the Butcher. At which I was much startled understanding him she had been dead upon a Hill or cast with her heels upward, and so had lost her; for I was then looking for her and 't was unexpected, Mother having partly bargained and the Butcher fetcht her away in the Night unknown. Had served this family above Ten years, above Nine since my dwelling in it.

Satterday May 9th, Brother Stephen Sewall visits me.—Monday, May 11th, 1685, I accompanied Mr. Moodey to Mr. Eliot's to persuade Mr. Benjamin to go to the Ordination of Mr. Cotton Mather, in which I hope we have prevailed; the mentioning of it drew Tears from the good Father so as to hinder his Speech. The Father was abroad and preached yesterday. Visited Mr. Dudley also.

Tuesday, May 12th, I weary myself in walking from one end and side of the Town to t'other to seek our lost Cow.—

Wednesday, May 13, 1685, Mr. Cotton Mather is ordained Pastor by his Father, who said, My son Cotton Mather, and in 's sermon spake of Aaron's Garments being put on Eleazer, intimating he knew not but that God might now call him out of the World. Mr. Eliot gave the Right Hand of Fellowship, calling him a Lover of Jesus Christ.

Wednesday, June 17th a Quaker or two goe to the Governour and ask leave to enclose the Ground [on the Common] the Hanged Quakers are buried in under or near the Gallows, with Pales: Governour proposed it to the Council, who unanimously denyed it as very inconvenient for persons so dead and buried in the place to have any Monument.

Thorsday, June 18. A Quaker comes to the Governour and speaks of a Message he had which was to shew the great Calamities of Fire and Sword that would suddenly come on New-England. Would fain have spoken in the Meetinghouse, but was prevented. Eliakim comes home this day, brings word that Capt. Henchman is coming away from Worcester with his Family.

Noyes this day of a French Pirat on the Coast, of 36 Guns.

Satterday, June 20th 1685. Voted. the 16th of July to be observed as a Fast.

Satterday, P. M. Carried my Wife to Dorchester to eat Cherries, Rasberries, chiefly to ride and take the Air: the Time my Wife and Mrs. Flint spent in the Orchard, I spent in Mr. Flint's Study, reading Calvin on the Psalms &c. 45. 68. 24.

Monday, July 6th. I am taken with a Feverish Fit; yet go to Court in the Afternoon, the County Court, where was read Major Pynchon's Letter to the Council; which is that 5 Men came to one of the Houses of Westfield (I think) about midnight 28th June, knockt at the door, the Man bid him come in, so in they came all Armed with drawn Swords, and threatened to run the man and his wife through if they stirred: so plundered that House, and another in like manner: told they had 60 Men in their Company and that if they stirred out of door, they would kill them; so stayd in a great part of Monday, then when thought the Coast was clear told the Neighbors and some were sent to Search after them; at last found them: one of the 5 snapt and missed fire, another shot, then one of ours shot so as to shoot one of theirs dead: another of the 5 fought one of ours with his sword, till another of ours knockt him down. One or two that were taken are brought to Boston, one at least is escaped. Major Pynchon his Works will cost near an hundred Pounds.

An Indian was branded in Court and had a piece of his Ear cut off for Burglary.

Wednesday, P. M., July 15. Very dark, and great Thunder and Lightening.

One Humphry Tiffiny and Frances Low, Daughter of Antony Low, are slain with the Lightening and Thunder about a mile or half a mile beyond Billinges Farm, the Horse also slain, that they rode on, and another Horse in Company slain, and his Rider who held the Garment on the Maid to steady it at the time of the Stroke, a coat or cloak, stounded, but not killed. Were coming to Boston. Antony Low being in Town the sad Bill was put up with [regard] of that Solemn judgment of God; Fast-day Forenoon. July 15, 1685. 2 Persons, 2 Horses.

July 21. This day about 31 Ministers meet, Mr. Higginson Prayes excellently: Governour gives the Question. Dine all together at Monk's. After Diner about 3 or 4 aclock, they give their Answere, i. e. Mr. Hubbard Speaks in behalf of the rest, that their Opinion was the Government ought not to give way to another till the Generall Court had seen and judged of the Comission; so should be called if not Sitting at the Arrival of a Comissioned Governour. But several expressed some Dissent: And after, shewed themselves extreamly dissatisfied, saying that Mr. Hubbard had greatly abused them and that he was not ordered by the Ministers that they knew to speak their minds, which six gave in under their Hands. The Meeting has been uncomfortable, and I doubt will breed great Animosities.

Wednesday, Augt. 5. rode to Dorchester Lecture with Cous. Nath. Dumer; was kindly entertained at Mr. Stoughton's after Lecture. Going thither I saw a few Feet of Ground enclosed with Boards, which is done by the Quakers out of respect to som one or more hanged and buried by the Gallows: though the Governour forbad them, when they asked Leave.

Friday, Nov[r]. 6. Mr. Willard calls in and tells me of a Thanks-Giving intended by the Ministers through the Colony upon the 3.[d] of the next Moneth: Go to the Governour to get his Approbation, which He doth not presently grant; but will speak of it in Council on Thorsday next; whether convenient for the Churches generally to attend such a Day without an Order from Authority, as usual. The difficulty of Printing an Order is, lest by putting in, or leaving out, we offend England. Having occasion this day to go to Mr. Hayward the Publick Notary's House, I speak to him about his cutting off his Hair, and wearing a Perriwig of contrary Colour: mention the words of our Saviour, Can ye not make one Hair white or black: and Mr. Alsop's Sermon. He alledges, The Doctor advised him to it.

Monday Nov[r]. 9. Mr. Cobbet buried about 4. in the Afternoon. Flight of snow. This day about 6 or 7 at night a Male Infant pin'd up in a sorry Cloth is laid upon the Bulk of Shaw, the Tabacco-Man: Great Search made tonight and next day to find the Mother. So far as I can hear this is the first Child that ever was in such a manner exposed in Boston.

Thorsday, Nov[r]. 12. Mr. Moodey preaches from Isa. 57. 1. Mr. Cobbet's Funeral Sermon; said also of Mr. Chauncy that he was a Man of Singular Worth. Said but 2 of the First Generation left.

After, the Ministers of this Town Come to the Court and complain against a Dancing Master who seeks to set up here and hath mixt Dances, and his time of Meeting is Lecture-Day; and 'tis reported he should say that by one Play he could teach more Divinity than Mr. Willard or the Old Testament. Mr. Moodey said 'twas not a time for N. E. to dance. Mr. Mather struck at the Root, speaking against mixt Dances.

Ecclips at night. County Court adjourned till this day 14 night. Governour's Hat blew off and fell flat on the Ground just as went to go in at 's Gate. Hath a new Border which began to wear Catechising day or Sabbath last, as I take it. Dept. Governour not in Town. New Almanack comes out this Day intituled New-England's Almanack, by Mr. Danforth.

Wednesday, Novr. 18. Uncomfortable Court day by reason of the extream sharp words between the Deputy Governour and Mr. Stoughton, Dudley and Others. Some Essay to have put a Sanction upon the Apointment for a Thanksgiving; but it fell throw. I argued 'twas not fit upon meer Generals, as (the Mercies of the year) to Comand a Thanksgiving and of Particulars we could not agree. Governour would have had one Article for the Peace of England, according to His Majesty's Proclamation.

Hollowells business heard, as to Land: about that grew the fierceness in discourse. Mr. G. Boroughs dined with us. Major Generall not well. Mr. Shove comes to Town today; but I see him not.

Thorsday, Novr. 19. Mr. Mather Preaches from Numb. 25. 11. Shewed that Love was an ingredient to make one zealous: those that received good People, received Christ, Mat. 25. Said that if the Government of N. E. were zealous might yet save this People. 2^{d} Part of 79th Ps. sung. Madam Usher, her Daughter and Husband in Mourning. Mr. Stoughton and Dudley called here. 'Tis reported that a Frigot is to come yet before Spring with a Comission for a Governour here, upon the place: Mr. Dudley is talked of and 'tis said Healths are drunk to the new Governour already, and were so Novr. 17. the day the Ship came in.

Friday Novr. 20th a very rainy and dark day, and in the Afternoon turns to a storm of Snow: Court is adjourned to Tuesday, February 16th at One of the Clock, except some Frigot or Ships Arrival from England with His Majesty's Comands that may call for one sooner; then the Secretary, or if he sick or dead, the Treasurer, to send forthwith to the Members of the Court, and to such others as Freemen may chuse to convene two days after the Date of such Signification, to which time the Court is adjourned in such Case. No Freemen made, nor Prayer. Ground covered with Snow by that time Court done, which is een quite dark. Mr. Stoughton and Dudley not here today. 'Twas Essayed again to have had a Sanction put on the Thanksgiving: but 'twas again pleaded, to do it without mentioning particular causes would be to impose too much on those Comanded: So fell.

Monday night Novr. 23, 1685. I go the Rounds with Cous. Quinsey and Isaac Goose, a very severe night for Cold, yet 'twas fair and comfortable: came home at 5. *mane.*

Novr. 26, Thorsday. Nurse Goose dyes about 2. or 3. aclock in the night; having lien sick about a Week: was here it seems Wednesday was Senight. Was helpfull to her self all along till this last sickness: washt her own Cloaths. She saw her great Grandchildren: was a good Woman.

Novr. 30. At night viewed the Eclips, which in the total obscuration was ruddy; but when began to receive some Light, the darkish ruddiness ceased. Horizon somewhat Hazy. Read in course the Eleventh of the Revelation.

Monday, Decembr. 7th 1685. About One in the Night my Wife is brought to Bed of a Son, of which Mother Hull brings me the first News: Mrs. Weeden Midwife.

Wednesday Decr. 9th 1685. Our Neighbour Gemaliel Wait eating his Breakfast well, went to do something in his Orchard, where Serjt. Pell dwells, there found him Self not well and went into Pell's his Tenant's House, and there dyed extream suddenly about Noon, and then was carried home in a Chair, and means used to fetch him again, but in vain: To the Children startled about him he said, here is a sudden Change, or there will be a great Change, to that purpose. Was about 87 years old, and yet strong and hearty: had lately several new Teeth. People in the Street much Startled at this good Man's sudden Death. Govr. Hinkley sent for me to Mr. Rawson's just as they were sending a great Chair to carry him home.

Satterday, Decr. 12, '85. Father Wait buried: Magistrates and Ministers had Gloves. There heard of the Death of Capt. Hutchinson's Child by Convulsions, and so pass to the Funeral of little Samuel Hutchinson about Six weeks old, where also had a pair of Funeral Gloves.

Sabbath-day, Decemb^{r}. 13th 1685. Mr. Willard baptizeth my Son lately born, whom I named Henry: David Stoddard, the son of Mr. Simeon Stoddard, was baptized next, and then Several other grown Children. Nurse Hill came in before the Psalm was Sung, and yet the Child was fine and quiet: Mr. Willard preached from John 15th 8. Herein is my Father glorified, that you bear much Fruit, so shall ye be my Disciples: which is the first Sermon my little Son hath been present at.

Monday, Dec. 14. This Monday a Jury is sumoned who sit on the Body of Joseph Johnson, and the verdict they find, a wound an inch or 2 above his Navel which they judge to be the cause of his Death, and that they were informed James Morgan did it with a Spit. So were Sworn in Court Decr 14. 1685., and James Morgan ordered to have Irons put on him. He comitted the Fact last Thorsday night.

Thorsday, Decr. 17th. Mr. Mather preacheth from Mat. 16., former part of the 25th Verse. For whosover will save his Life shall Lose it. At County-Court nothing done in Mr. Sergeant's Business: So he makes a Speech when the Court open, that if the Court did nothing they would give him a Record of it, that he might go elsewhere for he would not be kept out of 's Money; speaking warmly.

Mr. Francis Stepney, the Dancing Master, desired a Jury, so He and Mr. Shrimpton Bound in 50£ to Jan^{r}. Court. Said Stepney is ordered not to keep a Dancing School; if he does will be taken in contempt and be proceeded with accordingly. Mr. Shrimpton muttered, saying he took it as a great favour that the Court would take his Bond for £50.

Friday Dec. 18. Begun in Course to read the New Testament, having ended the Revelation the night before.

Satterday Dec. 19. Mr. Willard Prayes with my little Henry, being very ill.

Sabbath-day, Dec. 20. Send Notes to Mr. Willard and Mr. Moodey to pray for my Child Henry.

Monday, about four in the Morn the faint and moaning noise of my child forces me up to pray for it.

21. Monday even Mr. Moodey calls. I get him to go up and Pray with my extream sick Son.

Tuesday Morn, Dec. 22. Child makes no noise save by a kind of snoaring as it breathed, and as it were slept.

Read the 16th of the first Chron. in the family. Having read to my Wife and Nurse out of John; the fourteenth Chapter fell now in course, which I read and went to Prayer: By that time had done, could hear little Breathing, and so about Sunrise, or little after, he fell asleep, I hope in Jesus, and that a Mansion was ready for him in the Father's House. Died in Nurse Hill's Lap. Nurse Hill washes and layes him out: because our private Meeting hath a day of Prayer tomorrow, Thorsday Mr. Willard's Lecture, and the Child dying after Sunrise (wether cloudy), have determined to bury on Thorsday after Lecture. The Lord sanctify his Dispensation, and prepare me and mine for the coming of our Lord, in whatsoever way it be. Mr. Tho. Oakes our Physician for this Child. Read the 16th Chap. of the First Chronicles in the Family.

Thorsday, Decr. 24th 1685. We follow Little Henry to his Grave: Governour and Magistrates of the County here, 8 in all, beside my Self, Eight Ministers, and Several Persons of note. Mr. Phillips of Rowley here. I led Sam., then Cous. Savage led Mother, and Cousin Dumer led Cous. Quinsey's wife, he not well. Midwife Weeden and Nurse Hill carried the Corps by turns, and so by Men in its Chestnut Coffin 'twas set into a Grave (The Tomb full of water) between 4 and 5. At Lecture the 21. Psalm was Sung from 8th to the end. The Lord humble me kindly in respect of all my Enmity against Him, and let his breaking my Image in my Son be a means of it. Considerable snow this night.

Dec. 25. Friday. Carts come to Town and Shops open as is usual. Some somehow observe the day; but are vexed I believe that the Body of the People profane it, and blessed be God no Authority yet to compell them to keep it. A great Snow fell last night so this day and night very cold.

Satterday, Jan^{y}. [168⅚] Last night had a very unusual Dream; *viz.* That our Saviour in the dayes of his Flesh when upon Earth, came to Boston and abode here sometime, and moreover that He Lodged in that time at Father Hull's; upon which in my Dream had two Reflections, One was how much more Boston had to say than Rome boasting of Peter's being there. The other a sense of great Respect that I ought to have shewed Father Hull since Christ chose when in Town, to take up His Quarters at his House. Admired the goodness and Wisdom of Christ in coming hither and spending some part of His short Life here. The Chronological absurdity never came into my mind, as I remember. Jany. 1, 168⅚ finished reading the Godly Learned ingenious Pareus on the Revelation.

Friday, January 22. Joseph Redknap of Lin buried, being about 110 years old: was a Wine-Cooper in London, was about 30 years old at the Great Frost. Ralph King *teste*.

Sabbath, Jan^{r}. 24. Friday night and Satterday were extream cold, so that the Harbour frozen up, and to the Castle. This day so cold that the Sacramental Bread is frozen pretty hard, and rattles sadly as broken into the Plates.

Thorsday, January 28. Mr. Jenner having lodged at Capt. Clap's last night, with Mr. Belcher and others, come near twenty together to $Serj^{t}$. Bull's over the Ice and bring the News of the Rose Frigot ready to come and bring Mr. Randolph, who is to be Deputy Governour, and Mr. Dudley Governour. Jenner came from Ile Wight the 13, of November. When Mr. Jenner came in the Magistrates went all off the Bench to hear his News in the Lobby. Mr. Addington also came in. Isa. 33. 17. was preached from, by Mr. Cotton Mather. Thine eyes shall see the King, &c. whoes Sermon was somewhat disgusted for some expressions; as, sweet sented hands of Christ, Lord High Treasurer of Aethiopia, Ribband of Humility—which was sorry for, because of the excellency and seasonableness of the subject, and otherwise well handled. Doct. 'Tis a matchless priviledg to behold Christ in his Beauty. Mr. Eliot not at Lecture. Mr. Jenner rumors that the Oxford Frigot is to come in the Spring, and bring a Governour from England, and that one Vincent, Brother to the Minister, most talked of; which Mr. Dudley laughs at.

Sabbath-day, Febr. 14. Little Hull speaks *Apple* plainly in the hearing of his Grand-Mother and Eliza Lane; this the first word. At the Burial of Mr. Eyr's Child, Mr. Moodey discoursed of the grievous spreading of the Small Pocks in, and round about Portsmouth, at Exeter, &c.

Tuesday, Feb. 16, 168⅚. General Court meets. Dine 3 times. Is a discourse this day of a strange Beast killed at Middletown, or 4 miles off that place, last Dec., 10 foot long his Body, 10 foot his tail, as tall as a two year and vantage Horse; Had a dead Horse and two Dear lay at 's Den, and Indians waiting for him, at last saw him coming with another in 's Mouth, as a Cat carries a Mouse almost. Indian shot him down. [Sewall writes in the margin—all untrue.] Great disorder in the Town by Cock-skailing: I grant 2 warrants. Tho. Barnard has one, and James Barns the other, whereby several Companies broke up: but for want of a Law and Agreement shall find much ado to supress it.

Satterday, Febr. 20. I send for Edw. Cowel and blame him for his ill carriage at Richd. White's Wedding, Dec. 10. He denys the fact, and saith he came not nigh her (i. e. the

Bride) and stooped down only to take up his Hat taken off in the Crowd.

Sabbath-day, Feb. 28. A Jury is summoned to sit upon the Body of Sarah, the Daughter of Henry and Mary Flood, about 13 weeks old, for that said Mary was suspected of Murder. So now 3 in Prison for suspected Murder.

Tuesday, March 2. Brother St. and Wife visit us. Mr. Chickly is cast in his Attaint. Morgan, Indian and Flood put upon Tryal.

Wednesday, March 3^{d}. James Morgan is brought in guilty by the Jury, Saml Phips Fore-Man.

Thorsday, March 4. Mr. Moodey preaches. After Lecture, James Morgan is condemned to dye: He said was murdered; but spake not of Appealing, which I expected he might.

Friday 5. Joseph Indian is acquitted. James Morgan is sent to, and acquainted that he must dye next Thorsday, and ordered that Mr. Mather be acquainted with it who is to preach the Lecture. Note. Mr. Stoughton and Dudley voted not in the Judgment, and went off the Bench when Sentence was to be passed. Major Richards slid off too. Judgment was voted at George Monk's before rose from Table, on Thorsday.

Satterday, March 6. James Morgan sends a Petition by one Vaughan, signed with said Morgan's own hand, wherein he acknowledges his own sinfull Life, the justness of the Court's Sentence; and desires longer time to live, but 'tis not granted.

Tuesday, March 9th 168$\frac{5}{6}$. Mr. Tho. Kay our Maid's Father, dyes about 8. or 9. aclock. An Order is given for the Execution of Morgan next Thorsday; which the Marshal Generall acquaints him with.

Thorsday, March 11. Persons crowd much into the Old Meeting-House by reason of James Morgan; and before I got thether a crazed woman cryed the Gallery or Meetinghouse broke, which made the People rush out with great Consternation, a great part of them, but were seated again. However, Mr. Eliot, the Father, speaks to me that I would go with him back to the Governour, and speak that the Meeting might be held in our Meeting-House [the South] for fear of the worst. Deputy Governour forwarded it, so Governour proceeded, met Mr. Mather, paused a little and then went to our House, the stream of People presently following and deserting the Old: first part of the 51. Ps. Sung. Mr. Mather's Text was from Num. 35. 16. And if he smite him with an Instrument of Iron, &c. Saw not Mr. Dudley at Meeting, nor Court; suppose he might not be in Town. Mr. Stoughton here. Morgan was turn'd off about ½ an hour past five. The day very comfortable, but now 9. aclock rains and has done a good while.

Know not whether the mad woman said the House fell, or whether her beating women made them scream, and so those afar off, not knowing the cause, took it to be that; but the effect was as before; and I was told by several as I went along, that one Gallery in the old Meetinghouse was broken down. The mad woman was the Daughter of Goodm. Bishop, master of Morgan. She went in at the Southwest Dore, beat the women, they fled from her: they above supposed they fled from under the falling Gallery. Mr. Cotton Mather accompanied James Morgan to the place of Execution, and prayed with him there.

Friday, March 26, 1686. Court of Assistants. Go to the Governour's and accompany him to Court; was slow to go out till knew the Court pretty full: Deputy Governour and about ½ Duzen went down, among whom Mr. Stoughton: Mr. Dudley went not. At the Town-House debated what was best to do respecting Mr. Shrimpton: Mr. Stoughton related matter of fact. Governour had adjourned the Court from Thorsday to Monday, beside the Appointment to hear Mr. Sergeant, which was done Feb. 25. The Court not being full as the Governour alledged, several malefactors were call'd and sentenced, before which ended, Mr. Stoughton and Dudley came in; a while after the Governour said to Mr. Sergeant, Will you have your case called now, Here is but a thin Court,—which was somewhat grievous to Mr. Stoughton; At length Mr. Sergeant and Shrimpton called, Mr. Shrimpton in a great fury, said he was no Thief, &c. though called among them; and he perceived he was to Answer Mr. Sergeant and not the Court, because of the Governour's speech above; told the Governour he had wronged him much, which some apply to his Arbitratorship, some otherwise: said there was no Governour and Company, and the Governour had notice of it from Mr. Humphryes, and would not Answere: substance was what subscribed before in 's Paper given in more silently; but now spoken, in a great Croud with contemptuous Pride and Rage. Govr., Stoughton, Dudley, Davie, Fichards. Court cleared the Room, debated among themselves. None but the Governour Spoke to send Mr. Shrimpton to Prison, one reason was because he had given the Essence of it in writing long before, and nothing had been done to him: But would have spoken to him and the People, desiring the Governour to begin; Governour said he despised it, or the like, speaking to Mr. Davie who propounded it inconveniently: So went away angry, and rest followed him; So is extream Displeasure among the People, against Stoughton and Dudley chiefly: This 26th Shrimpton sent for, not coming, (was not at home) Court and Council is Adjourned to the next Thorsday after Lecture, and Marshal ordered to Summon him.

Satterday, March 27th Capt. Eliot, Mr. Wyllys, Allin, Frary go to the Governour's to comfort Him and strengthen his Hands, seeming to be extreamly concerned. I vindicated Mr. Stoughton, being the Senior Magistrate, all that ever I could; but I question whether it takes much place or no. Mr. Addington entered nothing, and professed before the Council that was so surprized and 'twas a sudden Gust, that scarce knew what he said: and all say 'twas extream sudden and tumultuous: I perceiv Sundry Oaths are taking, what avail they'll be of as to things done in Court, I know not.

Thorsday, April 1, 1686. Mr. Shrimpton comes before the Council, gives in a Paper shewing that March 22. he did say there was no Governour and Company in being in this place, which he still did averr, and was ready to prove if called to it. Council adjourned to April 15th and the Essex Magistrates writt to, to be here. Mr. Shrimpton said he never did disown a Government here, but honoured them. Mr. Secretary in writing the Letter writt *Henry,* in stead of *Samuel.* Am afraid little can or will be done, we shall only *sentire nos mori;* for Governour seemed to own before the People that the Charter was vacated in England, and insisted upon a Proclamation sent him: And the Deputy Governour said the Government must not be tumbled down till his Majesty call'd for it, or to that purpose: Such discourses and arguings before the People do but make us grow weaker and weaker. Said 'twas voided as much as London's; and they durst not since hold a Comon Council.

Thorsday, Apr. 15. After Lecture the Court meets, Mr. Shrimpton sent for, Evidences sworn. Considered how to hear him, as County Court, I voted for the County Court, and three more, or Assistants. When some were for Satterday, others for next Thorsday: first carried it because of Major Appleton and Pike: so Juries to be summoned then to appear. Mr. Shrimpton would not take any blame to himself as to substance of what had said, and pleaded that might be heard by the County Court, else refused to give Bond to appear. The Deputy Governour said his Case was Capital, which Mr. Stoughton earnestly spake against. In the hurry Deputy Governour Adjourned the Court, bid the Marshal Generall look to Mr. Shrimpton; Marshal Generall required a Warrant which Secretary would not grant because the Court Adjourned: So Mr. Shrimpton under no obligation to appear. Boston to chuse Jury-Men for the County Court, Friday 3 aclock all under one [ballot] and read the Nomination-Bill. This Thorsday 15. April, Capt. Ephraim Savage's Maid is known to have the Small Pocks, to the great saddening of the Town, besides all our other Deaths.

Warrants run for the Jury to appear 17th *Inst.* at 8 aclock *mane* to try a Case that concerns Limb, Life, or Banishment; and for a Grand jury. Doubt the terms of the Warrant extream inconvenient.

Thorsday, 15. April, *pomerid.* The Companies warned to Train. News is brought by Mary-Land that Mr. Randolph alone was come for N. England. Am told a Letter from Mr. Ive of Dec. 10. saith was then in the Downs waiting for a wind. So that the Report that the Devil Kirk was coming (as was said the Mariners called him) now abates.

Satterday, April 17, 1686. After much discourse an Indictment is drawn up, the Grand jury find the Bill *per* Pen Townsend, Foreman. Mr. Shrimpton appears not: so an Attachment ordered to goe out for him against next Thorsday, upon which the Marshal is to take Bond of him with Sureties of 1000. which if refuse to give, to carry him to prison. The Towns sent to as far as Weymouth sent their Jury Men very soon Satterday Morn; which was to me a very rare sight, seeing the warrants to arrive a Thorsday night. Mr. Stoughton and Dudley call'd here. Mr. Stoughton said would not come again till after the Election, [if it] should make me lose all my Votes.

Sabbath, Apr. 18. Capt. Ephr. Savage puts up a Bill to have God's hand sanctified in sending the Small Pocks into his Family.

Thorsday, Apr. 22. Court Assistants. Mr. Shrimpton gives no Bond, but is sent to Prison, Marshal did not light on him before. In the afternoon pleads against the illegality of the Indictment it having no Date: which suppose will be granted; is dismissed tonight on 's Parol to appear tomorrow. Acknowledged was ashamed of the manner of 's behaviour in the Country Court, but stood to the Substance, that no Governour and Company.

May 10th. Went to Charlestown and wished Mr. Cotton Mather Joy, was married last Tuesday.

Monday, 10th May, Night and Tuesday Morn, plenty of warm refreshing Rain which was extremly wanted.

Tuesday Morn. Mr. Mather's Maid, a Member of [blank] Church is brought to Bed of a Child. Nothing suspected before that I hear of. 'Tis said He has turn'd her out of 's House.

Friday, May 14. The Rose-Frigot arrives at Nantasket, Mr. Randolph up at Town about 8 *mane:* takes Coach for Roxbury: Major Pynchon and Mr. Stoughton are sent to the Magistrates to acquaint them with the King's Commands being come, and that Mr. Deputy, with whom he pleased to take with him, might go to Capt. Paige's and see the Commission, Exemplification of the Judgment and Seals. Mr. Shrimpton in the morn was sent for and told, by reason of the Governour's absence, and other business, should not now proceed with his Tryal, and that the Court would be adjourned and he should be acquainted with the time. Had a small Admiralty Case. Jury dismissed after Dinner. Major Pynchon has not took his Oath, I saw him not till came in with Mr. Stoughton.

Satterday, May 15. Govr. Hinkley, Major Richards, Mr. Russell and Self sent to by Major Dudley to come to Capt. Paige's, where we saw the Exemplification of the Judgment against the Charter, with the Broad Seal affixed: discoursed about their acceptance: had some thoughts of shewing their Seals to the Magistrates and Deputies, though not to them as a Court; but before we returned, the Magistrates were gone to the Governour's and from thence they adjourned till Monday one aclock. Major Generall came home and dined with me. Went to George Monk's and paid him in full, drank half a pint of Wine together.

Monday, May 17th 1686. Generall Court Sits at One aclock, I goe thither, about 3. The Old Government draws to the North-side, Mr. Addington, Capt. Smith and I sit at the Table, there not being room: Major Dudley the Præsident, Major Pynchon, Capt. Gedney, Mr. Mason, Randolph, Capt. Winthrop, Mr. Wharton come in on the Left. Mr. Stoughton I left out: Came also Capt. [of] King's Frigot, Govr. Hinkley, Govr. West and sate on the Bench, and the Room pretty well filled with Spectators in an Instant. Major Dudley made a Speech, that was sorry could treat them no longer as Governour and Company; Produced the Exemplification of the Charter's Condemnation, the Commission under the Broad-Seal of England—both: Letter of the Lords, Commission of Admiralty, openly exhibiting them to the People; when had done, Deputy Governour said suppos'd they expected not the Court's Answer now; which the Præsident took up and said they could not acknowledge them as such, and could no way capitulate with them, to which I think no Reply. When gone, Major Generall, Major Richards, Mr. Russell and Self spake our minds. I chose to say after the Major Generall, adding that the foundations being destroyed what can the Righteous do; speaking against a Protest; which some spake for. Spake to call some Elders to pray tomorrow which some think inconvenient, because of what past, and the Commissioners having several times declared themselves to be the King's Council when in the Town-House.

Wednesday, May 19. Capt. Eliot tells me that he hears Salem Troop is to be here on Friday, Capt. Higginson is Mr. Wharton's Brother in Law, and Capt. Gedney is of Salem, commands one of the Companyes. Mr. Higginson and Mr. Noyes steady for Submission; the former is the Captain's Father. My Son reads to me Isa. 22 in his course this morning. In the Afternoon Major Richards and Self sent for to Capt. Winthrop's and desired to have our Companyes in Arms next Tuesday, Boston Troop to bring the President from Roxbury; what was thought of the former notion is now laid aside.

Friday, May 21, 1686. The Magistrates and Deputies goe to the Governour's. I was going to them about 11. aclock, supposing them to be at the Town-House, and seeing a head through the Governour's Room, and, Brisco in the Street, I asked if Magistrates there; so went in and they were discoursing about delivering the Keys of a Fort which had been asked, seemed to advise him not to do it till the Gentlemen Sworn. Mr. Nowell prayed that God would pardon each Magistrate and Deputies Sin. Thanked God for our hithertos of Mercy 56 years, in which time sad Calamities elsewhere, as Massacre Piedmont; thanked God for what we might expect from sundry of those now set over us. I moved to sing, so sang the 17. and 18. verses of Habbakkuk.

The Adjournment which had been agreed before, Second Wednesday in October next at 8 aclock in the Morning, was declared by the Weeping Marshal-Generall. Many Tears Shed in Prayer and at parting.

This day the Præsident goes on Board the Frigot a little below the Castle, so the Flagg is hung out at the Main Top. About 4. or 5. P. M. She comes up with a fair wind, Castle fires about 25 Guns; a very considerable time after the Frigot fires, then the Sconce and Ships, Noddles Iland, Charlestown Battery, Frigot again, Ships with their Ancients out, and Forts their Flaggs. Not very many Spectators on Fort Hill and there about, I was for one, coming from the Warehouse. I waited on the Præsident in the morn to speak with him, and so accompanied Him to Town. Wednesday, Major Richards and I were sent for to Capt. Winthrop's to speak with us about attending with our Companyes on Tuesday; this was near night. Were advised to consult our Officers; Major Richards objected the discontent of the Souldiers and may be it might prove inconvenient. On Thorsday, before Lecture, at Capt. Paige's, I told the President thought I could do nothing to the purpose: On Friday waited on him on purpose and propounded Lieut. Hayward: when came home, after Dinner went to speak with Lieut. Hayward, found him at George's. There he was speaking with his Capt., the Præsident having spoken to him; he was to return an Answer to the Præsident. I hear no more of it, so I suppose 'tis left with him. On Wednesday Major spake of warning by Corporals not Drum.

Satterday, June 5th. I rode to Newbury, to see my little Hull, and to keep out of the way of the Artillery Election, on which day eat Strawberries and Cream with Sister Longfellow at the Falls, visited Capt. Richard Dummer, rode to Salem, where lodged 2 nights for the sake of Mr. Noyes's Lecture, who preached excellently of Humility, from the woman's washing Christ's feet. Was invited by Mr. Higginson to Dinner, but could not stay.

Friday, June 11. Waited on the Council, took the Oath of Allegiance, and rec'd my new Commission for Capt. Was before at a privat Fast at Deacon Allen's: so Capt. Hutchinson and I went about 5. aclock, and all the rest were sworn, Capt. Hutchinson at present refuses. I read the Oath myself holding the book in my Left hand, and holding up my Right Hand to Heaven.

Friday, June 18. My dear Son, Hull Sewall, dyes at Newbury about one aclock. Brother Toppan gets hither to acquaint us on Satterday morn between 5 and 6. We set out about 8. I got to Newbury a little after Sun-set, where found many persons waiting for the Funeral; so very quickly went; Mr. Woodbridge and Richardson there: Bearers Mr. Saml. Tompson, Jno Moodey, Jno Toppan, Johnny Richardson. Had Gloves. Gave no body else any because 'twas so late.

Sabbath-day Morn. Goodman Pilsbury was buried just after the ringing of the second Bell. Grave dugg over night. Mr. Richardson Preached from 1 Cor. 3, 21.22, going something out of 's Order by reason of the occasion, and singling out those Words *Or Death.*

On Monday I distributed some Gloves, and in the Afternoon about 6 aclock came with Deacon Coffin to Salem about 10 at night. From thence early in the Morn by reason of the flaming Heat, and got to Winnisimmet before the Ferry-men up, Got home about ¾ after seven, found all well. Hullie was taken ill on Friday Morn. Mr. Clark of Cambridge had a Son of 9 years old drowned the Tuesday before. Two women dy'd suddenly in Boston. James Mirick that lived just by my Father at Newbury, had his House suddenly burnt down to the Ground on Sabbath-day Even before this Friday.

The Lord sanctify this Third Bereavement.

July 27, 1686. Mr. Stoughton prayes excellently, and makes a notable speech at the opening of the Court. The Foreman of the Grand-Jury, Capt. Hollbrook, swore laying his hand on the Bible, and one or two more. So Mr. Ballard, Foreman of the Petit Jury, and one or two more. Others swore lifting up their hands, as formerly. Attorneys are sworn and none must plead as Attorneys but they.

July 28. A considerable Troop from Watertown come and fetch Mr. Bayly, some of ours also accompany them. Francis Stepney the Dancing Master runs away for Debt. Several Attachments out after him.

Friday, Augt. 20. Read the 143, 144 Psalms *mane,* and Sam Read the 10th of Jeremiah. I was and am in great exercise about the Cross to be put into the Colours, and afraid if I should have a hand in 't whether it may not hinder my Entrance into the Holy Land.

Sabbath-day, Augt. 22. In the Evening seriously discoursed with Capt. Eliot and Frary, signifying my inability to hold, and reading Mr. Cotton's Arguments to them about the Cross, and sayd that to introduce it into Boston at this time was much, seeing it had been kept out more than my Life-time, and now the Cross much set by in England and here; and it could scarce be put in but I must have a hand in it. I fetcht home the Silk Elizur Holyoke had of me, to make the Cross, last

Friday morn; and went and discoursed Mr. Mather. He judged it Sin to have it put in, but the Captain not in fault; but I could hardly understand how the Command of others could wholly excuse them, at least me who had spoken so much against it in April 1681, and that Summer and forward, upon occasion of Capt. Walley's putting the Cross in his Colours. Augt. 22. Balston arrives.

Monday, Augt. 23. At even I wait on the President and shew him that I cannot hold because of the Cross now to be introduc'd, and offer'd him my Commission, which he refus'd, said would not take it but in Council. Receiv'd me very candidly, and told me we might expect Sir Edmund Andros, our Governour, here within six weeks; for ought I know that might make him the more placid. Came over the Neck with Mr. Sherman. *Laus Deo.*

Friday, Septr. 3. Mr. Shrimpton, Capt. Lidget and others come in a Coach from Roxbury about 9. aclock or past, singing as they come, being inflamed with Drink: At Justice Morgan's they stop and drink Healths, curse, swear, talk profanely and baudily to the great disturbance of the Town and grief of good people. Such high-handed wickedness has hardly been heard of before in Boston.

Thorsday, Novr. 11. I deliver my Commission to the Council, desiring them to appoint a Captain for the South-Company; left it with them to put 'em in mind on't. As was coming home Capt. Hill invited me to his House where unexpectly I found a good Supper. Capt. Hutchinson, Townsend, Savage, Wing and sundry others to the number of 14 or 15, were there. After Supper sung the 46th Ps.

Novr. 18. Jno Neponet, alias Nemasit, executed. Mr. Eliot hopes well of him.

This day sent for my Coat home from Capt. Gerrishes, where I suppose I left it the 25th May, and now the cold wether made me look after it.

Friday, Novr. 19. Went to Capt. Gerrish and paid him

18d., which laid out for crying my Coat, from thence Eliakim calls me to Mr. Moodey, so we together viewed the Eclips. As to the time and digits the Cambridge Almanack rightest; had he not unhappily said 'twould not be visible. Clouds hindered between whiles that could not so well see how much the Moon eclipsed, but when near half darkened, and when emerging, had a good view.

This night Eliza Damon, servant to Nash the Currier, dyes about midnight of the small pocks, to our great startling, lest it should spread as in 1678. Had hop'd the Town was clear of it. But one that I know of dyed on't before, and that a great while since.

Monday, Novr. 29. This day Wm Clendon the Barber and Perriwig-maker dies miserably, being almost eat up with Lice and stupified with Drink and cold. Sat in the watch-house and was there gaz'd on a good part of the day, having been taken up the night before.

Decr. 8, 1686. Going to Cambridge-Lecture, a little beyond Daniel Champney's I saw a Rainbow to the North, being just about Noon: only Here. Simons with me just then; but Capt. Eliot and Mr. Tho. Oliver saw it, with whom rid over the Causeys. Mr. Oliver said he had not before noted a Rainbow in the North. Cloud rose suddenly very black and hail'd afterward. Ministers pray together at Boston this day.

Sabbath, Decr. 19, 1686. Day of the Fort-fight. As I was reading the Exposition of Habakkuk 3^d^, which this morn sung and read in the family, I heard a great Gun or two, as I supposed, which made me think Sir Edmund might be come; but none of the family speaking of it, I held my peace. Going to Mr. Bradstreet's, Tho. Baker told me Sir Edmund was below, which Winchcomb and Brisco confirmed; said they saw the Frigot with the Flagg in the main Top, and sundry gon down. President and Deputy come to Town; President comes and hears Mr. Willard, whoes Text was Heb. 11. 12. Therefore sprang there of one &c. 113. Psalm sung. Mr. Willard said he was fully persuaded and confident God would not forget the Faith of those who came first to New England, but would remember their Posterity with kindness. One Doct. Faith usually reaps the greatest Crops off the barrenest Ground. Between Sermons, the President and several of the Council goe down. Mr. Lee preaches with us in the Afternoon from Zech. 3. 9, 10.

Monday, Decr. 20, 1686. Governour Andros comes up in the Pinace, touches at the Castle, Lands at Govr. Leveret's wharf about 2 P. M. where the President, &c. meet him and so march up through the Guards of the 8 Companyes to the Town House, where part of the Commission read: He hath power to suspend Councillors and to appoint others if the number be reduced to less than Seven. He and Council to make Laws. Then took the Oath of Allegiance and as Governour, then about eight of the Council sworn. Court clear'd. Governour stood with his Hat on when Oaths given to Councillours. It seems speaks to the Ministers in the Library about accommodation as to a Meeting-house [for church services], that might so contrive the time as one House might serve two Assemblies.

Last Satterday, Mr. Cook not prosecuting his Appeal, Possession was given by Major Bulkly and Marshal Green, of the Farm to Capt. Paige and his wife. The Constables were ordered this day to come and take new Staves, little thinking the Government should have been before altered, or at this time. Mr. Nath. Oliver was the person first spyed the Frigot under sail about 7 *mane* Sabbathday, knowing her by the Flagg; he went to Capt. Davis, Capt. Davis to the President. Governour was in a Scarlet Coat Laced; several others were in Scarlet. Mr. Bradstreet and Mr. Danforth there, to meet the Governour at the Wharf. At Dinner Mr. Mather crav'd a Blessing. The day was serene, but somewhat cold. Major Richards made the South-Company change their Colours for the 8th Colours. Andrew Gardner led them.

Tuesday, Decr. 21. There is a meeting at Mr. Allen's, of the Ministers and four of each Congregation, to consider what answer to give the Governour; and 'twas agreed that could not with a good conscience consent that our Meeting-Houses should be made use of for the Common-Prayer Worship.

Dec[r]. 22. Kings-fisher comes up but neither salutes the Castle nor the Town. In the evening Mr. Mather and Willard thorowly discoursed his Excellency about the Meeting-Houses in great plainess, showing they could not consent. This was at his Lodging at Madam Taylor's. He seems to say will not impose.

Friday, Dec[r]. 24. About 60 Red-Coats are brought to Town, landed at Mr. Pool's Wharf, where drew up and so marched to Mr. Gibb's house at Fort-hill.

Satterday, Dec[r]. 25. Governour goes to the Town-House to Service Forenoon and Afternoon, a Red-Coat going on his right hand and Capt. George on the left. Was not at Lecture on Thorsday. Shops open today generally and persons about their occasions. Some, but few, Carts at Town with wood, though the day exceeding fair and pleasant. Read in the morn the 46. and 47. of Isa., and at night Mr. Norton from Jn° 9.3. Neither this Man nor his Parents.

Thorsday, Dec[r]. 30. The Council meets. Gentlemen from Plimouth and Rhode-Iland here and take their Oaths without any Ceremony, perhaps for sake of the Quakers, who have promised to deliver up their Charter. Mr. Lee preaches the Lecture from Isa. 4. 5, 6. But the Governour and most of the Councillours absent. Mr. Stoughton, Gov[r]. Hinkley, Mr. Usher and some other at Lecture.

Friday, Jan. 7th. I went to Capt. Winthrop's upon business, and the Governour happen'd to be there, Capt. Winthrop had me up to him, so I thankfully acknowledged the protection and peace we enjoyed under his Excellencie's Government. Capt. Wing waited on him at the same time about a Man slain at Worster yesterday by a Logs rolling upon and over him which he just before had cut off. Capt. Davis carries his wife out of Town for fear of the Small Pocks, she being with Child. This day Dame Walker is taken so ill that she sends home my Daughters, not being able to teach them.

Tuesday, January 18, $168\frac{6}{7}$. Between two and three in the Afternoon, for near an hour together, was seen in a clear Skie such a Rainbow, Parelions and Circles as ware on January 2. $168\frac{4}{5}$. In the night following falls a snow, not much. I was at the North-end when I first saw it. People were gazing at it from one end of the Town to tother.

Thorsday, January 20. Mr. Lee preaches the Lecture Eccles 7. 13. From whence exhorted to quietness under God's hand: about middle of Sermon fire was cry'd, which made a great disturbance, by many rushing out. 'Twas only a chimney I think. Spake of the inverted Rainbow, God shooting at somebody. And that our Times better than the former, and expected better still, Turks going down, a sign on't: Jews call'd, and to inhabit Judea and old Jerusalem.

Sabbath, January 30th $168\frac{6}{7}$. About ¾ past eight at night my wife is delivered of a Son, Eliza. Weeden, Midwife. Was fine moderate wether though had been very severe for near a week together before. My wife sent not for the Midwife till near 7. at night. But one staid at home with her, though was not well most part of the day. The child large, so my wive's safe delivery is much to be heeded, considering our former fears. 'Twas much another had not intercepted the Midwife, to whom went from us.

Feb. 6, $168\frac{6}{7}$. Between 3. and 4. P. M. Mr. Willard baptiseth my Son, whom I named Stephen. Day was Louring after the storm, but not freezing. Child shrunk at the water but cried not. His Brother Sam. shew'd the Midwife who carried him, the way to the Pew, I held him up. Thomas Bumsted was baptiz'd at the same time. This day the Lord's Super was administered at the middle and North Meeting-Houses;

the ratling of the Guns during almost all the time, gave them great disturbance. 'Twas never so in Boston before.

Feb. 15, 168$\frac{6}{7}$. Jos. Maylem carries a Cock at his back, with a Bell in's hand, in the Main Street; several follow him blindfold, and under pretence of striking him or 's cock, with great cart-whips strike passengers, and make great disturbance.

Friday, 22. Two persons, one array'd in white, the other in red, goe through the Town with naked Swords advanced, with a Drum attending each of them and a Quarter Staff, and a great rout following as is usual. It seems 'tis a chaleng to be fought at Capt. Wing's next Thorsday.

Satterday, Ap. 23. Eight Companies Train: Many persons: some officers have red paper Crosses fastened to their Hats. The Governour rode by and among the Souldiers, accompanied by the President, Mr. Davie and others. Major Lidget the Chief Commander, Col. Shrimpton, he, and Luscomb on Horse-back. Gave a Volley or two on the Comon, march'd out about one aclock to the Market place. The Rose fired and others. Companies gave three Vollyes, broke off about 3. in the afternoon. In the night a Bonfire or two were made on Fort-hill. After followed fire-works with Huzzas, ended about 11. or 12.

Monday, Apr. 25. Another Challenge goes with his naked Sword through the Street with Hitchborn Drummer, and a person carrying a Quarter-Staff.

May 26. Marshal Green visits me, and tells that he is wholly left out of all publick employment. Sam[l]. Gookin Sheriff for Middlesex. Said Green told me he knew not of it till today, and that he was undone for this world. It seems the May-pole at Charlestown was cut down last week, and now a bigger is set up, and a Garland upon it. A Souldier was buried last Wednesday and disturbance grew by reason of Joseph Phips standing with 's hat on as the Parson was reading Service. 'Tis said Mr. Sam[l]. Phips bid or encouraged the Watch to cut down the May-pole, being a Select-Man. And what about his Brother and that, the Captain of the Fisher and he came to blows, and Phips is bound to answer next December, the Governour having sent for him before Him yesterday, May 26. 1687.

Friday, May 27, between 5. and 6. Father Walker is taken with a Lethargy as was shutting up his shop to goe to their privat Meeting: His left side was chiefly struck with a kind of Palsy: His speech came to him something between 6. and 7. He told me there was plenty of Lavander in the Town where he was Prentice. He overheard some discourse about the May-Pole, and told what the maner was in England to dance about it with Musick, and that 'twas to be feared such practices would be here. Told me he had been liable to be overtaken with Sleep for three-score years, and that 'twas his Burden which he something insisted on. Had a blistering plaister to his neck, Drops of Lavander in 's mouth and his neck chaf'd with Oyl of Amber.

Wednesday, June 22. Went to Muddy-River. Mr. Gore finishes compassing the Land with his plain Table; I do it chiefly that I may know my own, it lies in so many nooks and corners. Went to Cambridge-Lecture.

June 28, 1687. Went to Roxbury and heard Mr. Cotton Mather preach from Colos. 4. 5. Redeeming the Time. Shew'd that should improve Season for doing and receiving good whatsoever it cost us. His Excellency was on the Neck, as came by, call'd Him in and gave Him a glass of Beer and Claret and deliver'd a Petition respecting the Narraganset Lands.

July 1, 1687. Went to Hog-Iland; had Eliakim thither: went to see where to make a Causey to land handsomly: brought home a Basket of Cherries: As went, saw a Surveyor with two red-coats, and another measuring and surveying Noddles-Iland. Came home about ½ hour after four aclock. About 6. aclock Abigail Saunderson is buried, who died yesterday.

July 8. Carried my wife to Cambridge to visit my little Cousin Margaret, they were going, so went to Mr. Leverett's Chamber, the Library, Hall, Sir Davenport and Mitchel's Chamber, and so home well, blessed be God. Little Stephen hath a Tooth cut two or three dayes agoe.

Monday, July 11. I hire Ems's Coach in the Afternoon, wherein Mr. Hez. Usher and his wife, and Mrs. Bridget her daughter, my Self and wife ride to Roxbury, visit Mr. Dudley, and Mr. Eliot, the Father, who blesses them. Go and sup together at the Grayhound-Tavern with boil'd Bacon and rost Fowls. Came home between 10. and 11. brave Moonshine, were hinder'd an hour or two by Mr. Usher, else had been in good season.

Tuesday, July 12. I go to Mr. Usher's about 5. *mane,* Wan having been here: about 7. or eight we goe on Board, the Ship being under Sail. Go with them to Alderton's Point, and with our Boat beyond, quite out of the Massachusetts Bay, and there catch'd fresh Cod. Went to Nantasket, in which way lost my hat, and for fear of running the Boat on the Rocks, left it. From Nantasket, in less than an hour and half sail'd home between 7. and eight. Goe in the Ship Mr. Wharton, Sam. Newman, Mr. Charles Morton, Mr. Wooddrop, Mrs. Bridget Usher, and her Daughter Mrs. Bridget Hoar, and others. Had an extraordinary good wind. Mr. Usher wept at taking leave of 's Wife and Daughter. Before went from Mr. Usher's, Mr. Moodey went to Prayer in behalf of those going to sea, and those staying behind, in a very heavenly manor.

Satterday, July 16. At night a great Uproar and Lewd rout in the Main Street by reason of drunken raving Gamar Flood, came from about Wheeler's pond, and so went by our House into Town. Many were startled, thinking there had been fire, and went to their windows out of Bed between 9. and 10. to see what was the matter.

Monday, July 18. Was startled in the morn as was at prayer in the Kitchen, at a sudden unusual noise; which prov'd to be two Cows running into our little Porch; the like to which never fell out before, that I know of.

July 18. Mr. Mather had two Venice Glasses broken at our Meeting.

Tuesday, July 26, 1687. About Nine aclock my dear Son Stephen Sewall expires, just after the Judges coming to Town; died in his Grandmother's Bed-Chamber in Nurse Hill's Arms. Had two Teeth cut, no Convulsions. Mr. Willard pray'd with him in the Morning, Mr. Moodey coming in when at Prayer.

Wednesday, July 27, 1687. Between 6. and 7. after Noon, The Body of my dear Son Stephen is carried to the Tomb by Jn° Davie, Saml. Willard, Joseph Eliot and Samuel Moodey. Samuel Clark and Solomon Rainsford put him into Tomb. Sam. had the head; Solomon's foot, on a loose brick, slipt, and he slid down the steps and let go the Coffin; but the end rested upon Jony's stone set there to show the Entrance, and Sam. held his part steadily; so was only a little knock. I led my wife, Brother Stephen led Mother Hull, Sam. led Hanah, Billy Dumer led Betty, Cous. Quinsey led his wife, Cous. Savage and Dummer went together. Got home between 7. and 8. Mr. Torrey visited us but could not stay the Funeral. Sam. and his sisters cryed much coming home and at home, so that could hardly quiet them. It seems they look'd into Tomb, and Sam said he saw a great Coffin there, his Grandfathers.

Augt. 24, 1687. Bartholomew-day. Indulgence for Liberty of Conscience published here.

Augt. 25. Mr. Mather preaches from the 5th verse of Jude, shewing that persons deliver'd, yet through Unbelief left to eminent Judgments. Praised God for the Liberty good People enjoy in England. Said, 'tis marvellous in our Eyes. Mr. Dudley tells me His Father and Mr. Stoughton are petitioning for Patents. After Lecture, I visit Mr. Benjamin Eliot, who is much touch'd as to his Understanding, and almost all the while I was there kept heaving up his Shoulders: would many times laugh, and would sing with me, which did; he read three or more staves of the Seventy first Psalm, 9 verses, his Father and Jn° Eliot singing with us; Mr. Benjamin would in some notes be very extravagant. Would have sung again before I came away but 's Father prevail'd with him to the contrary, alledging the children would say he was distracted. Came with me to the Gate when took horse.

Friday, Sept. 9th. Mr. Cook and I set out for Portsmouth. Dine with Brother Sewall at Salem, call on Mr. Phillips. Lodge at Brother Gerrishes.

Satterday, call on Major Pike at Mr. Wears, of Hampton, stay a good while. Our Horses well baited, in this time the Judges got before us, overtook them at the Ordinary at Diner. Din'd with them at the Sheriff's cost. Went, But Mr. Cook and I cast behind by alighting to take off our Coats, so rode alone till overtook Mr. Hutchinson, who staid for us. Went into Town another way than they did, so miss'd of the Invitation and lay at the Ordinary in the Porch of the great Chamber alone.

Monday, Sept. 12. The Court sits. Our case is deferr'd till March next. Was no Declaration filed, no Jury out of the Province of Main, and we had no time to provide. Court was kept at Partridge's and there we dine at Sheriff's cost again, unwittingly. Lodge at Mr. Vaughan's.

Tuesday, 13th. Breakfast at Mr. Grafford's. After, a Fellow plays Tricks. Cook, Hutchinson and Self ride to Bloody Point, so to Hilbon's point over the Ferry; visited Mr. Pike while Mr. Hutchinson and Broughton came over; Boat would not carry all. Mr. Pike not at home, but his wife and two Sons. Call'd at Major Waldron's, where Mr. Cook lodg'd, but Hutchinson and Self rode to the Salmon-falls, George Broughton being our Guide, who was accidentally at Otisses. Lodge at Wm Love's in a very good House and Bed.

Wednesday, See the Mill, get a Cut, visit Mrs. Rainer and her Daughter Broughton. Breakfast there. Ride into Swamp to see a Mast drawn of about 26 Inches or 28; about two and thirty yoke of Oxen before, and about four yoke by the side of the Mast, between the fore and hinder wheels. 'Twas a very notable sight. Rode then to York, through very bad way, Jn° Broughton Pilot. Saw Mr. Sawyer's singular Saw-mill. Lodg'd at Cous. Dumer's with Mr. Martin. Rode to Wells on Thorsday 15th, to view the Records. Din'd at the Ordinary, (call'd at Mr. Wheelrights in the way.) Then I rode with Jn° Broughton to the Salmon-falls, got thether about 8; Lodg'd at Love's.

Friday 16. See Hobs his Hole, Quamphegen. Stay a little at George and Jn° Broughton's: by then at Capt. Wincoll's; by this time Mr. Cook come. Din'd at Wincoll's. Came to Hampton, by that time 'twas dark. Supped there, then to Newbury. Mr. Cook and I lodge at Brother Gerrishes.

Satterday, 17. Ride homeward. Dine at Mrs. Gedney's: whether send for my Brother. Major sends a Letter by me to his Excellency: we ride round by Charlestown, and get home between 7. and 8. finding all well, blessed be God. Note, The Friday we set out, at night, a Shallop riding at anchor in the Sea was run over by a Brigantine, and two Men drown'd.

Tuesday, Oct. 4. Take a view of the Meadow, ride to Joseph Morse's; set an H on a sear Pine, which said Morse shewed me that it was certainly our Bound-Tree, and another little green Pine with Stones at the Roots. It wet, and so rode home. This Night Horse breaks out.

Wednesday, Oct. 5. Ride near round the Farm, Goodm. Holbrook shewing me the Bounds in Company of Joseph Moss and Moses Adams.

Thorsday, Oct. 6. Joseph Moss and Goodm. Whitney shew me the Stone-wall, what was wanting to finish it, that so the Meadow might be secured. About Noon my Unkle and Goodm. Brown come from Braintrey. On my Unkle's Horse after Diner, I carry my wife to see the Farm, where we eat Aples and drank Cider. Shew'd her the Meeting-house. In the Even Capt. Prentice's Negro brings my Horse. In the Morn Oct. 7th Unkle and Goodm. Brown come our way home accompanying of us. Set out after nine, and got home before three. Call'd no where by the way. Going out, our Horse fell down at once upon the Neck, and both fain to scrabble off, yet neither receiv'd any hurt. Laus Deo.

Oct. 17, 1687. Weare Arrives, in whom comes the Governour's Lady. Lands about eleven aclock at Forthill; Takes Coach in the narrow way that leads by Mr. Gillam's; Governour, his Lady and one more ride together. Many Guns fired. Mr. Stoughton here.

Oct. 18. Carried Mother Hull behind me to Roxbury-Lecture; Mr. Joseph Eliot preached. Mr. Stoughton, Moodey, Allen, Hobart, Brown and Self there. House not very full because of the rawness and uncertainty of the day. Got home about ½ hour after Three. Belcher arrives this day, who it's said is Deputy to Sir Wm. Phipps, Provost Marshal. Mr. Eliot said the King was turn'd a Puritan, and he was ravish'd at it; supose 'twas from something he had heard as to som Nonconformists, Aldermen and Lord Mayor. As came home from Roxbury, I met the Governour's Lady riding in her Coach hitherward. The same day the Governour's Lady arriv'd, word came that Capt. Phips was Knighted, so have two Ladies in Town.

Friday, Oct. 21. I went to offer my Lady Phips my House by Mr. Moodey's, and to congratulate her preferment. As to the former, she had bought Sam. Wakefield's House and Ground last night for 350£. I gave her a Gazett that related her Husband's Knighthood, which she had not seen before; and wish'd this success might not hinder her passage to a greater and better Estate. Gave me a cup of good Beer, and thank'd me for my Visit.

Oct. 27. Mr. Joseph Eliot preached the Lecture from 1 Cor. 2. 2. parallels the diseases of New England with Corinth;

among others mentions itching ears, hearkening after false Teachers, and consequently sucking in false Principles, and despising, sitting loose from the true Teachers. Advis'd to fly into the Arms of a crucifi'd Christ, because probably might have no whether else to goe. This morn, Mr. Sims thanks me for my kindness to Goodm. Huchins.

Wednesday, Jan. 11th. Sam. falls ill of the Measles: Joshua Gee, come in Capt. Legg, visits me, and returns thanks for my kindness to him when Captive in Algier.

Thorsday, Jan. 12. Eliakim falls ill of the Measles. Joshua Gee dines with us. Mr. Allen preaches the Lecture.

Friday, Jan. 13. Betty Lane falls sick of the Measles. Get Mehetabel Thirston to help us. Sabbath only Mother and self at Meeting: Betty vomits up a long worm: Mehetabel goes home sick.

Friday, Jan. 13. Joshua Gee with Joseph Bridgham, Jno Barnard and Dyar, come to agree with me what I must have for my Money disbursed in London: said Gee presents me with a pair of Jerusalem Garters which cost above 2 pieces 8-8 [Spanish dollars] in Algier; were made by a Jew.

Friday, Jan. 20. Coming from Charlestown Lecture, I saw Mr. Wears Ship lying on her Larbord side, fell so on Wednesday by reason of Melasses between Decks, as she lay at Scarlet's Wharf. Are now by Boats and empty Buts trying to right her again. Is much damage to Sugar that was laden, the water coming into her: besides what damage the Ship may receive. Many people looking at this odd sight. This is the Ship my Lady [Andros] arriv'd in, Octr. 17th and in which Mr. Mather hath bespoke his passage for London.

Satterday, Jan. 21. My dear Daughter Hanah is put to bed, or rather kept in Bed, being sick of the Measles. Droop'd ever since Thorsday.

Sabbath, 22d. Hanah's Measles appear very full in her face: had a restless night, read in course the 38th Psalm. My Lady Andros was prayed for in Publick; who has been dangerously ill ever since the last Sabbath. Today I hear that Mr. Brown of Salem, the Father, dyed on Friday last in the afternoon. One of a Dutch Church in London is admitted to the Lord's Supper with us. About the beginning of our afternoon Exercise, the Lady Andros expires.

Monday, Jan. 23. The Measles come out pretty full on my dear Wife, which I discern before I rise. She was very ill in the night.

Tuesday, Jan. 24. Betty Sewall keeps her Bed; but is not so full as her Sister Hanah. Capt. Nicholson sat with me an hour or two on Monday night.

Tuesday, Jan. 24th. About noon, the Physician tells me the Measles are come out in my face, and challenges me for his Patient.

Jan. 31. Mr. Randolph, in his Action against Mr. Increase Mather, is cast. Mr. Hale being subpœna'd by Mr. Randolph, pleaded he might not lay his hand on the Bible; must Swear by his Creator, not Creature. 'Twas granted that he only lift up his Hand as customary in New England. Col. Shrimpton lent Mr. Mather his Coach to ride home: He abode there the time of the Tryal, to be at hand if need were.

Friday, Feb. 10, 1687/8. Between 4. and 5. I went to the Funeral of the Lady Andros, having been invited by the Clark of the South Company. Between 7. and 8. (Lychus [Lynchs? *i. e.,* links or torches] illuminating the cloudy air) The Corps was carried into the Herse drawn by Six Horses. The Souldiers making a Guard from the Governour's House down the Prison Lane to the South-Meetinghouse, there taken out and carried in at the western dore, and set in the Alley before the pulpit, with Six Mourning Women by it. House made light with Candles and Torches. Was a great noise and clamor to keep people out of the House, that might not rush in too soon. I went home, where about nine aclock I heard the Bells toll again for the Funeral. It seems Mr. Ratcliffs Text was, Cry, all flesh is Grass. The Ministers turn'd in to Mr. Willards. The Meeting-House full, among whom Mr. Dudley, Stoughton, Gedney, Bradstreet, &c. 'Twas warm thawing wether, and the wayes extream dirty. No volley at placing the Body in the Tomb. On Satterday Feb. 11, the mourning cloth of the Pulpit is taken off and given to Mr. Willard. My Brother Stephen was at the Funeral and lodged here.

March 28, 1688. Capt. Davis spake to me for Land to set a Church on. I told him could not, would not, put Mr. Cotton's Land to such an use, and besides, 'twas Entail'd. After, Mr. Randolph saw me, and had me to his House to see the Landscips of Oxford Colledges and Halls. Left me with Mr. Ratcliff, who spake to me for Land at Cotton-Hill for a Church which were going to build: I told him I could not, first because I would not set up that which the People of N. E. came over to avoid: 2^{d}. the Land was Entail'd. In after discourse I mentioned chiefly the Cross in Baptism, and Holy Dayes.

March 30, 1688. Obadia Gill, John Atwood and Joseph Davis are by a Writt from the Sheriff imprisoned, because they paid not the 13^{s} 4^{d} which each was fined, Feb. 8., for not laying their Hand on the Bible: Judgment run thus—refusing to take the Oath as by Law is required. Though they offer'd to take the same Oath, the oath the others did, that Ceremony set aside. They pay the Fine and charges and Ly not in Prison one night. Mr. Larkin sought after Mr. Mather this week to Arrest him. Mr. Mather on Tuesday was taking Physick and so was free, and since hath purposely avoided him.

Satterday, March 31. I, Daniel Maio and another hand plant Six Chestnut Trees at Hog Iland.

Ap. 2, 1688. Mr. Robert Sanderson rides with me to Neponset and gives me Livery and Seisin of his 8th of the powder-mill Stream, Dwelling-House and Land on each side the River, Mr. Jno. Fayerwether, Desire Clap, and Walter Everenden, witnesses, having the Deed there and exhibiting it, when he gave me Turf, Twigg and Splinter. Mr. Thacher's

Son, Tho., dies this morn. Lodge at Unkle Quinsey's with Cous. Dan[l]. Gookin, who has a Son born last Satterday.

Satterday, Apr. 7th 1688. Capt. Arthur Tanar sails about 10 aclock, a shallop follows quickly after, which 'tis said is to prevent Mr. Mather's getting on Board: 'tis certain all the Town is full of discourse about Mr. Mather. Carie sails a little after. Many Guns fired at Madam Craven's going off.

Friday, March 30. I am told Mr. Mather left his House and the Town and went to Capt. Phillips's at Charlestown.

Apr. 13, 1688. Grafted a Stock next Jn[o] Wait's, pretty high out of the Cows reach, with cions from Mr. Moodey's Orange Pear, and grafted Two Apletree Stocks with Mr. Gardener's Russetings; the Cow having eaten last year's Grafts all save one Twigg. Mr. Moodey, Willard, Cotton Mather, Capt. Townsend, Mr. Eyre were here last night. It seems Mr. Watter and Elisha Odlin were fined last Wednesday, 13. 4[d]., apiece, for refusing to lay their hand on the Bible in Swearing.

April 18. The news about Lima's Ruine comes abroad. Mr. Cotton Mather mentions it on the 19th at the Lecture. Above 60.000 persons perished, and now there is a Pool of Water where it stood, if the news be true.

May 10. Mr. Dudley and his Son call here. I speak to him about the mode of swearing, if no remedy might be had, of which had no encouragement, but said Lifting up the Hand was the handsomest way.

May 23, Wednesday, 1688. Went to Hog-Island with Brother Stephen Sewall, Brother Topan and Sam. Shepard: Upon the Hill we agreed that Sam. Topan should be bound to Brother Stephen for five years from September next, to be bound to Brother only during his Life. Brother Topan chose it rather than that he should be bound to a Trade as a Taylor, or the like; Hopes by going to Sea or the like after his Time is out, may get a livelihood.

Monday, May 28. News comes of his Excellency lying at

Newbury last night, so sundry Gentlemen ride out to meet Him coming home this day.

Wednesday, May 30. Eliakim sets forth with his Brother Williams for Conecticut. Mr. Joseph Eliot here, says the two days wherein he buried his Wife and Son, were the best that ever he had in the world.

Friday, June 1, 1688. Went to Watertown Lecture in Company of Mr. Moodey and Capt. Townsend. Text 1. Cor. 11. 31. If we would judge, &c. Mr. Dudley, Blackwell, Mr. Danforth, Councillor Usher, Mr. Russel Graves, and many more there, Madam Phipps for one, who was ready to faint at word was brought in by the Coach-man of Sir William's being spoke with at Sea. By that time we got home, we heard that Sir William came in his Pinace from Portsmouth this day. Many of the Town gone to complement Him.

June 22. I goe to Hogg-Island with Mr. Newgate to see if could agree about his Marsh: Father Griggs and Sam[l]. Townsend there. When came back, went and bid Sir William welcome to Town, who landed an hour or so before me, being come with his Frigot from Portsmouth. This day Mrs. Joyliff and Mrs. Grecian goe to his Excellency, and expostulat with Him about his Design of meeting first on Sabbath-days in our Meetinghouse.

Satterday, June 23. Capt. Frary and I goe to his Excellency at the Secretaries Office, and there desired that He would not alter his time of Meeting, and that Mr. Willard consented to no such thing, neither did he count that 'twas in his power so to doe. Mr. West said he went not to ask Mr. Willard Leave. His Excellency asked who the House belong'd to; we told Him the Title to the House was on Record. His Excellency turned to Mr. Graham and said, Mr. Attorney we will have that look'd into. Governour said if Mr. Willard not the Parson, so great an Assembly must be considered. We said He was Master of the Assembly, but had no power to dispose of the House, neither had others, for the Deed expressed the Use 'twas to be put to. Governour complain'd of our long staying Sabbath-day senight; said 'twas the Lord's Supper, and [he] had promised to go to some other House on such dayes; Mr. Randolph said he knew of no such promise, and the Governour seemed angry, and said He would not so break his word for all the Massachusetts Colony, and therefore, to avoid mistakes, must give in writing what we had to say; we answered, Mr. Randolph brought not any writing to those he spake to. Governour said we rent off from the old Church against the Government, and the Land the House stood on was bought clandestinely, and that one should say he would defend the work with his Company of Soldiers. Mention'd folks backwardness to give, and the unreasonableness; because if any stinking filthy thing were in the House we would give something to have it carried out, but would not give to build them an house: Said came from England to avoid such and such things, therefore could not give to set them up here: and the Bishops would have thought strange to have been ask'd to contribute towards setting up the New-England Churches. Governour said God willing they would begin at Eight in the Morning, and have done by Nine: we said 'twould hardly be so in the winter. Mr. Graham said if they had their Service by Candle-Light what was that to any: And that the Service appointed by the Church for morning could not be held after Noon.

Thorsday, July 12. Mr. Jn° Hubbard tells me there is a Writt out against me for Hog-Island, and against several other persons for Land, as being violent intruders into the Kings Possession. George Keith [a Quaker] doth this day send a Challenge to the 4 Ministers of Boston, in an open letter by Edward Shipen, to dispute with them about the false Doctrine they delivered. Wild arrives, 9 weeks from the Downs; Mr. Bromfield comes in him.

Satterday, July 14th Jeremiah Belcher comes and brings me the Information Mr. Sherlock left with him on Thorsday last in the Afternoon, when he served on him a Writt of Intrusion. I try'd to goe to the Island yesterday but could not, wind and Tide being against me, and one Oar broke. Went from Winisimmet to the Point, but none fetch'd me over. Wind is out [from the east], and so Sir William comes up and Capt. Belcher.

To Sir Edmund Andros Knight, Capt. General and Governour in Chief of His Majesties Territory and Dominion of New-England in America, the humble Petition of Samuel Sewall of Boston, Sheweth.

That whereas your Petitioner stands seized and possessed of a certain Island or Islands, comonly called and known by the name of Hogg-Island, lying scituat near Boston aforesaid, in the present tenure and occupation of one Jer. Belcher, having been peacably and quietly possessed by your Petitioner and his Predecessors for the space of fourty years or upwards by past: And whereas the said Belcher hath been lately served with a Writt of Intrusion at His Majesties Suit, And your Petitioner not being willing to stand Suit, but being desirous of His Majesties Confirmation for the said Island or Islands:

He therefore humbly prays your Excellencies favour that he may obtain His Majesties Grant and Confirmation of the said Hogg-Island, with the members and Apurtenances thereof, unto your Petitioner his Heirs and Assigns forever under the Seal of this His Majesties Territory. To be holden of His Majesty, His Heirs and Successors, upon such moderat Quit-Rent as your Excellency shall please to order.

And your Petitioner shall ever pray.

SAM SEWALL.

Presented the above written Petition to the Governour with my own hand July 24th 1688.

July 26th. 'Twas read in the Council, and an order made upon it for a Survey.

Monday, July 30th. With many others I went to Dedham to accompany his Excellency in his way to New-York and Jersy: who goes to take the Government of those places.

Thorsday, Augt. 9th. Mr. Moodey, Willard, Mather, Capt. Townsend here, Mr. Thacher was here before. This day I goe for Mrs. Weeden, my wife having been ill a week or more, and now ready to conclude her time to Travail was come. Midwife staid and went to Bed here; in the night was call'd away by another woman about 2. *mane*. It seems the Monday the Governour went hence towards New-York, Five Indians were killed at Spectacle Pond not far from Springfield, four taken Captive, two escaped. They that did the Murder are some of our late Enemies who have since lived under the protection of the French.

Sabbath, Augt. 12. My wife stayes at home as last Sabbath, but that Mother goes to Meeting and the Children only bear their Mother Company: who hath much pain, yet holds up still.

Augt. 14, 1688. About ½ hour past Nine at Night Stephen Greenleaf comes in and brings my Mother Sewall; they set sail from Newbury about 10. in the morning, had a brisk Norwest Gale, turn'd up from Dear-Island and lay aground a pretty while before they could fleet in. Cous. Greenleaf sups with Mother. I give him the Catechise, Day of Doom, &c. bound together in a good Cover, in part for Mother's passage.

Wednesday, Augt. 15th. About 4. *mane,* I rise to make a fire, and to call the Midwife, Charlestowns Bell rung for 5. as came away from Mrs. Weeden's House. Very cool day. My Wife is brought to Bed of a Son between 8. 9. while the Service-Bell was ringing. Cous. Anne Quinsey first tells me of it.

Thorsday, 16th. Put up a Bill for Thanksgiving. About 9. in the night news comes from Salem, by a Vessel from Holland, that the Queen was deliver'd of a Prince, June 10th. So from 11. to 1. or 2. is Drumming, Bonfire, Huzas, small and great Guns, Ringing of Bells, at which many startled for fear of fire or an Alarm; because the thing was so sudden, People knew not the occasion.

Sabbath, Augt. 19th 1688. Town is full of the news of 5. English persons killed at Northfield; So the Councillors sent for; and by that means Mr. Stoughton at our House in the afternoon to hear Mr. Willard, who after Sermon, baptized my young Son, whom I named Joseph, in hopes of the accomplishment of the Prophecy, Ezek. 37th and such like: and not out of respect to any Relation, or other person, except the first Joseph. The Lieut. Governour goes this day to Woburn to secure some Indians there, now busied in gathering Hops. It seems were met together and praying when secured, or just before.

Friday, Augt. 24. I carried my Mother over Winisimet Ferry to Salem, there met with Mr. Noyes. Left my Horse at Salem and came home in Mr. Grafton's Sloop the *Lark*. Loosed from the Wharf at Winter-Island about 4. P. M. and got into my own House at Boston about 11. at night. Wind was East if not somewhat Southerly, so, very bare till we got past Marblehead Neck. Had Moon-shine. The Widow Bordman, and Mr. Kitchin's daughter by Mary Bordman, came Passengers, Landed at Scarlet's Wharf. Got to Salem about noon. Left my Horse for Mother to goe to Newbury.

Wednesday, Augt. 29. Mr. Torrey comes to our House, Mr. Sherman there at the same time, who hath bespoke a passage for England in Mr. Gillam. When he was gon Mr. Torrey and I had pretty much Discourse together about England and going thether. I had been wishing to speak with him.

Thorsday, Sept. 6th. The Duke of Albemarl's Yott arrives, fires in Lecture time. In the even Mr. Cotton Mather comes and prayes with my little sick Joseph.

Sept. 7th. Visit sick Tho. Gardener, the son, bespeak 3 Barrels of Aples of the Father and Andrew; goe to Simon Gates's, from thence to Cambridge to see my little cousin Margaret; visit Mr. Brattle, and then Mr. Leverett, Fellows of the Colledge. Come home and find my own Child somewhat better as is hop'd.

Sept. 15, 1688. Corrected Sam. for breach of the 9th Commandment, saying he had been at the Writing School, when he had not.

Sept. 17th I speak to Mr. Gillam for a passage in his Ship. This day Capt. Frary sees a Souldier with an Indian Squaw in the Com and open Sun.

Sept. 19th The rain hinders my going to Salem, and so to Newbury. Eldridge comes in, who sais the Amsterdam Gazett reported that Mr. Mather's Petition is granted, said Eldridge sais that one Ales was come out of the Downs, who brings Mr. Palmer of New-York, Chief Judge of the Teritory of New England.

Sept. 20. Mr. Lee preaches from Ezek. 47. 11. Shew'd that Edom was on the South side of Asphaltites, and probably they would not be converted. Jews understood it of Italy, called that Edom. This a Prophesy of the great abundant enlargement of the Church not yet accomplished, 'twas now hastening; but then also, some wicked hardened Wretches. Had not heard of an Edomite converted; though that of the 10th Generation implied there might be such a thing. Mr. Mather's last Sermon was on the same Text. Pray'd for Bristow before and after Sermon.

Sept. 21, 1688. This day I ride to Newbury with Mr. Lorie and Penhallow, to visit my friends, and ask them about my going for England; met with my fellow-Travailers at Mr. Moodey's by accident the night before. Brother Stephen there with whom I Lodge. Visit Mr. Wodbridge and Mrs. Noyes.

Monday, Sept. 24th. Come to Brother Moodey's and dine with him, his wife, Mother and James Noyes; then Brother brings me going to Rowley-Mill; I call at Mr. Payson's; drive a Nail in Mr. Gerrishes Meetinghouse, gave 2s. Visit Mr. Higginson.

Sept. 25th. Visit Mr. Nathl. Mather, sick at Salem at Mr. Swinerton's. Come home in Company Major Gedny and Brown, a very fair wind over, went in and drunk at Brookins, came home and found all well, blessed be God.

Satterday, Sept. 29th. Lydia Moodey comes hether to dwell, helping my wife to nurse the Child Joseph.

Monday, Oct. 1. A Whiping Post is set up by the middle Watch-house. Brother Stephen visits us.

Wednesday, Oct. 3d. Have a day of Prayer at our House: One principal reason as to particular, about my going for England. Mr. Willard pray'd and preach'd excellently from Ps. 143. 10:, pray'd. Intermission. Mr. Allen pray'd, then Mr. Moodey, both very well, then 3d.—7th verses of the 86th Ps., sung Cambridge Short Tune, which I set. Then had Govr. Bradstreet and his wife, Mr. Moodey and wife, Mr. Allin and Mr. Willard and wife, Cous. Dumer and wife, and Mrs. Clark her sister, Cousin Quinsey and wife and Mrs. Scottow, should have reckon'd formerly Mother Hull and Self. My wife was so lately very ill of the Ague in her face, she could not come down out of the Chamber. Fifteen sat down together. Mr. Addington, Mr. Eyre, Capt. Townsend and several others here beside the Meeting.

Friday, Oct. 5. Mrs. Anger of Cambridge is buried: Was Sister to Mrs. Topan of Newbury. Went to Mrs. Williams's Meeting where Mr. Moodey preached. About 9. night, Thomas, an Indian and very usefull Servant of Mr. Oliver, hang'd himself in the Brewhouse.

Satterday, Oct. 6. The Coroner sat on him, having a Jury, and ordered his burial by the highway with a Stake through his Grave.

Wednesday, Oct. 10th Went on Board the America, Mr. Isaac Addington one of the Owners, introducing me: took up the Starboard Cabbin, and when came back, met Capt. Clark and gave him Earnest 20s; then went to Mr. Moodey's to a Meeting. At night read in course the Seventh of the Romans. Received a Letter from Mr. Taylor this day, and writt to him before I had received it. Both of us concluded alike from Joseph's Blessing, Deuteronomy.

Tuesday, Oct. 16. Little Hanah going to School in the morn, being enter'd a little within the Schoolhouse Lane, is rid over by David Lopez, fell on her back, but I hope little hurt, save that her Teeth bled a Little, was much frighted; but went to School; one Stebbin took her in, who lives next Solomon Rainsford's Shop up the Lane, on the left hand as goe up. This day the Ground-Sills of the Church are laid; the stone foundation being finished. Visit Cousin Dummer sick abed.

Wednesday, Oct. 24, 1688. Mr. Bayly and his wife, Mr. Moodey and his wife and Cous. Richard Dumer dined with us. In the afternoon coming out of Town, I met Mr. Ratcliff, who ask'd me if I were going for England; he ask'd when, I said in Capt. Clark. He pray'd God Almighty to bless me, and said must wait upon me. Capt. Clark tells me at the Coffee-House, that he will sail next week, or Monday come senight at out-side.

Monday, Oct. 29. Went to Hogg-Island, had Sam., Hanah and Betty thether, Mr. Oliver's two daughters, Mr. Johnson's daughter, Mr. Balston's daughter: Mr. Oliver himself went; Sam[l] Marshall and his boy carried us. Landed at the Point because the water was over the Marsh and Wharf, being the highest Tide that ever I saw there. Cous. Savage came and din'd with us on a Turkey and other Fowls: had a fair wind home, Landed at Gibbs his Wharf, got home about Sun-set. Visited Mr. Smith who lies very ill.

Oct. 30. We have the news of Herbert Wanton and Blagg being cast away on the Isle of Pines. Very high Tide to day, in so much I feared 'twould have carried away the Island-Dam, and sent on purpose to see: All was firm and sound, blessed be God.

Wednesday, Oct. 31. Went to the Funeral of Mrs. Gookin: Bearers, Mr. Danforth, Mr. Russell, Sewall and Hutchinson, Eliakim, Mr. James Taylor, and Mr. Edw. Bromfield. Note. The Tide was over the Causey, and Mrs. Willard, whom Mr. Pain carried, fell into the water, so that she was fain to goe to

Bed presently in stead of going to the Grave, the Horse verg'd to the right, till fell into the Ditch. Mr. Hutchinson's Coach-Horses also plung'd.

Joshua Gee Lanches to day, and his Ship is called the Prince. Bant sails. Capt. Clark treats his Owners and Passengers: I was invited but the Funeral took me up. I help'd to ease the Corps into the Grave. Mr. Torrey goes home. More mischief done at the Eastward by the Indians. Mr. Alden dispatch'd again with Souldiers.

Satterday, Nov. 3. Mr. Offly and Mr. Clark come and speak to me about laying in for the Cabbin. Yesterday was Cous. Quinsey's Meeting where Mr. Moodey preach'd.

Nov. 7. Brother Stephen comes to Town and brings my Letter of Attorney and other writings. I go with him to the Governour's where the witnesses are sworn, and after that I ask his Excellency if He has any service for me to Hampshire or Coventry: He ask'd where; I said in England. He said none in particular; Ask'd whom I went in; said in Capt. Clark. He said 'twas very well, and passed away out of the Porch.

Nov. 16. The Upholsterer tells me the Ship is loaden too much by the head and sails badly. About 11 M. The Widow Glover is drawn by to be hang'd. Mr. Larkin seems to be Marshal. The Constables attend, and Justice Bullivant there.

Satterday, Nov. 17. Brother Stephen and I with Mr. Pole and Capt. Clarke goe on Board the America. It rained before we got aboard, and all the way as we came from the Ship; had a glass of good Madera. Brother comends the Ship, dines with us and returns to Salem.

Thorsday, November 22, 1688. Set sail out of Boston Harbour about an hour by Sun, with a very fair wind. Friday, Nov. 23, *mane,* the wind came up at North-East to our great discomfort. Beny Harris reads the 21 of the Proverbs, which is the first Chapter I heard read on Shipboard. I much heeded that verse, He that wandereth out of the way of Understanding shall remain in the Congregation of the dead. At night I read the first of the Ephesians, and go to prayer. Saturday, Nov. 24, wind holds North-East, we go away East-South-East and the like, hoping to shape clear of Nantucket Shoals. Mr. Clark reads the two first Chapters of Isaiah, and Capt. Clarke prayes. Sabbath, Nov. 25, Strong East wind. In the even reef the Mainsail. I read the 74th Psalm, being that I should have read at home in the family. Read four or five verses out of Dr. Manton on the first of James: very suitable for me. Sung the 23^{d} Psalm. Monday, Nov. 26, sail generally East-South-East. Mate takes an Observation, and finds that we are in the Latitude of 40^{D} and 13^{M}. Tuesday Nov. 27, sail East-South-East, and sometimes East and North. Ait my wives Pastry, the remembrance of whom is ready to cut me to the heart. The Lord pardon and help me. Wednesday, Nov. 28, rains hard in the morning, the other Tack is brought on board, and we sail North-North-East. Just at night the wind blows very hard, just in our teeth, so ly by under the Mizzen, the other sails being furled. Scarce any sleeping all night, things in the Cabbin were so hurled to and again. Thursday, Nov. 29, wind comes up at North, or thereabouts, so steer East-N.-East. This is the first day of a fair wind since our coming out; goe away with fore-sail on our course. Clouds and no observation. About 12 at night, the Ship being under a hard Gale of wind, the whipstaf is somehow loosed from the Goose-neck, which puts us into great consternation: and the word is given, Turn out all hands. Several go into Gunroom and steer there for awhile, and by God's blessing no great harm. Some of the men said if she had not been a stiff ship would have been overset. Friday, Nov. 30th, one Cassemate being left down and the wind astern, a Sea is shipped into the Cabbin to our great startling and discomfort. Mrs. Baxter, who lay athwart ships at the bulkhead, the most wet. Very high wind and by flaws, we ly under our foresail not quite hoisted, and sail East. 'Tis a very laborious day by reason of hail, snow, wind and a swoln sea all in a foaming breach. A little before night the foresail is reefed, and Main Top-Mast took down to prepare for the tempestuous night, which proves very stormy, sore flaws of wind and Hail. Satterday, Decemb. 1, wind very high, frequent storms of Hail and Rain in fierce Gusts. About an hour by sun we are put into great confusion, the iron of the Whipstaff coming out of the said Staff. Some goe down and steer below, but fain at last to take in the foresail and ly by till the staff was fitted. The good Lord fit us for his good pleasure in this our passage.

Sabbath, Dec. 2, goe with our fore courses, and just before night hoist the Top-sail, sailing East-N.-E. Read out of Dr. Preston and Manton, prayed and sung Psalms. Monday, Dec. 3, calm in the morn for some hours, then a South-west wind and Top-sails out. Rain at night. Reef the Mainsail because now the wind very high. Caught two Petterils which Mr. Clark intends to preserve alive. Note, my Erasmus was quite loosened out of the Binding by the breaking of the water into Cabbin when it did. Was comforted in the even by reading the 4. 5. 6. 7. verses especially of the Ephesians. About 8 at night the Mate tells me he saw three Corpressants, upon the top of each mast one. Tuesday, Dec. 4. *mane,* a violent North-East storm rises, so all sails taken in and ly by: very troublesome by reason of the frequent seas shipt and throwing the things in the Cabbin into confusion. Mrs. Mar [c ?]y's Chest broken and her things powred out. I put on a clean shirt this morn. Can't dress victuals to day. Wednesday, Dec. 5, wether is moderated: but the wind so contrary that we sailed E.S.E. and South-East. Thorsday, Xr. 6th wether is comfortable, but wind, E.N.E., so we sail N. or N. and by West. Mrs. Baxter is taken ill with a Flux. Kill a Shoat. Friday, Dec. 7th, very fair day: sail N. East. Breakfast on one of my wives Plum Cakes. Read Dr. Preston, Saints Support of sorrowful Siners. One of the Geese dyes yesterday, or to day. Mrs. Baxter is better.

Satterday, Dec. 8, very mild wether. Sail N.E. and E.N.E.

In the afternoon veer'd out about 100 Fathom of Line, but found no bottom. Suppose ourselves very near the Banks of New-found-Land, by reason of the multitude of Gulls. Guner trims me. Sabbath, Dec. 9. South, and South-w. wind; very temperat whether. Just at night Rain and N.W. wind. Cloudy all day. Monday, Dec. 10th North Wind. Tuesday, Dec. 11. N. and N. and by W. Pleasant wether. Last night I prayed to God and was somewhat comforted. This day the Captain takes a List of 's Letters. Wednesday, Dec. 12. West wind. Very pleasant wether. Thursday, Dec. 13. Strong S.W. wind. Ship runs between 6 and 7 Knots. Cloudy, dusky day. Friday, Dec. 14. Fast wind. See Birds, and a number of Fishes called Bottle-noses. Some say they are Cow-fish, or Black-fish. Satterday, Dec. 15. N.W. wind. Very pleasant morn. A little before night is a calm, after that the wind comes up at South-East, or thereabouts. Sail East N. East.

Sabbath, Dec. 16. Very high wind and swoln sea, which so tosses the ship as to make it uncomfortable; wind after, so Cabbin shut up and burn Candles all day. Shifted my Linen this day, Shirt, Drawers, N. Wastcoat, Binder: only fore course [four courses?] to last with. Monday, Dec. 17. Strong N.W. wind. Tuesday, Dec. 18, wind N. N. West: many flaws: storms of Hail. Afternoon was a Rainbow. Killed the Sheep to day. Dream'd much of my wife last night. She gave me a piece of Cake for Hannah Hett; was in plain dress and white Apron. Methoughts was brought to bed, and I through inadvertency was got up into the upermost Gallery, so that I knew not how to get down to hold up the Child. We are in about 48D N. Latitude.

Wednesday, Dec. 19, pleasant, west and southwest wind. Have an Observation. Was a Rainbow in the morn, and in the even Mr. Sampson set the Sun by the Compass. This morn was refreshed in prayer from the Instance of Jonah and God's profession of 's readiness to give his Spirit to those who ask.

Thorsday, Dec. 20, strong North wind. Are in 48 D. 36, M. Lat. At night the wind veers a little to the Eastward of the North.

Friday, Dec. 21. Little wind and that is Northerly. See many Porpuses. I lay a [wager] with Mr. Newgate that shall not see any part of Great Britain by next Saterday senight sunset. Stakes are in Dr. Clark's hand. In the night wind at North-East. Satterday, Dec. 22, wind is at North-East, at night blows pretty fresh. This day a Ganet was seen, and a Purse made for him that should first see Land, amounting to between 30 and 40^{s}. N. England Money. I gave an oblong Mexico piece of Eight. Starboard Tack brought on board, and sail, N. E., N.N.E. and North by E.

Sabbath, Dec. 23. Pretty strong East, N. East wind. Sail N. and by E. Saw a Ship about noon some two Leagues to Leeward of us. A Ganet seen this day. Towards night the Capt. sounds and finds a sandy bottom. The water between 70 and 80 Fathoms deep.

Monday, Dec. 24, wind remains right in our Teeth. See a Ship to Leeward most part of the day which stood the same way we did: but we worsted her in sailing. Tuesday, Dec. 25, see two Ships, one to windward, 'tother to Leeward. About 10, m. a Woodcock flies on board of us, which we drive away essaying to catch him. Wind at North-East. Ly by under the Mainsail all night. Wednesday, Dec. 26. This morn perceive the Rails of the Ships head and the Lion to be almost beaten off, which cost considerable time and pains to fasten again. Ly by with no Sails. A Rainbow seen this day. Thorsday, Dec. 27, begin to sail again a little, winding East, N. East. Friday, Dec. 28, wind contrary, yet keep sailing sometimes N. East, sometimes goe South and by West upon the other Tack. Saw three Ships in the Afternoon, which, suppose are bound for England as we are. Satterday, Dec. 29. Have an Observation; are in 49^{D} and 50^{M}. See a Ship.

Sabbath, Dec. 30th. Spake with a Ship 7 weeks from Barbados, bound for London, tells us he spake with an English Man from Galloway, last Friday, who said that the King was dead, and that the Prince of Aurang [Orange] had taken England, Landing six weeks agoe in Tor-Bay. Last night I dreamed of military matters, Arms and Captains, and, of a suddain, Major Gookin, very well clad from head to foot, and of a very fresh, lively countenance—his Coat and Breeches of blood-red silk, beckened me out of the room where I was to speak to me. I think 'twas from the Town-house. Read this day in the even the Eleventh of the Hebrews, and sung the 46th Psalm. When I waked from my Dream I thought of Mr. Oakes's Dream about Mr. Shepard and Mitchell beckening him up the Garret-Stairs in Harvard College. Monday, Dec. 30th, contrary wind still, speak with our Consort again Tuesday, Jan. 1. [1689.] speak with one who came from Kenebeek [?] in Ireland 8 day's agoe: says there are Wars in England. Pr. of Aurang in Salisbury Plain, with an Army Landed with fourscore and 5 Men of War and above two hundred Fly Boats, has took Plymouth and Portsmouth, &c. and is expected at London daily. Read Hebrews 13th Wednesday, Jan. 2. Last night about 12 aclock the Wind comes fair, so that by morning the word was, Steady, Steady. The Lord fit us for what we are to meet with. Wind veered from East to South, and so Westerly. This day eat Simon Gates's Goose. Thorsday, Jan. 3, wind comes East again. A gray Linet and a Lark, I think, fly into the Ship. Friday, Jan. 4, wind not very fair. Some say they saw a Robin-Redbrest to-day. Satterday, Jan. 5th, wind is now come to be about Southwest. Sounded and found a red, blackish sand about 50 Fathoms deep. Have a good Observation. This day I finished reading Dr. Manton. Blessed be God who in my separation from my dear Wife and family hath given me his Apostle James, with such an Exposition. Page 8. "Honour God in your houses, lest you become the burdens of them, and they spue you out. The tendernes of

God's Love! He hath a James for the Xns. of the scattered Tribes.

Satterday, Jan. 5th 1688 [9] Sounded twice to day. Found 50 Fathom first, then about 70. odd. Wind Souwest. A flock of Sparrows seen today. Psa. 84, or some such small Birds.

Sabbath, Jan. 6. See Capt. James Tucker, Comander of the Betty of London, about 120 Tons, whom spake with, this day sennight. Saith he saw the Light of Silly last Thorsday night. We carry a light and keep company. Monday, Jan. 7th, Mr. Clark goes on Board our Consort, and brings Oranges and a Shattuck [shaddock]. So steer in the night E. and East and by South. We had no Observation. Capt. Tucker saith he had by a forestaff, and Latitude 49.30. Reckons we shall be abrest with the Lizard by morning. Wind So west. Tuesday, Jan. 8, *mane,* a brisk west wind. We sound and have 55 fathom: speak with our Consort, who saith he had Lizard Soundings, and would now have us steer East and by N. They were a little to windward of us, and a little astern. By and by they all gathered to their Starboard side, and looking toward us made a horrid Outcry, Land! Land! We looked and saw just upon our Larboard Bow, horrid, high, gaping Rocks. Mr. Clark imagined it to be the French Coast. We asked our Consort. He said, Silly! Silly! Trim'd sharp for our Lives, and presently Rocks all ahead, the Bishop and Clarks, so were fain to Tack, and the Tack not being down so close as should be, were afraid whether she would stay [not miss stays]. But the Seamen were so affected with the breakers ahead that the Mate could not get it altered, or very little. But it pleased God the Ship staid very well, and so we got off and sailed in Bristow Channel toward Ireland, winding Nore, N. West, and N.N.W., westerly. Just when saw the Rocks it cleared a little, and when fix'd in our course thicken'd again. Blessed be God who hath saved us from so great a Ruin. Saw the Light-House, that look'd slender, about the height of a man, and a Rock with a cloven top, not altogether unlike a Bishops

Mitre, which I therefore take to be the Bishop. Wind would have carried us between Silly and the Lands End, but durst not venture and could not speak to our Consort, who probably knew better than we. And we Tacking, he Tacked.

Tuesday, Jan. 8, 168⁸⁄₉. About Noon our Consort being astern, Tacked, and we then Tacked, and stood after him, hoping to wether Sylly and its Rocks. Just before night we were in much fear by reason of many Rocks, some even with and some just above the water under our Lee, very near us, but by the Grace of God we wethered them. In the next place we were interrogated by the Bishop and his Clarks, as the Seamen said, being a Rock high above the water, and three spired Rocks by the side of him, lower and much lesser, which we saw, besides multitudes at a remoter distance. The breach of the Sea upon which made a white cloud. So I suppose the former Rocks near the Land of Sylly not the Bishop. Sailed Souwest, and S.W. by S. At night our Consort put out a Light, and about 8 o'clock began to hall away South-East. We imagined we saw some Glares of the Light of Sylly, but could not certainly say.

Wednesday, Jan. 9th As soon as 'twas light the word was they saw of Man of War, which put us into as great a consternation almost as our yesterday's Danger. Puts out his Ancient [ensign]; coming nearer speaks with us: is a Londoner from the Canaries, who by dark wether for several days had not made the Land, and lost his Consort last night. We told him we came from Sylly last night. He told us that five weeks agoe a Ship told them the Prince of Aurange was Landed in England before they came from Portland. This was at Canaries. Said also, the King not dead. Suppose ourselves abrest with the Lizard. Our Guner said he saw it. Sail along 3 of us pleasantly, *Laus Deo*.

In the night the Londoner carries two Lights, one in 's poop, the other in 's round Top.

Thorsday, Jan. 10, 168⅞. Very fast wind, sail along with four or five more ships. About Ten o'clock saw the Isle of Wight plain, which is the first Land next to Sylly that I have seen. Next to that saw high white Cliffs: but then Clouds and Fogg took away our Sunshine and Prospect. The Isle of Wight makes a long space of Land, Hills and Valleys.

Friday, Jan. 11. A prety while before day, a vehement North wind comes up, so that fain to ly by, and great confusion by reason that the 6 or 7 Ships were so near together that ready to fall fowl one of another. In the morn see that we are over against Beachy [Head]. In a while Tack about to try to gain the Wight, but cannot. A little before night tack again; Seven Cliffs. Make thus cold wether.

Jan. 12. Meet with a Pink 14 days from Liverpool: tells us Prince of Aurange landed about the 29th Nov. [really on the 5th] in Torbay, with 50 Thousand Men, Six hundred Ships: Sea-Commanders all yielded to him: no bloud shed: King and Prince of Wales gone to France somwhat privatly. Bought three Cheeses of him. He sent us some Bottles of very good Beer, and we him one of my Bottles of Brandy. About 12 o'clock the wind springs up fair, and about 6 in the even we take our leave of Beachey. Saith the occasion of Prince's coming in, that apprehends King James has no Legitimate Son, that that of Pr. Wales is a Cheat. Told us there were Englishmen found dead, drowned, tied back to back: so put us in great fear, because he intimated as if French Men of War were cruising with English Commissions. Sabbath, Jan. 13. Goe ashoar at Dover, with Newgate, Tuttle and Sister. Hear 2 Sermons from Isaiah, 66. 9.—Shall I bring to the birth? Monday morn, Jan. 14th, view the fort at the west end of the Town and the Castle: went into the Kings Lodgings.

A small River runs that helps to clear the Dock of Shingle: the Peers also defending. Houses of Brick covered with Tile generally: Some very good Buildings. A handsome Court-

House and Market-place, near which the Antwerp Tavern, where we drunk coming out of Town.

Got this night to Canterbury time enough to view the Cathedral, and Kentish Husbandry as went along.

Jan. 15. To Chatham and Rochester, which make a Long Street of Good Houses. A fair Assize-House now building, just over against which we lodged at a Coffee House: no room in the Inn. Dined at Sittingburne.

Wednesday, Jan. 16th. To Dartford, where had a good Goose to Dinner. 'Tis a considerable place. A river runs into the Thames under a Stone Bridge of four Arches. To Southwark, where we drink and reckon with the Coachman. Hire another Coach for 18^{d} to Cousin Hull's. Thorsday, Jan. 17th, went to the Exchange. Jan. 30th, went to the Temple and to White-hall. Saw Westminster Abbey: Henry 7^{ths} Chapel. Heard Dr. Sharp preach before the Commons, from Psa. 51.—Deliver me from Blood guiltinesse, &c Saw St. James's Park.

Feb. 7. A Minister who lives at Abbington earnestly invites me to his House with Mr. Mather, and he will goe and shew us Oxford. Mr. Brattle shewed me Gresham Colledge, by Mr. Dubois his kindness and Cost. Afterward went to Smithfield, and the Cloisters of the Blew Coat Boys [at Christ's Hospital]. Gresham-Colledge Library is about one Hundred and fifty foot long, and Eighteen foot wide.

Feb. 9, $168\frac{8}{9}$. Guild-Hall I find to be Fifty yards long, of which the Hustings take up near seven yards, Measuring by the same yard-jointed Rule, Mr. Brattle and I find the breadth to be Sixteen Yards.

Feb. 11th. Mr. Brattle and I went to Covent-Garden and heard a Consort of Musick. Dined to-day with Madam Lloyd and Usher.

Feb. 12. Saw three Waggons full of Calves goe by together. At the Star on the Bridge, Mr. Ruck's, saw the Princess pass in her Barge, Ancients and Streamers of Ships flying, Bells Ringing, Guns roaring. Supped at Mr. Marshal's.

March 19. Saw Paul's, which is a great and excellent piece of work for the Arches and Pillars and Porches. The Stairs are five foot ½ long and four Inches deep, winding about a great hollow Pillar of about six foot Diameter. March 20. Went and saw Weavers Hall and Goldsmiths Hall. Went into Guild-Hall and saw the manner of chusing the Mayor. About 16 were put up, though I think but four were intended. Pilkington and Stamp had by much the most Hands, yet those for fatal Moor and Rayment would have a Pole, which the Court of Aldermen in their Scarlet Gowns ordered to be at four o'clock. They sat at the Hustings. Sheriffs in their Gold Chains managed the Election.

April 20. Went on foot to Hackney through Brick-Lane, about ½ a mile long, and dined with Mr. Tho. Glover his Son, Read, Thompson, their wives, Mr. French, and several Grandchildren. Eat part of two Lobsters that cost 3.9[d] apiece, 7[s]:6[d] both.

April 23. With Mr. Mather waited on the Lord Wharton, and Sir Edward Harly.

London, April 26, 1689.

Honoured Sir, Hat in Hand, &c, Necessity puts men upon hard Shifts to find out some pretence or other for making their addresses to those from whom they may expect relief. There was Capt. John Hull, of Boston in N. E., with whom in his life-time you had some Correspondence by way of Merchandize. He died in Sept. 1683, leaving a Widow and a Daughter, who is my wife; by whom I had an Estate that might afford a competent Subsistence according to our manner of living in N. E. But since the vacating of the Charter, and erecting a Government by Commission, the Title we have to our Lands has been greatly defamed and undervalued: which has been greatly prejudicial to the Inhabitants, because their Lands, which were formerly the best part of their Estate, became of very little value, and consequently the Owners of very little Credit. Sir, I am glad that you are returned again to England, to your Country, Possessions, and dear Relations, and to a Seat in Parliament. I hope your former Distresses will help you to sympathise with others in the like condition. I, and several besides me, are here far removed from our Wives and Children, and have little heart to goe home before some comfortable settlement obtained, whereby we might be secured in the Possession of our Religion, Liberty and Property. I am informed some favorable Votes have been passed in the House of Commons, wherein N. E. was mentioned. I entreat your forwarding of such Votes as you have Opportunity, in doing which you will be a Partner with God, Who is wont to be concerned in relieving the Oppressed. I shall not take up more of your time from your momentous Employments. My hearty Service presented to you, I take leave, who am, Sir, your humble Servant, SAM. SEWALL.

April 29. went to Greenwich with Mr. Mather, Whiting, Brattle, Namesake: Supped at the Bear. Went through the Park to Mr. John Flamsted's, who shewed us his Instruments for Observation, and Observed before us, and let us look and view the Stars through his Glasses.

April 30. Come to Deptford, where breakfast with Cheesecakes: from thence to Redriff upon the River's Bank, where Dr. Avery's Cousin had us to a Gentleman who showed us many Rarities, as to Coins, Medals, Natural and artificial things: from thence by water to Tower-Stairs, about 10 o'clock.

April 29. In the morn saw the Westminster Scholars; 3 of them made Orations in Hebrew, Greek, Latin, before the Dean and Delegates. Cambridge Delegates sat now on the right hand, for they take turns. Sub-Dean also had an Epistle; as did the Dean and Delegates. The grave Dr. Busby sat by.

Tuesday, May 7th went to Windsor, 8th Eaton, Hampton Court, and so home.

Thursday, May 9, went to H. Court, to wait on the King and Council. Mr. Mather not there: said he was feverish, yet I perceive was at Change. Sir Robt Sawyer spake of the Quo Warranto in Charles the First's time, and supposed we had no Charter: asked if any had seen it. I said I had seen a Duplicate. Dr. Cox craved Day; so are to appear agen next Thorsday, and just as we were going out, by Sawyer's means were called back, and then he spake of the Quo-Warranto for Misdemeanors, and we are ordered to attend the Attorney General with our Charter. As we came home were entertained by Mr. Stephen Mason with Cider, Ale, Oysters and a Neat's Tongue, being ten of us, or 11. This house is at Clapham, wherein Col. Bathe did dwell.

Tuesday, May 14th, Mr. Richard Wharton dyes about 10 *post merid.* He rid to Town the Wednesday before in order to goe to Hampton-Court last Thorsday. Monday, May 6, was at Westminster pleading against Mr. Blathwayt, in behalf of N. E. Mr. Brattle and I came down by water with him. Wednesday, May 15, went and dined with Fish at Capt. Kelly's upon Mr. Partrige's Invitation. Capt. Hutchinson, Clark, Appleton, Brattle, Hull, in company. Went to a Garden at Mile End and drunk Currant and Rasberry Wine, then to the Dog and Partrige's, and plaid Nine Pins. At the house a Souldier was shot by his drunken companion the night before.

May 18, goe to Hampton Court in company of Capt. Hutchinson and Jo. Appleton; Mr. Mather, Sir Sam. Tomson, Mr. Whiting, and Mr. Joseph Tomson ridd in another Coach. Cost 21s apiece, besides money to the Drivers. Were dismissed *sine Die.* Mr. Ward and Hook our Council. Entertain Mr. Humphrys too. Just now about a virulent Libel comes out against N. E., the day Mr. Wharton was buried.

Monday, May 20. Meet to answer the Print, and in the evening another accosts us, called an abstract of our repugnant Laws, full of Untruths almost as the former. To comfort me when got home, met with a Letter from my dear Brother, by the way of Bilbao, dated the 12 March; all friends and my wife and Children well, but New England bleeding.

May 31. Went to Mr. Papillon to speak to him in behalf of N. E., who entertains me candidly, and promises to promote our Interest, and would have me take off [dissuade] those who may think contrarily. May 31. Is a Fast kept at Dr. Annesly's: they began with singing and sang 4 or 5 times. After all, had a Contribution. When came home, found a Letter from Cousin Quinsey, giving an account of the Health of my Wife, Children and friends, on the 26 March.

June 3, 1689. Capt. Hutchinson, Mr. Brattle and I went to Newington to visit Mr. Saltonstall, at his son-in-law Horsey's. I gave him two of Mr. Cotton Mather's Sermons. As came home saw one Elisabeth Nash, born at Enfield, about 25 Years old, just about Three foot high, not the breadth of my little finger under or over. Her Hands show Age more than anything else. Has no Brests. By reason of her thickness and weight can goe but very sorrily. Can speak and sing but not very conveniently, because her Tongue is bigger than can be well stowed in her Mouth. Blessed be God for my Stature, unto which neither I, nor my Dear Mother, my Nurse, could add one Cubit.

June 4. Green Hastings, i.e. Pease, are cry'd at 6[d] a Peck, in little carts. Cous. Hull, Mrs. Perry and Bedford come from Portsmouth. I meet them at the Cross Keys in Gracious Street.

June 15. Being at Mrs. Calvin's alone in a Chamber, while they were getting ready dinner, I, as I walked about, began to crave a Blessing, and when went about it remembered my Cloaths I had bought just before, and then it came into my mind that it was most material to ask a blessing on my Person: so I mentally pray'd God to bless my Flesh, Bones, Blood and Spirits, Meat, Drink and Aparrel. And at Dinner, paring the Crust of my Bread, I cut my Thumb, and spilt some of my Blood, which word I very unusually, or never before, have used in prayer to my present remembrance.

June 16. Last night I dreamed of my Wife, and of Father Hull, that he had buried somebody, and was presently intending to goe to Salem.

June 20th Writ to Cousin Stoeke, answering his of the 10th *inst.* Last Sabbath day night dreamed of the death of my dear Wife, which made me very heavy.

Wednesday, June 26. Mr. Mather, his Son, Cousin Hull and self, set out for Cambridge, 45 miles: got thither by 7 o'clock, with one set 4 Horses. Lay at the Red Lion in Petit Curie.

Thorsday, June 27, Mr. Littel, Fellow of Emanuel Colledge, shows us the Gardens, Walks, New Chapel, Gallery, Library of the Colledge, in it a Bible MS. of Wickliffe's Translation. Mr. John Cotton and Hooker had been Fellows, as appeared by Tables hanging up. Dr. Preston, Head of it. The Street where it stands is called Preacher's Street, from Black Friars formerly resident there. Note. Said Fellow had in 's Chamber, Sir Roger Le Strange, Jesus Salvator and K. Charles, 2[d], hanging up together. Saw St. John's Colledg, which stands by the River. Hath a good Library and many Rarities, among which was a petrified Cheese, being about half a Cheese. Trinity Colledge is very large, and the new Case for the Library very magnificent, paved with marble checkered black and white; under, stately walk on brave stone; the Square very large, and in midst of it a Fountain. In the Hall many Sparrows inhabit, which is not known of any Hall beside. At meal-Times they feed of Crums, and will approach very near Men. King's Colledge Chapel is very stately. Went on the top of the inward Stone Roof, and on the top of the outward Lead-Roof, and saw the Town, and Ely about 10 miles off. Below, on the side, under little Arches, is the Library. Mr. Littel dined with us at our Inn: had a Legg Mutton boiled and Colly-Flowers, Carrets, Rosted Fowls, and a dish of Pease. Three Musicians came in, two Harps and a Violin, and gave us Musick. View the Publick Library, which is in form of an L, one part not fil'd with books, some vacant shelves to bespeak Benefactors. Saw the Divinity School over which the Regent House is. The School fair and large. Public Acts are kept in St. Marie's Church, over against which the Schools are. Just before night our Landladie's Son had us along Bridge-Street, and shewed us Sidney-Colledg as I take it, and be sure Magdalen Colledg on the other side of the River, on which side there is none but that. Went to the

Castle-Hill, where is a very pleasant Prospect, the Prison and Sessions House just by, which is very ordinary, like a Cow-House. Cattell having free egrees and regress there. Gallows just by it in a Dale, convenient for Spectators to stand all round on the rising Ground. In sum Cambridge is better than it shows for at first; the meanness of the Townbuildings, and most of the Colledges being Brick.

June 28. Mr. Harwood and I step'd out and saw Queen's Colledge, which is a very good one, in the Garden a Dial on the Ground, Hours cut in Box. The River has there also a quicker Stream, being a little below the Mill: have several Bridges to go over to their Groves. Over against it stands Katherine Hall, the New Buildings of which are some of the goodliest in Cambridge. By it, the Printing Room, which is about 60 foot long and 20 foot broad. Six Presses. Had my Cousin Hull and my name printed there. Paper windows, and a pleasant Garden along one side between Katherine Hall and that. Had there a Print of the Combinations. As came Homewards, saw Audley Inn, or End. I can't tell which is the right name. 'Tis a stately Palace. Din'd at Safron-Walden: went out and saw the Safron Roots, which are Ten Shillings a Bushel, about an Acre might yield an hundred pounds and more. Were just dugg up to be planted at Abington, a little place not far off. Have a fair Church. I writt out the Lord Audley's Epitaph. Went into the Vault and saw the Earl of Suffolk's Coffin, who died January last: stands on Tressels, and may see it in the outside at the Grate. Outside is black Velvet, and a small plate of Coper, telling time of 's Death: rest is garnished. Lodg'd at Hockerred, pertaining to Bishop-Stafford. In the even, Mr. Sam. Mather and I viewed Trisday's Well and Castle Hill. Set out on Satterday, about 4 *mane,* breakfasted at Eping. Got to Mr. Croper's about Eleven aclock. He keeps a Coffee House. While Mr. Mather read the Votes I took Thorsdays Letter and read the News of Boston, and then gave it Mr. Mather to read. We were surpris'd with joy. At Change Capt. Hutchinson shew'd me Capt. Byfield's Letter, which comes by Toogood. They had the News on Change that day we went to Cambridge.

June 7. Goe and hear Mr. Stretton, and sit down with him at the Lord's Super. He invites me to diner. Text, Hosea, 2. 14. Before Sermon read the 32 Psalm, the 50th of Jeremiah, the 12th of Matthew. Had one plate of bread, about 5 Bottles of Wine, and two Silver Cups. At night about 10 aclock, a great fire breaks forth in Mincing Lane. I was hardly asleep between 10 and 11, before there was a sad Alarm and Noys of Carrs to carry away Goods. A Woman lately brought to Bed was fain to be remov'd to another House. I went and sat a little while with Mr. Mather in Fan [Fen] Church Street.

July 8. Went with Mr. Brattle and swam in the Thames, went off from the Temple Stairs, and had a Wherry to wait on us: I went in in my Drawers. I think it hath been healthfull and refreshing to me.

July 9. Cousin Brattle, his wife and Daughter, Mrs. Shinkfield, Mr. Crossman, were invited to Diner by Cous. Hull. Afterward, He and I went to Stepney, saw Thomas Saffin's Tomb, one end of 't joins to the wall. 50s was given for the Ground. Tis a very large burying-place. Were to be ten buried this night: we saw several Graves open and the Bones thick on the Top. Saw a Bowling Green where is 3 or 4 Sets of Bowls. The Lord help me aright to improve my Flesh, Bones and Spirits, which are so soon to become useless, and it may be expos'd in one part or other of God's Creation.

Monday, July 15th. I rid to Tyburn, and saw Eighteen Persons, 16 Men and 2 Women, fall. They were unruly in the Prison, which hasten'd the Execution. Din'd in Great Russell Street, view'd the House and Walks of Lord Montague: then ridd to Hemsted. Montague House makes a goodly Shew that way. Hempsted is a most sweet and pleasant place for Air and shady Groves. Bought the Gazett there. From thence ridd to Highgate, which is about a Mile.

July 17. Mr. Mather, on Change, told Capt. Hutchinson and Sam. Apleton that he had put in their Names as Witnesses to Sir Edmund's [Andros] raising Money without an Assembly. Ask'd where was Capt. Hutchinson. I shewed and went with him to him, and Mr. Mather ask'd him to be at Westminster at such a time, but said not a word to me. Afterwards I went home, and then went to Mr. Whiting's and told him that I could testify, and Mr. Walker that collected the Money was in Town. He seem'd little to heed it, and said I might be there: he knew not that I could testify: but he seems plainly to be offended, and for my part I can't tell for what. A Moneth or two agoe Mr. Mather spake something about it, and I said I could not tell whether 'twere so convenient then, because we hop'd every day for the Parliament Act to come forth, and thought Sir Edmund might have friends there, and such a thing as this might make them more desperately eger to hinder the Bill. But now the Bill is even despair'd of, and our friends in N. E. are in for Cakes and Ale, and we must doe all we may and swim or sink with them.

Monday, July 29, Standing in the Shop about 7. *mane,* Mr. John Usher comes to the door, which surpriseth me. Foy is at Pezans. Mr. Usher came to town Satterday night. Sir William [Phips] and Lawson arriv'd; all friends well. He knew not of his coming away till a day or two before. Is very confident, and hopes to be going home in seven weeks, or to be at home in little more than that time. I go and acquaint Mr. Mather, who had heard nothing of it. He hastens to tother end of the town. The Lord save N. E. I spoke to Mr. Usher not to do harm, as knowing the great King we must finally apear before: because he spake of going to the King. King is proclaim'd at Boston. Mr. Cook had like to have been kill'd with a fall from his horse. This 29th July the Jews have great joy by reason of a Priest come to Town in the Harwich Coach, they having not had one a long time. Mr. Ekins his Wife and Daughter here.

July 31. N. E. Convention printed here, 500 Copies. Visited Mr. James, but found him not at home: Sat a little while with 's Daughter, but he came not in. Left Him N. E. Revolution and Convention.

Aug. 11. Sung, or rather wept and chatter'd, the 142 Psalm, in course. Mrs. Perry ill, kept her Bed yesterday.

Tuesday, Aug. 13. Came with Capt. Hutchinson, Mr. Brattle, Partridge, Apleton from Salutation at Billingsgate to Woolige, where din'd with Mr. Sam. Allen; saw the King's Ropeyard and the Canon in the Waren. Ropeyard nine score paces long. From thence to Graves-End in the even. Went on board the America about 10 aclock, hurting my shin against the end of a Chest going into the Cabbin, from which I supose in the night issued a pretty deal of Blood, and stain'd my Shirt, which startled me when rose in the morning at Graves-End, where I lodg'd with Mr. Brattle.

Aug. 14th. Mr. Mather comes down, and chides us severely that none staid for Him, and seeing the Ship not gone, goes to London again. I gave him my Letter by Cous. Hull, which had writt to inform him, not knowing of 's coming, and beg'd his pardon, thinking I might be more servicable here and at Deal, than at London.

Aug. 15. Write to Cous. Quinsey by Bant, with Invoice and Bill of Lading, Mr. Vaughan's Cheese, his and Bro. Sewall's Anotations: Wife's Stockings. Mr. Brattle and I ride to Chatham, dine at the Crown, see the Dock and 33 Spiners of Rope-yarn, goe on board the Britania, so to Sittingburn, lodge at the George: rains hard in the night. In the morn a good Ring of 6 Bells entertains us: no whether for the Ringers to work.

Aug. 16. From Sittingburn to Canterbury in the Rain, dine at the Crown: Mr. Powell: send for Cou. Fissenden, his Sister dead since my being there, and my Landlady at the red Lion dead. Bought each of us a pair of Gloves of Mr. Chiever. From Canterbury to Sandwich with the Post. Sandwich a large place and wall'd about, 10 miles from Canterbury, in a very flat, level country; Crek comes up to it. From thence to Deal 5 miles, built on the Beach. Land we ride over is call'd the Downs, and the Castle, Sand-Down Castle. Lodge at the 3 Kings. Mrs. Mary Watts, a widow, our Landlady.

Satterday, Aug. 17. Goe to the new Meeting house that is building for Mr. Larner in the 3[d] and lower street of Deal, towards the north end, which is, within the Walls, 34 wide and 41 foot long: 2 Galleries, one at each end, of 4 Seats apiece. Roof is double with a Gutter in the middle: built with Brick covered with Tile. Went to see Sand-Down Castle: but a Coach was there to bring out a Corps. The little Sand-Cliffs and iner Sand Hills, something like Plum Iland little hills, give name no Question to that part of the Sea now call'd the Downs. Deal is built between the 2 forlands, about 5 mile from the North-forland, 3 parallel Streets, the upermost built on the very Beach, daring the Sea.

Aug. 27. Tuesday. Exceter sumons all aboard about 4 p. m. Came to us in the Ship-Arbour, Mr. Lamin. Got aboard between 6 and 7. The shifting the wind was unexpected. No publick Prayer in the even. Very sore night for Thunder and Lightning. Were about to sail at midnight and the wind chopt about, and blew so hard that were glad to drop another Anchor again.

Aug. 22—26. Enclos'd in Cou. Hull's to me. Mr. Mather, Sam, Mr. Brattle and I came aboard first in a boat: gave 3[s]: Others came aboard in the night.

Satterday, Sept. 14th. Went on Board when the Ship under sail, but wind veer'd against us, so came again to Deal.

Sept. 15. Sabbath-Day. Went aboard: the Fleet sail'd, Wind N. West, veer'd fairer and fairer: in the Night was much Lightening and loud Thunder. Exceter convoy. Sail by Dover, Folkston, Rumney.

Monday, Sept. 16. is rainy, so can't well see the Land.

Tuesd. Sept. 17. Come up with Portland, wind at north, or thereabouts, and very strong. We are almost the farthest of all from the Shoar, and had lost the Exceter in the night: find her in the morning. Am ready to wish myself with Mr. Mather and my Namesake, recovering of the Small Pocks at Deal. After, sail with the Barclay-Castle, and on Wednesday morning, betwen 8 and 9. fair wether. Came to an Anchor in Plimouth Sound, the Tide being made strongest against us, and the wind but bare.

Wednes. Sept. 18. About 6. p. m. the Ship being got up higher, we went ashoar. Mr. Brattle and I lodg'd together at the house of one Mr. John Jenings near the Key. Note. In coming up a Privateer fell foul of us, took off our Ancient-Staff, much discompos'd our wooden Guns, put Will's [Merry's] Thumb out of joint, and some other damage.

Sept. 24. Mr. Brattle, Dr. Edwards and I walk to Stone-house, 1½ Mile from Plimouth, a Causey thither. Visit Capt. Hutchinson and Mr. Partridge, who lodge there in a very mean Chamber.

Sept. 25. Went with Mr. Bedford, who shewed us the Cittadel, and Sir Nicholas Staning, the Lieut. Governour, who gave order that he should have us into his house, and then came in himself, and drank to us in a Glass of Ale, that being the drink I chose and Mr. Brattle. Two Men were laid Neck and heels. In the afternoon went aboard and fetch'd ashoar my Trunk: Landlady's Brother and Daughter went with us.

Sept. 26. Went with Capt. Hutchinson, Brattle and Partridge to Milbrook in Cornwall, and there din'd well for 6[d] apiece. Went by the Beach and came home the uper Way by Maker Church, which is a large fair one upon the Hill, and so a very good Mark for Seamen. Go over Crimble Passage to Mount Edgcomb. Milbrook is part in Devonshire and part in Cornwall. Dr. Edwards came after us, and overtook us coming home. Milbrook People goe to Maker Church.

Sept. 28. Mr. Brattle and I walk out and see the Course of the Water brought by Sir Francis Drake, Ano, 1591, as apears by an Inscription. We are told it is brought so winding about, that notwithstanding the Hilliness of the Country, no Troughs are used to carry it over Valleys. Many very good Overshut Mills driven by it. Upon another Conduit is engraven, *Redigit desertum in Stagnum,* 1593. It's brought 9 or 10 miles, from Ruper Down, deriv'd from a River as one goes to Tavistock, comonly call'd Testick.

Oct. 5. The Ships inward bound sail for London. Dr. Edwards in Weare. Went to Grimble [Cremil] Passage. Spake to Mr. Jacobs when came home. Saw an Ensign buried. The Company was drawn up in one Rank, Pikes, next the House of Mourning. When ready to goe, rank'd six, came to funeral Posture: Colours cover'd with Mourning went after Pikes, then Captain, then Parson and Corps. Posted the Pikes *ex adverso,* mutually, when Service saying. Gave 3 Volleys, but saw not the Colours open all the while. The Tattoo with which the Watch is set goes thus:—

Dūrrera dūm
Dūrrera dūm
Dūrrera dūm
Dūrrera dūm
Dūm dūm Dūm dūm Dūrrera dūm
Dūm dūm Dūm dūm Dūrrera dūm
Dūrrera dūm

About three Sets of Drums take it one after another.

Thorsday, Oct. 10. Set Sail out of Plimouth Sound with a fair wind, East, N.E. Capt Allen having left the Ship I was about to leave it too, but he returning I returned.

Oct. 11. Pleasant wether. Two Rogues to windward of us, which the Man of War keeps off but can't come up with them: in the night a meer Calm.

Sabbath, Oct. 13. The Convoys leave us when scarce 40 Leagues from Silly. Night very tempestuous.

Oct. 14. Make a shift to sail West, and West and by South. A Scattering day. I broke my white Plate.

Tuesd. Oct. 15. Is a strong West wind, or West by South. Saw a Rainbow or two this day. Sail to the Northwest.

Oct. 16. The wind is just in our Teeth. Last night presently after going to bed, turn'd out in some Consternation because of a Squawl, and danger of runing on 2 or 3 Ships. Many Porposes, or Hering Hogs seen this day.

Nov. 13. Are in 43. Latitude. Sound, but find no bottom; so supose we are Southward of the Bank, 4 p. m. Birds and coldness of the Water are indications that we are near it.

Nov. 14. Fair Wind and Wether. Sound, but find no bottom. Wether so mild that eat at the Table on the Deck, 4 or 5 times together.

Friday, Nov. 15. 9 *Mane*. Sound, and find ground in 45 or 50 fathoms. Bring the Ship to and put out fishing Lines. Mr. Fanevill only catches a good Cod, which had several small Fish in him, supose to be Anchoves, however, very much resemble that Fish. Very foggy wether. Judge are on the Southermost point of the Bank. And now we have tasted afresh of American Fare. Lord, give me to taste more of thyself everywhere, always adequately good. Nov. 16. N.W.NN.W. Nov. 17. North Wind. Calm.

Wednesday, Nov. 20. East Wind. Sail 6 and 7 Knotts. Note. Last night about 2 aclock, Mr. Partridge came into Cabin and told us the Ships were come up with us, which made several suspect them to be Rogues, and put us in fear lest they should be Enemies. The small Arms are charg'd. But in the morning, by putting out our Ancients, find them to be Jersey-Men, our Friends. The best Sailer spake with us: he shortens sail for his partner, who sails heavy and hath sprung a Leak. Thinks we are the hindermost of all the Fleet. So, by the good Hand of God, that which cause of Fear and thoughtfulness to us, is turned into matter of Pleasure and

Comfort. Blessed be his Name. Yesterday Observed: found the Latitude 41 and 25 Minutes.

Nov. 20, 1689. If it should Please God, who is Righteous in all his Ways, and Holy in all his Works, to put an End to my Life before I come to Boston, my Desire is that the Rev. Mr. John Hale, of Beverly, have given him the Sett of Pool's Synopsis which I bought of Mrs. Mills, quarto 5 Volumes: And that Mr. Charles, the Son of the Reverend Mr. Israel Chauncy, of Stratford, have given him another Sett of Mr. Pool's Synopsis Criticorum, in five Books: And that the Money laid out with the Winthrops, on account of the Land the South Meeting House stands on, be given the persons concerned, that so I [who?] have done them no good, may doe them no hurt. Provided no damage hapen by a Bond I have given the Winthrops, or one of their Husbands, a Copy of, which is in my Papers. And that my dear Brother, Mr. Stephen Sewall, have given him my new Cloath-colour'd suit with the Chamlet Cloak. And if I have not done it already in my Will, left at Boston, I desire that my Namesakes, Sam. Toppan and Sam. Sewall of Newbury, have Five pounds apiec given them by my dear Mother and Wife, unto whom my other Friends are equally known as to my Self. I desire my dear Wife to accept of my Watch as a Token of my Love. And as to the things mentioned on this and the other side of this Leaf, I leave them to the Discretion and good liking of my dear Mother and Wife, to doe them or leave them undone, because the Estate is theirs. As witness my Hand.

SAM SEWALL.

Nov. 24. Supose are now in the Latitude of Cape Cod, or near it: Sound, but find no bottom: Wind at West, but by night veers to the Southward, so as to ly West Norwest. Very pleasant wether, but no Observation.

Nov. 28. Stand to the Norward, N.W. and N.W. and by Nor. E. Have a good Observation: are in the Latitude of 42 and 50, which, it seems, is the Latitude of Cape Anne. Hoist up the Top Sails, to see if can make the Northern Land. See a small Boat gone adrift. About 3 p. m. Samay goes up the Shrouds and on the Top Sail Yard spies Land, and takes the Purse. The Mate Wallis and Guner say 'tis Pigeon-Hill on Cape Anne. Guner, who is a Coaster, saith also that he sees Newbury Old Town Hill, and Rowly Hill. All see it plain on the Deck before Sunset. Pleasant wether, clear skie, smooth sea. Sail N.W. Blessed be God who has again brought me to a sight of New-England.

Nov. 29. Most pleasant day. Find the Land we saw yesterday to be Agamenticus Hills. Canot wether Cape Anne, so goe into Piscataqua River: land at the Great Island: from thence to the Bank in the night. Capt. Hutchinson and I lodge at Mr. Crafford's. Send Madam Vaughan her Cheese.

Satterday, Nov. *ult.* Ride to Newbury. Friends there exceeding glad to see me, being surpris'd at my coming that way.

Dec. 2. Came to Boston: Staid so long at the Ferry that it was between 9. and 10. before I got into my own House. Mr. Cook only came with me from Govr. Bradstreets.

Thorsday, Dec. 5. Capt. Hutchinson and I took our Oaths; Govr. Bradstreet there: Deputies treated us at Wing's after Lecture, as Major and Capt. Apleton, Mr. Eps and others had done at Ipswich as came along.

Friday, January 3. I treated the Magistrates at James Meers; viz: Dept. Governour, Mr. Winthrop, Richards, Russel, Johnson, Apleton, Hutchinson, Cook, Hawthorn, Smith, Philips, Shrimpton, Addington, Swain, with Mr. Willard, Belcher Bromfield; I think all these there.

Jan. 9th. Tho. Hawkins, Pirat. was Tried and found guilty.

Jan. 10th. It falls to my Daughter Elisabeth's Share to read the 24. of Isaiah, which she doth with many Tears not being very well, and the Contents of the Chapter, and Sympathy with her draw Tears from me also. Mr. Dudley went home yesterday, or the night before; but it seems refuseth to pay the Guards except the Council will order the Sum.

Sabbath, Jan. 12. Richard Dumer, a flourishing youth of 9 years old, dies of the Small Pocks. I tell Sam. of it and what need he had to prepare for Death, and therefore to endeavour really to pray when he said over the Lord's Prayer: He seem'd not much to mind, eating an Aple; but when he came to say, Our father, he burst out into a bitter Cry, and when I askt what was the matter and he could speak, he burst out into a bitter Cry and said he was afraid he should die. I pray'd with him, and read Scriptures comforting against death, as, O death where is thy sting, &c. All things yours. Life and Immortality brought to light by Christ, &c. 'Twas at noon.

Friday, 17. Return homeward. Call and see Mr. Torrey and his wife; Cous. Hunt and her Sons Jn° and Daniel. Lodge at Unkle Quinsey's, coming in the night from Weymouth for fear of Snow. Got home between 11. and 12. Went after diner to the Town-House, to Mr. Addington, from thence to Mr. Browning's, from thence with Mr. Cotton Mather to the Prisoners who were condemned on Friday. Spoke to, and pray'd with Pounds and others; then with Coward, Johnson and others. Gave him [Mr. Mather] two Duzen Books bound, *viz.* Right thoughts. &c. Sermons to his Father Philips, and on the Ark.

Monday, Jan. 27. Five were order'd to be executed, but, chiefly through Mr. Winthrop's earnestness in Reprieving, only Tho. Johnson dies. Had join'd in reprieving Pounds and Buck at the Governour's, and then got away; but Mr. Winthrop, Addington, Shrimpton followed me to my house with another Writing for Hawkins, which Winthrop and Shrimpton had signed, and got me to sign: He was ready to be turn'd off before it took effect, which gave great disgust to the People: I fear it was ill done. Governour, Winthrop, Shrimpton, Addington, Phillips, repriev'd Coward, and most seem'd to desire that he and his 3 companions might be spar'd. Some in the Council thought Hawkins, because he got out of the Combination before Pease was kill'd, might live as well as Coward; so I rashly sign'd, hoping so great an inconvenience would not have followed. Let not God impute Sin.

Feb. 8. and 9th Schenectady, a village 20 miles above Albany, destroy'd by the French. 60 Men, Women and Children murder'd. Women with Child ripp'd up, Children had their brains dash'd out. Were surpris'd about 11. or 12 aclock Satterday night, being divided, and secure.

In the Storm of Snow that then fell Skipar Dotey, his Son Jn°, and Elkana Watson, were cast away on Ba[rn]stable Bar. Bodies not found, and 'tis fear'd they are murder'd by a free Negro and Indians.

Feb. 24. Monday, Govr. Bradstreet and Lady, Mr. Stoughton, Major Hutchinson and wife, Mr. Willard, Mr. Moodey and wife, Mrs. Mather, Maria, Mr. Allen and wife, Cous. Dumer and wife, Cous. Quinsey and wife, Mr. Cotton Mather, Mr. Tho. Brattle, who with Mother, wife and Self. made Twenty, Marshal Green waited: Sat all well at the Table. Mr. Cotton Mather returned Thanks in an excellent maner: Sung part of the Six and fiftieth Psalm, in Mr. Miles Smith's version, Thou knowst how long I have from home—to the End. Mr. Mather was minded to have that Translation: I set it to Windsor Tune. N.B. The bitterness in our Cups, was that, the Massacre at Schenectady by the French; the amazing news on't was by Post brought to Town this day. Govr. Bradstreet brought the Papers and read them before and after diner. At last, Mr. Danforth, Major Richards, Major General Winthrop, Col. Shrimpton, Mr. Addington came in, and dispatcht Orders to the Majors to stand upon their Guard, To Capt. Price, Senr. Capt. in Salem Regiment.

Just about diner time Mr. Nelson comes in and gets me to subscribe 100. to the Proposals against the French. I thought 'twas time to doe something, now were thus destroy'd by Land too. Mr. Danforth looks very sorrowfully. Mr. Stoughton thinks best to prosecute vigorously the business against the Eastern French.

TO THE CONSTABLES OF BOSTON,

AND EVERY OF THEM.

You are required in their Majesties Names to Walk through the several parts of the Town this day, and take effectual care to suppress and dissipate all unlawful Assemblies, or tumultuous gathering together of people for the Shailing or throwing at Cocks, and such like Disorders, tending to the disturbance of their Majesties Liege People, and breach of the Peace, contrary to the wholsom Laws on that behalf made and provided, particularly, those entituled Cruelty, and Prescriptions. Hereof you may not fail. Dated in Boston the fourth day of March 16$\frac{89}{90}$. Annoque Reg. and Reginæ Willielms and Mariæ — Secundo.

SIMON BRADSTREET *Govr.*
WAIT WINTHROP
ELISHA HUTCHINSON } *Asist^st.*
SAM SEWALL
ISAAC ADDINGTON

I gave the preceding Warrant to Thomas Banister, Constable, who said he would take effectual Care about it. Another was given to Capt. Prout, to be deliver'd to a Constable at the North end of the Town, only it was given on Monday night at James Meer's and so the Governour had not sign'd it.

March 4, 16$\frac{89}{90}$. Sam. Haugh, 14 years old last February, chuses me for his Guardian. Solomon Raynsford introducing of him with a pretty handsome Speech for my acceptance. Dept. Governour was by and told him he must now hearken to me and take me for his Father. George Monk brought in a Dish of Fritters, but Major Hutchinson, Mr. Addington and my self eat none of them, only Major Richards (of the Court) did eat.

March 18, 16$\frac{99}{90}$. I gave New-Roxbury the name of Woodstock because of it's nearness to Oxford, for the sake of Queen Elizabeth, and the notable Meetings that have been held at the place bearing that Name in England, some of which Dr. Gilbert inform'd me of when in England. It stands on a Hill, I saw it as went to Coventry, but left it on the Left hand. Some told Capt. Ruggles that I gave the name, and put words in his Mouth to desire of me a Bell for the Town.

Friday, March 21, $16\frac{89}{90}$. Madam Bradstreet, Mrs. Moodey, Mrs. Mather and my wife ride in the hackney Coach to Dorchester, dine with Mr. Stoughton. It should have been on Wednesday, when the news came indistinctly in the afternoon of the Surprisal of Salmon Falls. This Friday morn before they went to Mr. Stoughton's, the dolefull news came that between 80. and 100. persons were kill'd and carried away, were taken by surprise about break of day: no Watch kept: are about half French, half Indians. Hopewood Capt. of the Indians, Artel [Francois Hertel] of the French. Hampshire General got 100. Men and came up with the Enemy about Sun-set and fought them till night took away the sight of them. One Frenchman taken making up his pack who gives an account as above.

This day Capt. Townsend is appointed Comander in Chief.

Satterday, March 22. Sir William Phips offers himself to go in person; the Governour sends for me, and tells me of it, I tell the Court; they send for Sir William who accepts to goe, and is appointed to Comand the Forces; Major Townsend relinquishes with Thanks. Sir William had been sent to at first; but some feared he would not goe; others thought his Lady could not consent. Court makes Sir William free, and Swear him Major Generall, and several others. Adjourn to Boston, Wednesday 14 night one aclock.

March 24, $16\frac{89}{90}$. Eight Companies and Troops Train. I goe into the field, pray with the South Company, Exercise them in a few Distances, Facings, Doublings; before which Thanked them for their Respect in mentioning me when in England, warning the Company in my Name; and told them the place

I was in required more Time and Strength than I had, so took leave of them.

March 25. Drums are beat through the Town for Volunteers.

April 4, 1690. Major Richards, Hutchinson, Col. Shrimpton, Mr. Addington and my self went to the Castle to view what Capt. Fayerwether had done, and what was proper for him further to doe in making Batteries, and putting the place into yet a more defensible posture. Went to Dear-Island, and saw how the sea wash'd it away. Then went to Apple-Island, to the Castle again, and there din'd; suffer'd no Guns to be fired; but the Captain caus'd the Flagg to be hoisted all the while we were there, in token of Respect. Cost us 5^s 8^d apiec.

April 24. Set sail, leaving our Horses and taking our Bridles and Saddles in the Sloop.

Satterday, April 26. got into Oyster Bay [L. I.], the wind being Contrary, and there anchored.

April 27. Went ashore, rid to Hempsted through Jerico, to hear Mr. Hubbard, but he was at York: Staid at Mr. Jacksons, read Chapters, and Mr. Stoughton prayed excellently.

April 28. Rid to Jamaica, there din'd with Mr. Prudden, Pastor of the Church there. From thence to Brookland [Brooklyn], where Mr. Edsal met us with a File or two of Troopers, got to the Ferry about 12. aclock. Went over and din'd with the Governour. Lodg'd at Mr. Mariot's; but were so disturb'd that were overcome by the Governour's importunity and lodg'd at his House. Major Gold and Mr. Pitkin met us there for Conecticut.

May 5. Got on board our Sloop, leaving Capt. Du Peyster's Diner. Wind sprung up fair, got well throw Hell-Gate, went ashore at Dr. Taylor's near the White Stone, wooded and watered: Sailed again with a fair wind.

On Wednesday Morn, May 7th there was a Fogg, which put us to our shifts, not knowing which way to sail; but it pleased God to clear the Air, so as we saw our Course, Block-Island, Point-Judith, and got in about noon, being their Election day. Gov[r]. Bull furnish'd us with Beds for the voyage; Din'd at Mr. Hedge's. Henry Bull chosen Governour, Major Green of Warwick, Dept. Governour. Rid to Bristow, lodg'd at Capt. Byfield's.

May 8. Rid to Billinges, where Mr. Lee met us in his way homeward, gave an account of the wellfare of my family, having din'd with my Mother and wife at Cous. Dummer's. Pray'd with us.

May 9. Friday, Rid to Dedham and there refresh'd, so home by 12. or thereabouts; visited Mr. Eliot and Mr. Walters by the way. Mr. Stoughton and I waited on the Governour and I on the Council with Gov[r]. Leisler's Letter.

Found my Family all well, save Sam's sore in his neck, and Hanah droops as though would have the Small Pocks. Note. I have had great heaviness on my Spirit before, and in this journey; and I resolved that if it pleas'd God to bring me to my family again, I would endeavour to serve Him better in Self-denial, Fruitfullness, Not pleasing Men, open Conversation, not being solicitous to seem in some indifferent things what I was not, or at least to conceal what I was; Endeavouring to goe and come at God's call and not otherwise; Labouring more constantly and throwly to Examin my self before sitting down to the Lord's Table. Now the good Lord God of his infinite Grace help me to perform my Vows, and give me a filial Fear of Himself, and save me from the fear of Man that brings a Snare.

May 10. Hanah takes a Vomit, her Grandmother earnestly desiring it. Has the Small Pocks very favourably, keeps her Bed but three or four days; about 50 or 60 in her face; pretty many on her Wrists.

May 19th Begins to keep below with her Brother, and Sister Betty.

May 26. Mr. Cotton Mather prays with Eliakim.

May 28. Small Pocks apear.

Sabbath, June 1. Betty and Joseph are taken. Betty very delirious.

Monday, June 9th Joseph hath a very bad night, as also the night before.

June 10th. He grows better and the Small Pocks doe aparently dye away in his face.

Wednesday, June 11th. We put Sam. to Bed, having the Small Pocks come out upon him, as the Physician and we judge. Betty is so well as to Goe into Mother Hull's Chamber, and keep Jane Company, between 9 and 10. *mane.*

June 17th Tuesday. Sam. rises and sits up a good while very hearty and strong. Blessed be God. This day one of my Shirts goes to lay out a Man dead at Nurse Hurds of this distemper, being a Stranger.

Sabbath, Augt. 10th Went to see Cous. Quinsey; read the 102, Psal. and begin 103. pray'd, and so went home. Put up a Bill at his request. Just after Contribution in the Afternoon, was call'd out, Cousin being very bad, so far as I could perceive. He desired me to pray, which I did: Afterward sent for Mr. Willard, and He pray'd, then Cousin pull'd his hand out of the Bed, and gave it to Mr. Willard. Seem'd to pray himself; but I could hear little except Jesus Christ; breath'd quick and hard, till at last abated and He quietly expired about Seven aclock. Mother Hull and I being there. I have parted with a cordial fast Friend, such an one as I shall hardly find. The Lord fit me for my Change and help me to wait till it come. Cousin was concern'd what he should doe for Patience, but God graciously furnish'd him, and has now translated Him to that State and place wherein He has no occasion for any.

Tuesday, Augt. 12. About 7. P.M. we lay the Body of Cous. Daniel Quinsey in my Father's Tomb. Mr. Serjeant, Dumer, H. Usher, Davis, Williams, Coney, Bearers. I led the

Widow, then the Children, next, Mr. T. Brattle, Mrs. Shepard, H. Newman, Mistress Margaret, Mr. Willard, Mother Hull, Mr. Parson, my wife and so on. Note. My wife was so ill could hardly get home, taking some harm in going in Pattens, or some wrench, so had a great flux of Blood, which amaz'd us both, at last my wife bad me call Mrs. Ellis, then Mother Hull, then the Midwife, and throw the Goodness of God was brought to Bed of a Daughter between 3. and four aclock, Aug. 13th 1690. *mane*. Mrs. Elisabeth Weeden, Midwife. Had not Women nor other preparations as usually, being wholly surpris'd, my wife expecting to have gone a Moneth longer.

Augt. 17. Mr. Willard keeps his Sabbath at Roxbury, and so the Baptism of my little Daughter is deferred to the next Lord's Day.

Sabbath-day, August the four and twentieth, 1690. I publish my little Daughter's name to be Judith, held her up for Mr. Willard to baptize her. She cried not at all, though a pretty deal of water was poured on her by Mr. Willard when He baptized her: Six others were baptized at the same time; Capt. Davis's Son James, and a grown person, Margaret Clifford, two of them. I named my Daughter Judith for the sake of her Grandmother and great Grandmother, who both wore that Name, and the Signification of it very good: The Lord grant that we may have great cause to praise Him on her account and help her to speak the Jews Language and to forget that of Ashdod. Nehem. 13. 24. And that she may follow her Grandmother Hull, as she follows Christ, being not slothfull in Business, fervent in Spirit, serving the Lord. Her Prayers and Painstaking for all my Children are incessant, voluntary, with condescension to the meanest Services night and day: that I judg'd I could in justice doe no less than endeavour her remembrance by putting her Name on one of her Grand-Daughters. I have now had my health and oportunity to offer up Nine Children to God in Baptisme. Mr. Tho. Thacher baptized the two eldest; John and Samuel; Mr. Samuel Willard baptized the Seven younger. Lord grant that I who have thus solemnly and frequently named the name of the Lord Jesus, may depart from Iniquity; and that mine may be more His than Mine, or their own.

Augt. 29, 1690. I watch at night with about 30. men. Word was Skenectady. Nathan Clarke of Newbury buried this week, died Augt. 25.

Sept. 1, 1690. Eight Companies Train. Governour dines at Mr. Pain's with the South Company. Capt. Frary exercises the Company. Joseph is carried into the Comon to take the air and see the men.

Thorsday Sept. 11th Being crowded in the Pue, by reason Mr. Hutchinson and Sergeant constantly sit there and claim Propriety, so Mr. Usher is forced to take my place; having also found that sitting so near the out-side of the House causeth me in Winter-time to take cold in my head, I removed into Gallery, and sat with Dept. Governour, Mr. Russel, Major Hutchinson, where had very convenient sitting.

Sept. 14th I Watch, Word was Salmon-Falls, had a very comfortable night; only between 3. and 4. were disquieted by Guns fired at Charlestown, and Drum beat: But I did not observe a continual Beat of the Drum, so caus'd not an Alarm; and about day a Messenger was sent over who told us the occasion was some Indians seen in their back fields. Run-away Servants they apear to be; by which means the Town was generally rais'd: But throw God's goodness Trouble at Boston prevented.

Sept. 17th. Fast at Mr. Mathers.

Sept. 18th. Mr. Willard's Edward dies of a Convulsion Fit.

Sept. 20. Is buried at Roxbury in Mr. Eliot's Tomb, I was at the Funeral. Rain and Thunder this day after a great deal of dry wether which made it extream dusty. Mr. Walter went to Prayer: Mrs. Willard sick, and not at the Grave. My little Judith languishes and moans, ready to die.

Sabbath, Sept. 21. About 2 *mane,* I rise, read some Psalms and pray with my dear Daughter. Between 7. and 8. (Mr. Moodey preaches in the Forenoon,) I call Mr. Willard, and he prays. Told Mr. Walter of her condition at the funeral, desiring him to give her a lift towards heaven. Mr. Baily sat with me in the Afternoon. I acquainted Him. Between 7. and 8. in the evening the child died, and I hope sleeps in Jesus.

Sept. 22. In the even, Mr. Moodey, Allen, Mather come from Mrs. Clark's Funeral to see us. Mr. Moodey and I went before the other came, to neighbor Hord, who lay dying; where also Mr. Allen came in. Nurse Hord told her Husband who was there, and what he had to say; whether he desir'd them to pray with him: He said with some earnestness, Hold your tongue, which was repeated three times to his wive's repeated intreaties; once he said, Let me alone, or, be quiet, (whether that made a fourth or was one of the three do not remember) and, My Spirits are gon. At last Mr. Moodey took him up pretty roundly and told him he might with the same labour have given a pertinent answer. When were ready to come away Mr. Moodey bid him put forth a little Breath to ask prayer, and said twas the last time had to speak to him; At last ask'd him, doe you desire prayer, shall I pray with you, He answer'd, Ay for the Lord's sake, and thank'd Mr. Moodey when had done. His former carriage was very startling and amazing to us. About One at night he died. About 11. aclock I supposed to hear neighbour Mason at prayer with him, just as I and my wife were going to bed. Mr. Allen prayed with us when came from said Hord's.

Sept. 23. Tuesday, between 5. and 6. Sir Moodey carries the Body of my dear Judith to the Tomb, Solomon Rainsford receives it on the Stairs and sets it in. On the Coffin is the year 1690. made with little nails. Govr. Bradstreet and Lady, Mrs. Moodey, Mather, the Mother, Mr. Winthrop, Richards here, with many others; Ministers, Willard, Moodey, Mather.

As we were going, one [blank] of Watertown came up with

the Bearer, and talk'd to him on horseback, Mr. Moodey bid him he gon about his business; at that he was in a rage and threaten'd to strike him, and said he was a pittyfull Dogg and we were all pittyfull Doggs. I thought of David and Shimei and said nothing to him. The Lord prepare me to undergo evil Report, and to be vilified by men; but not for evil-doing. I led my wife, Sam. his Grandmother, Hanah Betty, Jane Toppan managed Joseph. Before we went, Children read the 18. 19. and 20th Chapters of John, being in course for family reading.

Wednesday, Nov. 26th. Mr. Willard and I rid to Dorchester, from thence with Mr. Stoughton and Danforth, the Minister, to Braintrey, where met Mr. Torrey. I sign'd a Lease to Nehem. Hayden; Mr. Stoughton, Unkle Quinsey and his Son Witnesses. Mr. Torrey is for a Fast, or at least a Fast first. Mr. Willard for a Thanksgiving first. Mr. Torrey fears lest a Thanksgiving should tend to harden people in their carnal confidence. Cousin Gookin grows worse of her brest rather than better. Were wet coming home; met Mr. Caleb Moodey and N. Godoing on Crane's plain, riding to meet the Son of said Moodey, who came home in Jarvis and landed at Cape-Cod Harbour. When came home went to Capt. Hill's to the Meeting. I read the 11th Sermon of Mr. Flavell to the end of the 3d Excellency; 6 first Lines I composed with my own hand in London concerning God's being the Centre and Rest of the Soul. No body ask'd for the Meeting, so I invited them to our house.

Nov. 27. As 2d Bell is begun to be rung for Lecture, the Cleper falls out, the staple that held it being broken. At night Goodm. Williams rings the South-Bell for 9 aclock, at which many people started, fearing there had been fire. No ringing at the Old Meting-House on the Sabbath, Nov. 30, nor 9 aclock Bell since Thorsday, that I have heard.

Nov. 29. Menval had a hearing before the Council as to Money of his in Sir William's hand: very fierie words between

Sir William and Mr. Nelson. When Sir William went out semed to say would never come there more, had been so abus'd by said Nelson, and if Council would not right him, he would right himself.

Dec. 29, 1690. Mr. Addington and I goe to Sir William Phips's, where Mr. Moodey and Mr. Mather in his Border: had very sharp discourse; Mr. Mather very angrily said that they who did such things as suffering Sir William to be arrested by Meneval, were Frenchmen, or the people would say they were, &c.

Dec. 30. Council orders the Writt against Sir William to be null.

Jan. 7th. Mr. Addington and I went to Mr. Cotton Mather, and expostulated with him about the discourse at Sir William's, and the Remonstrance brought to the Council by Capt. Greenough and Mr. Coleman the Tuesday following: and hope 'twill tend to promote Charity and Peace.

Satterray, Jan. 10, 169⁰⁄₁. Betty with her Sister and others were riding in a sled, and the Indian who drove it struck Betty with his Goad on the side of the head so as to make it bleed pretty much and swell, but thanks be to God, no danger now the fright is over, and heals.

Sabbath, Jan. 11th. At night the House of Joshua Gardener, at Muddy-River, is burnt, and two of his Children; the Lord help us to repent that we do not likewise perish. Twas my turn to Watch. I sent Eliakim; the north watch saw the light of the fire.

Jan. 21, 169⁰⁄₁. Meeting at Mr. Woodmancies in Major Wallies house. A cry of fire was made which much disturb'd us in the middle of Sermon; it prov'd to be Mr. Pole's Chimney, which made a great light. Snow on the houses which prevented danger. Sermon, Brother Emons read, was about Hungring and Thirsting after Righteousness. Mr. Burroughs on the Beatitudes. Sung 2d part 45. Psal. Mr. Burroughs referring to the time of the new Jerusalem. Very Cold.

March 19, 169⁰⁄₁. Mr. C. Mather preaches the Lecture from Mat. 24., and appoint his portion with the Hypocrites: In his proem said, *Totus mundus agit histrionem.* Said one sign of a hypocrit was for a man to strain at a Gnat and swallow a Camel. Sign in 's Throat discovered him; To be zealous against an inocent fashion, taken up and used by the best of men; and yet make no Conscience of being guilty of great Immoralities. Tis supposed means wearing of Perriwigs: said would deny themselves in any thing but parting with an oportunity to do God service; that so might not offend good Christians. Meaning, I suppose, was fain to wear a Perriwig for his health. I expected not to hear a vindication of Perriwigs in Boston Pulpit by Mr. Mather; however, not from that Text. The Lord give me a good Heart and help to know, and not only to know but also to doe his Will; that my Heart and Head may be his.

Apr. 20th 1691. Being pressed with the sense of my doing much harm and little good, and breach of Vows at my return from New York, this time twelvemonth, that is, not heedfully regarding to go at God's Call, I kept a Fast to pray that God would not take away but uphold me by his free Spirit. When I came to look, I found it to be the very day of the week and year as much as could be that I set out for New York, which made me hope that twas a token for good that God would pardon that Sin and Sins since committed. Pray'd for Sister Dorothy, my family, New England, that God would fit me for his good pleasure in doing and suffering. Treaty with Indians to be the 1st May, &c.

May 4. Eight Companies Train; I went not into field; in the evening Major and Captains came hether to desire me not to lay down my place, Mr. Cotton Mather being here, set in with them. Mr. Mather staid and went to prayer with us, and had the very expressions us'd by the Dept. Governour when He deliver'd me my Comission; viz: Let us serve our

Generation according to the Will of God, and afterwards fall asleep.

May 20th. Election-day, very fair and comfortable wether. Led the South-Company into the Comon, there pray'd with them, so march'd with Capt. Hill to the Governour's. Guard consisted of two Files on each Flank, &c.; had put four Drums, made extream bad Volleys at night. After being treated by the Governour, the 122. Psalm was sung, Mr. Allen got me to set the Tune, which was Windsor; it brought to mind the Psalm sung in that very Room in 1686, which Mr. Nowell read. Note. Throw what heartlessness I scarce know, but I went not for Mr. Morton to bring him to the Meetinghouse, nor to fetch him from Mr. Eyre's to diner, which now I look upon it, troubles me much. Mr. Hutchinson and Addington not sworn this day.

Augt. 28. Friday. Fast at Charlestown, where I am. After my coming home when 'tis almost dark, Jane Toppan comes in from Newbury and brings the very sorrowful News of the death of Cous. Sam. Toppan last Tuesday night about nine of the Clock; buried the Wednesday night following, because of the Heat. No Minister with him: Mr. Shove prayd not with him at all, went not to him till was just dying: suppose might be afraid of 's school. Sam. bewail'd his not minding Spiritual things more, and that times were such as that things of that nature were scoff'd at. About Monday night last as Joseph was going into Cradle, He said, News from Heaven, the French were come, and mention'd Canada. No body has been tampering with him as I could learn. The Lord help us to repent that we may not perish, as probably Eliakim and those with him have done; and now poor Cousin Sam.

Oct. 16. Ordered the Clark to warn the Officers to meet me at Serg^{t}. Bull's. After the meeting at Mr. Willards went thether. Serj^{t}. Bull, Rainsford, Odlin; Corp^{l} Wheeler, Weare, Banister, Jno and Isaac Marion there. I acquainted them with my inability to serve longer as a Captain, and my desire the Company might be setled.

Sabbath, Oct. 25. Capt. Frary's voice failing him in his own Essay, by reason of his Palsie, he calls to me to set the Tune, which accordingly I doe; 17, 18, 19, 20, verses 68th Psalm, Windsor Tune; After the Lord's Supper 6, 7, 8, 9, verses 16th Low-Dutch. P.M. 2½ staves of 141. Ps. St. Davids, Jehova, I upon Thee call. After Evening Exercise, 2d part 84th Ps. Litchfield; I knew not that had the Tune till got to the 2d Line, being somewhat surprized, though design'd that Tune. I would have assisted Capt. Frary but scarce knew what Tune he design'd; and the Tune I guess'd at, was in so high a Key that I could not reach it.

Sabbath, Oct. 25, 1691. Boston, N. E. I pray'd this morn that God would give me a pardon of my Sins under the Broad Seal of Heaven; and through God's goodness have receiv'd some Refreshment and Light; I hope I doe thirst after Christ; and sensible of my own folly and Loathsomness that I value Him no more, and am so backward to be married by Him.

Wednesday, Oct. 28, 1691. My wife is brought to Bed of a Daughter about 8. in the morning; Elisabeth Weeden, Midwife. Rose about 4. m.

Sabbath. Novembr 1. A very pleasant day. Mr. Willard baptiseth my Daughter Mary, was enlarged in Prayer, none else baptised. Capt. Eliot not being abroad, I set the Tune again; Martyr's, St. Davids, Oxford.

Thorsday, Nov. 19th 1691. Sam. goes to Cambridge with Mr. Henry Newman, who is to carry him to morrow Nov. 20, to Mr. Neh. Hobart's at New Cambridge.

Nov. 18th. Last night the Governour was taken with the Stone, so the Council meet at his House; He was at the Townhouse yesterday but then the Wether hinder'd the Council's meeting.

Tuesday, Dec. 1, 1691. Brother Wm Moodey brings Sister

Gerrish to see us; she is great with child, looks to ly in the latter end of February, with her eighth.

Dec. 2. Very stormy day of Snow and Rain; by the fire I speak earnestly to Sister to make sure of an Interest in Christ, being alone.

Friday, Dec. 4. Brother Moodey and Sister Gerrish take their journey homeward, intend to call at Salem, notwithstanding the Small Pocks.

Monday, Dec. 7th. I ride to New-Cambridge to see Sam. He could hardly speak to me, his affections were so mov'd, having not seen me for above a fortnight; his Cough is still very bad, much increas'd by his going to Cambridge on foot in the night. Mr. Hobart not at home. Mr. Lawson was by accident there, and so had the benefit of his Company home. Got well home before 6. aclock, set out from home after 12. Staid there about 1½ hour. Laus Deo.

January, 2, 169½. Tim° Dwight dies about 10. *mane*.

Boston in N. E. January 2, 169½. I had been at Mrs. Collucott's, and coming home between 12. and 1. I call'd to see Tim° Dwight, and as I stept into the Room, saw him laid out under the sheet.

Monday, Jan. 4th Went to the Funeral of Tim. Dwight. Cous. Dumer, Capt. Jn° Walley, Capt. Wing, Rowse, Tho. Savage, Goldsmith, Robt Saunderson, Bearers. Mr. Joyliff and I went next the Relations; by the Dock-head Mr. Willard struck in: no Minister before; buried at the new burying place; something troublesom going, by reason of the great Snow fell yesterday. 38 years old. Lord grant that I may be ready, when the Cry shall be, Behold, the Bridegroom cometh.

Tuesday, Jan. 12, 169½. Major Hutchinson and I visit Major Johnson, Mr. Hez. Usher and Sol. Phips in Company. He is very glad to see us. Call'd at Betty Gardener's as came back. This week's Rain and Sun have thaw'd the ways as if it were March. Major Johnson has kept house about 18 weeks. Takes his disease to be the burning Ague mentioned in the Scripture. This night [blank] Hamlen, formerly Plats, before that, Crabtree, a middle-aged woman, through some displeasure at her Son whom she beat, sat not down to Supper with her Husband and a Stranger at Table: when they had done, she took away, and in the Room where she set it, took a piece of grisly meat of a Shoulder of Mutton into her mouth which got into the top of the Larynx and stopt it fast, so she was presently choak'd. Tho. Pemberton and others found it so when they opened her Throat. She gave a stamp with her foot and put her finger in her mouth: but Pemberton not at home, and di'd immediately. "What need have all to Acknowledge God in whose Hand their breath is, &c." Sam. Worden, and another woman, die the same night, and widow Oliver de Sweet, the next day.

Jan. 24th 169½. Govr Bradstreet comes to Meeting this Afternoon, which as I remember has not done in January till now.

Tuesday, Jan. 26, 169½. News comes to Town by Robin Orchard, of Dolberry's being arrived at Cape Cod; Sir William Phips made Governour of the Province of New England. Foy (in whom went Mr. Lee) taken into France; Quelch and Bant also. Six weeks passage from Plimouth. This day, almost at the same Time, news was brought of an Attack made by the Indians on York.

Jan. 25, 169½. I asked Mr. Willard at Mr. Eyre's whether the Times would allow one to build an house; answer'd, I wonder you have contented your selvs so long without one; but I little thought what was acted that day at York. Got Mr. Eyre to come home with me about 8. at night to advise me.

Satterday, Feb. 27. Between 4. and 5. *mane,* we are startled at the roaring of a Beast, which I conjectur'd to be an Ox broken loose from a Butcher, runing along the street, but proved to be our own Cow bitten by a dog, so that were forc'd to kill her; though calved but Jan. 4th and gives plenty of

Milk. Hapy are they, who have God for their Spring and Brest of Suplies. Exceeding high wind this day at North East.

Sabbath, Feb. 28. Day is so Stormy that Governour went not to meeting. Madam Bradstreet not well.

April 11th 1692. Went to Salem, where, in the Meeting-house, the persons accused of Witchcraft were examined; was a very great Assembly; 'twas awfull to see how the afflicted persons were agitated. Mr. Noyes pray'd at the beginning, and Mr. Higginson concluded.

May 14th 1692. Sir William arrives in the Nonsuch Frigat: Candles are lighted before He gets into Townhouse. Eight Companies wait on Him to his house, and then on Mr. [Increase] Mather to his. Made no volleys because 'twas Satterday night.

Monday, May 16. Eight Companies and two from Charlestown guard Sir William and his Councillors to the Townhouse, where the Comissions were read and Oaths taken. I waited on the Dept. Governour to Town, and then was met by Brother Short and Northend, who inform'd me of the dangerous illness of my father, so I went with them, and was not present at the Solemnity; found my father much better. At Ipswich, as we were going, saw a Rainbow just about Sunset, in Company of Brother Northend.

July 20th 1692. Fast at the house of Capt. Alden, upon his account. Mr. Willard pray'd. I read a Sermon out of Dr. Preston, 1st and 2d Uses of God's Alsufficiency. Capt. Scottow pray'd, Mr. Allen came in and pray'd, Mr. Cotton Mather, then Capt. Hill. Sung the first part 103. Ps., concluded about 5. aclock. Brave Shower of Rain while Capt. Scottow was praying, after much Drought. Cous. Daniel Gookin sups with us, and bespeaks my marrying of him to morrow.

July 27, 1692. A plentifull Rain falls after great Drought.

July 30, 1692. Mrs. Cary makes her escape out of Cambridge-Prison, who was Committed for Witchcraft.

Thorsday, Augt. 4. At Salem, Mr. Waterhouse brings

the news of the desolation at Jamaica, June 7th. 1700 persons kill'd, besides the Loss of Houses and Goods by the Earthquake.

Augt. 19th 1692. This day George Burrough, John Willard, Jno Proctor, Martha Carrier and George Jacobs were executed at Salem, a very great number of Spectators being present. Mr. Cotton Mather was there, Mr. Sims, Hale, Noyes, Chiever, &c. All of them said they were inocent, Carrier and all. Mr. Mather says they all died by a Righteous Sentence. Mr. Burrough by his Speech, Prayer, protestation of his Innocence, did much move unthinking persons, which occasions their speaking hardly concerning his being executed.

Augt. 25. Fast at the old [First] Church, respecting the Witchcraft, Drought, &c.

Monday, Sept. 19, 1692. About noon, at Salem, Giles Corey was press'd to death for standing Mute; much pains was used with him two days, one after another, by the Court and Capt. Gardner of Nantucket who had been of his acquaintance: but all in vain.

Sept. 20. Now I hear from Salem that about 18 years agoe, he was suspected to have stamped and press'd a man to death, but was cleared. Twas not remembered till Ane Putnam was told of it by said Corey's Spectre the Sabbath-day night before the Execution.

Sept. 21. A petition is sent to Town in behalf of Dorcas Hoar, who now confesses: Accordingly an order is sent to the Sheriff to forbear her Execution, notwithstanding her being in the Warrant to die to morrow. This is the first condemned person who has confess'd.

Thorsday, Sept. 22, 1692. William Stoughton, Esqr., John Hathorne, Esqr., Mr. Cotton Mather, and Capt. John Higginson, with my Brother St., were at our house, speaking about publishing some Trials of the Witches. Mr. Stoughton went away and left us, it began to rain and was very dark, so that getting some way beyond the fortification, was fain to come back again, and lodgd here in Capt. Henchman's Room. Has been a plentiful Rain, blessed be God. Mr. Stoughton went away early in the morn so that I saw him not. Read the 1 Jn° 1. before went to bed.

Satterday, Oct. 15th Went to Cambridge and visited Mr. Danforth, and discoursed with Him about the Witchcraft; thinks there canot be a procedure in the Court except there be some better consent of Ministers and People. Told me of the woman's coming into his house last Sabbath-day sennight at Even.

Friday, Oct. 21. Went to Salem and visited my sick Brother, who has had a Fever all this moneth; Is very desirous to live, and makes vows to serve God better, if his life be spared: was much affected at my coming in.

Oct. 23. At night, Mr. Cook, Oakes and Wiswall arrive, got to their houses almost before any body knew it; have been 8 week and 5 days from Plimouth. Went and saw my Landlord and Landlady Jennings; their Son in Jamaica has a Plantation spoiled by a Mountain thrown upon it by the late Earthquake.

Oct. 26, 1692. A Bill is sent in about calling a Fast, and Convocation of Ministers, that may be led in the right way as to the Witchcrafts. The season and maner of doing it, is such, that the Court of Oyer and Terminer count themselves thereby dismissed. 29 Nos. and 33 yeas to the Bill. Capt. Bradstreet and Lieut. True, Wm Huchins and several other interested persons there, in the affirmative.

Oct. 28th Lieut. Governour coming over the Causey is, by reason of the high Tide, so wet, that is fain to go to bed till sends for dry cloaths to Dorchester; In the Afternoon, as had done several times before, desired to have the advice of the Governour and Council as to the sitting of the Court of Oyer and Terminer next week; said should move it no more; great silence, as if should say do not go.

Oct. 29. Mr. Russel asked whether the Court of Oyer and Terminer should sit, expressing some fear of Inconvenience by its fall. Governour said it must fall. Lieut. Governour not in Town today. Several persons drowned on Friday 28th. Major General comes home Oct. 28. even, having been gon a Moneth. Deputies doe this day Treat the lately returned Agents Oct. 28.

Nov. 4, 1692. Law passes for Justices and Ministers Marrying persons. By order of the Comittee, I had drawn up a Bill for Justices and such others as the Assembly should appoint to marry: but came new-drawn and thus alter'd from the Deputies. It seems they count the respect of it too much to be left any longer with the Magistrate. And Salaries are not spoken of; as if one sort of Men might live on the Aer. They are treated like a kind of useless, worthless folk.

Nov. 6. Joseph threw a knop of Brass and hit his Sister Betty on the forhead so as to make it bleed and swell; upon which, and for his playing at Prayer-time, and eating when Return Thanks, I whipd him pretty smartly. When I first went in (call'd by his Grandmother) he sought to shadow and hide himself from me behind the head of the Cradle: which gave me the sorrowful remembrance of Adam's carriage.

Nov. 22, 1692. I prayd that God would pardon all my Sinfull Wanderings, and direct me for the future. That God would bless the Assembly in their debates, and that would chuse and assist our Judges, &c., and save New England as to Enemies and Witchcrafts, and vindicate the late Judges, consisting with his Justice and Holiness, &c., with Fasting. Cousin Anne Quinsy visited me in the Evening, and told me of her children's wellfare. Now about, Mercy Short grows ill again, as formerly.

Thorsday, Dec. 22, 1692. After Lecture, the Governour delivers Mr. Stoughton his Comission as Chief Justice of the Superiour Court, and to Major Richards, Winthrop, Sewall as Justices, and the Secretary gave each of us an Oath singly that would impartially administer Justice according to our best skill. I would have stayed till Mr. Danforth took his; but the Governour granted it not.

Major General tells me, that last night about 7 aclock, he saw 5. or 7 Balls of Fire that mov'd and mingled each with other, so that he could not tell them; made a great Light, but streamed not. Twas our privat Meeting; I saw nothing of it. Order comes out for a Fast. I carry one to Mr. Willard. Mrs. Willard talks to me very sharply about Capt. Alden's not being at the Lord's Supper last Sabbath-day.

Sabbath, Jan. 22, 169⅔. A very extraordinary Storm by reason of the falling and driving of the Snow. Few Women could get to Meeting. Our two Maids and my self there. A child named Alexander was baptized in the Afternoon. Major General not abroad in the Afternoon. Govr. Bradstreet very sick.

Jan. 27, 169⅔. Mr. Elisha Cook, Mr. Isaac Addington and I saw and heard Simon Bradstreet Esqr. sign, seal and publish a Codicil now anexed to his Will, written by said Addington at said Bradstreets direction, and read to him several times. Signd and seald it sitting up in his Bed. After told us that if his Estate should exceed Two hundred pounds more than was mentioned in the Will, would have his Executors distribute it according to the direction of his Overseers, and Wife, I think. Said, the reason why would sell the little farm, was because 'twas a ruinous thing, and yielded but 8£ *per* anum in Country-pay. Call'd for Ale and made us drink.

Jan. 28. Went in with Mr. Cotton Mather to Mr. Bradstreets, and heard him pray.

March 9, 169⅔. Joseph puts his Grandmother and Mother in great fear by swallowing a Bullet which for a while stuck in his Throat: He had quite got it down, before I knew what the matter was. This day in the Afternoon One of Mr. Holyoke's Twins falls into the Well and is drownd, no body but a Negro being at home; was a very lovely Boy of about 4 years old. Satterday, March 11, about Sunset He is buried. When I come home from the funeral, my wife shows me the Bullet Joseph swallowed, which he voided in the Orchard. The Lord help us to praise Him for his distinguishing Favour.

Wednesday, March 22, 169⅔. Our kitchin chimney fell on fire about noon, and blaz'd out sorely at top, appeared to be very foul: the fire fell on the shingles so that they began to burn in several places, being very dry: but by the good Providence of God, no harm done. Mr. Fisk was with us, and we sat merrily to dinner on the Westfield Pork that was snatch'd from the fire on this Occasion. Mother was exceedingly frighted; and is ready to think we are called to remove. This very morning had as 'twere concluded not to build this Summer; because my wife is loath to ly in at another place. What we shall now doe, I know not. Rid to Dorchester.

Apr. 26, 1693. Wednesday. The old Kitchen is pulled down.

Satterday, Apr. 29. The little Hall is Removed, and joined to Matthias Smith's house.

Friday, May 5. Alexander Millar and Frank, Cous. Savages Negro, begin to digg the Cellar. Mrs. Goose is brought to bed of a daughter.

Tuesday, May 16, 1693. The first stone is laid in the new building, being the great Stone that lay at Capt. Wyllys's Corner, and is now our Corner-Stone next Father Walker's.

May 20. The Corner stone next Fort-Hill is laid; The Corner next Wheeler's Pond had the other half; being the white split Rock on the Comon.

May 20. The Governour comes home from Sea. Major Converse went out after the Enemy with 200 and odd men, yesterday was senight; designed for Tackonnick.

Tuesday, May 23, 1693. The Corner Stone next Cotton-Hill is laid, which fell as it were cheerfully and willingly into his place; I gave the workmen a piece of Eight.

Satterday, May 27. The foundation of the Cellar is finished, by stones gotten out of the Comon.

Monday, June 12, 1693. I visit Capt. Alden and his wife, and tell them I was sorry for their Sorrow and Temptations by reason of his Imprisonment, and that was glad of his Restauration.

Monday, June 26. The Brick-Work is begun; the South-end of the house being carried up several foot high.

July 15, 1693. I went to Mr. Goose, and told him his wife could not conveniently sit any longer in my wives Pue, and therefore desired her to look out another place.

Monday, Augt. 7. About 4. *mane* I go for the Midwife; About 4. P.M. My Wife is brought to Bed of a Daughter. Thanks be to God. This day Sarah Noyes a young woman of about 21 years dies. Tis very cool and comfortable wether after about a weeks time of excessive Heat. Clouds gather thick, and a little Rain in the Evening.

Wednesday, Augt. 9. There falls a plentifull Rain after a long distressing Drought. *Laus Deo.*

Augt. 14. The plates and sumers of the lower Chamber Floor are laid.

Satterday, Augt. 12. Capt. Eliot comes sick from Muddy-River.

Wednesday, Augt. 16. Dyes about 2. at night.

Augt. 17. Is buried. Major Hutchinson, Sewall, Joyliff, Walley, P. Allen, Bridgham, Bearers. Buried in the new burying place. Tis a sudden and very sore Blow to the South Church, a Loss hardly repaired. On the Sabbath, Mr. Willard being in before me, I did not mind D. Eliot's absence, and wondered I heard not his voice beginning the Ps., and Capt. Frary waited when I should begin it. We shall hardly get another such a sweet Singer as we have lost. He was one of the most Serviceable Men in Boston, condescending to his friends. One of the best and most respectfull Friends I had in the World. Lord awaken us. Scarce a Man was so universally known as He. Dyed in the 61. year of 's Age. Was one of the first that was born in Boston.

Satterday, Sept. 9. I return from Point-Judith, having been gon from home ever since the 28. of August. At my return, find little Jane not well.

Sept. 12. Call Mr. Willard to pray with little Jane. Went to Roxbury-Lecture, Mr. Hobart came home with me, who also pray'd with Jane; both excellently. By Dr. Oakes advice, I give her a little Mana. Methinks she looks like Henry in his Sickness. The good Lord prepare her and us for the issue, and help us to choose the things that please Him. Nurse Judd watches.

Sept. 13, 1693. Between 12. and 1. at night following that day, Little Jane expires, much as Henry did, in neighbour Smith's lap, Nurse Hill and I being by.

BOSTON, NEW ENGLAND.

*1. John Sewall, the Son of Samuel and Hanah Sewall, was born Apr. 2^{d} 1677, died Sept. 11th 1678.

2. Samuel Sewall, was born June 11th 1678.

3. Hannah Sewall, was born Feb. 3^{d} $16\frac{79}{80}$.

4. Elisabeth Sewall, was born Dec. 29th 1681.

*5. Hull Sewall, was born July 8th 1684. Died at Newbury, June 18th 1686, is buried there.

*6. Henry Sewall, was born Dec. 7th 1685. Died Dec. 22^{d} 1685.

*7. Stephen Sewall, was born Jan 30th $168\frac{6}{7}$. Died July 26th 1687.

8. Joseph Sewall, was born Aug 15th 1688.

*9. Judith Sewall, was born Aug. 13th 1690. Died Sept. 21st 1690.

10. Mary Sewall, was born Oct. 28th 1691.

*11. Jane Sewall, was born Aug. 7th 1693. Died Sept. 13th 1693.

All the above-named Eleven Children have been by their father, Samuel Sewall, (holding them in his arms,) Offered up to God in Baptisme, at the South-Meeting-House in Boston. The Rev^{d}. Mr. Thomas Thacher baptised John and Samuel; and the Rev^{d}. Mr. Samuel Willard baptised the other Nine, upon the Sabbath Day in the Solemn Assembly of God's Saints.

Sept. 15, 1693. The body of Jane Sewall was laid in the Tomb, between 4. and 5. P.M. John Willard carried the Corps. Lord teach me to profit. I led my wife; Cous. Dumer, Mother; Sam. his Sister; Jane, Elisabeth;

Oct. 11th Carried my daughter Hanah to Salem in Company of Mr. Hathorne and Sam. Wakefield; got thether about 8. at night.

Oct. 12. Carried her to Rowley, Wm Longfellow rid before her; I staid Lecture at Ipswich, where unexpectedly heard Mr. Edward Tomson preach a very good Sermon from Felix's procrastination.

Oct. 13. Rid home, having much adoe to pacify my dear daughter, she weeping and pleading to go with me.

Wednesday, Oct. 18. Jno Barnard raises the Roof of the brick House, no hurt done, through God's goodness.

Tuesday, Nov. 21, 1693. Our House is covered and defended against the wether.

Nov. 24. The first Snow falls.

Friday, Jan. 5th. Being in the chamber of the new House next Tiler's, I fell down, and razed off the skin of my right Legg upon the shin bone, putting my self to much pain; I was fain to fall across the Joysts, to prevent falling through, which I was in great danger of.

Satterday, Jan. 13, 169¾. The Floor of the lower Chamber towards the North-East, is laid; I drove a Nail.

Monday, Jan. 15, and Jan. 16, the Floor of the Hall-Chamber is laid. The Ice is clear gon out of the Docks as in March.

Jan. 19, 169¾. Kitchen floor is finished. This day Mrs. Prout dies after sore conflicts of mind, not without suspicion of Witchcraft.

Satterday, Jan. 27. The Hall Floor is finished.

Jan. 30, 169¾. The Kitchin Casements are Glazed and set up.

April 2, 1694. Monday. Artillery Training; Bastian and I set seeds of White-Thorn at Saunder's Pasture, north end. In the Afternoon, all the Town is filled with the discourse of Major Richard's Death, which was very extraordinarily suddain; was abroad on the Sabbath, din'd very well on Monday, and after that falling into an angry passion with his Servant

Richard Frame, presently after, fell probably into a Fit of Apoplexy, and died. On Tuesday night was opened and no cause found of his death; noble Parts being fair and sound.

Friday, April 6. Major Richards is buried in his Tomb in the North Burying Place; Companyes in Arms attending the Funeral. Bearers, Stoughton Danforth; Russell, Brown; Sewall, Addington; Major General and Mr. Foster led the Widow. Mr. Torrey was not there because 'twas Friday. Coffin was covered with Cloth. In the Tomb were fain to nail a Board across the Coffins and then a board standing right up from that, bearing against the top of the Tomb, to prevent their floating up and down; sawing and fitting this board made some inconvenient Tarriance.

Oct. 20. This week the upper Floors are laid with boards that had only this Summer's seasoning.

Sabbath, Oct. 28, 1694. There is a very High boisterous and cold Norwest Wind, my dear Mother Hull for fear the wind should bear her down, does not put on her Cloak: but wears two Scarvs and so catches cold; however, grows indispos'd so that canot eat nor sleep; kept from the Catechising and Lecture. I left word with Mr. Oliver that Mother desired his Brother to come and see her, which he did Nov. 1. and left directions. Mr. Moodey prays with her.

Nov. 1, 1694. Capt. Dobbins refusing to give Bail, the Sheriff was taking him to Prison, and Sir William Phips rescued him, and told the Sheriff He would send him, the Sheriff, to prison, if he touch'd him, which occasioned very warm discourse between Him and the Lieut. Governour.

Nov. 3, 1694. 1. past m. Mr. Willard prays and the Governour adjourns the General Court to the last Wednesday in February next, P.M. Several of the Council desired a dissolution, lest some Emergency should require the Calling of an Assembly, and this Adjournment bind our hands; but the Governour would not harken to it. Onset of the Enemy, Packets from England, were mention'd. Before the Adjournment,

Governour expostulated with the Speaker about copying out and dispersing a Letter of Sir H. Ashurst's; then said, This Court is dissolv'd to such a time: being put in mind of his mistake, said, I mean Adjourn'd.

Wednesday, Nov. 7. First day of the Court's meeting this week, Capt. Dobbins is call'd. He utterly refuseth to give Bail, confesseth himself to be in the Sheriff's Custody. Between the Sheriff and Keeper is carried to Goal, which makes great Wrath. He pleaded Justification for it, produced two Warrants under the Governour's Hand and Seal, and an Act of Parliament: Court adviseth.

Sixth-day, Nov. 9, 1694. Lieut. Governour and Council dine at James Meers's; The Treat was intended for the Governour; but is so offended at Capt. Dobbins Imprisonment, that He comes not, nor Mr. Mather the Father, nor Son, nor Capt. Foster; so chair at the uper end of the Table stands empty. Note. Mr. Cotton Mather was sick of a grievous pain in his face, else He had been there, as He told me afterward.

Fifth-day, Nov. 15th. Is a Council at the Governour's House about taking Mr. Jackson's Affidavits; defer it till after Lecture that Capt. Byfield may have notice to be there.

Mr. Walter preaches a very good Sermon from Ps. 73. 27. They that are far from Thee shall perish: shewd the misery of the unregenerat: the Hapiness of Believers, by reason of their manifold Nearness to God. Governour did not go to Lecture. After Lecture was much debate at the Townhouse, and at last Mr. Jackson's Affidavits were all read over, and his Oath given him by the Lieut. Governour and Council.

Seventh-day, Nov. 17th 1694. Just about Sunset or a little after, the Governour goes from his House to the Salutation Stairs, and there goes on board his Yatcht; Lieut. Governour, many of the Council, Mr. Cotton Mather, Capts. of Frigatts, Justices and many other Gentlemen accompanying him. 'Twas six aclock by that time I got home, and I only staid to see them come to sail. Guns at the Castle were fired about seven: Governour had his Flagg in main Top. Note. Twas of a seventh day in the even when the Governour came to Town, and so tis at his going off, both in darkness: and uncomfortable, because of the Sabbath.

Nov. 21. My wife grew so ill that I got up between three and four in the morn. Call Mrs. Weeden; proves a rainy day.

Nov. 21, 1694. My wife is brought to bed of a Daughter between 9. and 10. of the Clock in the morn. Mr. Torrey prayd with Mother and me in the Kitchen of the new house for that mercy; Mother desiring Him, saying that my wife was in great and more than ordinary Extremity, so that she was not able to endure the Chamber: I went also to acquaint Mr. Willard, and as I came back, I met Mrs. Perce, who wish'd me joy of my Daughter, as came in at the Gate. Mr. Torrey was prevail'd with to go into Chamber and Return Thanks to God. Women din'd with rost Beef and minc'd Pyes, good Cheese and Tarts. Grows to a very great Storm.

Nov. 22. I put up a Bill for to Thank God for delivering my wife in childbearing; there was no other. Mr. Cotton Mather preached from Isa. 32. 2. taking occasion from the Storm. Lieut. Governour not at Meeting. Mr. Torrey and Fisk lodge here.

Sabbath, Nov. 25, 1694. I named my little Daughter Sarah, Mr. Willard baptiz'd her. Lydia Cornish, and Joseph Scot were baptiz'd at the same time. Mr. Torrey said, call her Sarah and make a Madam of her. I was strugling whether to call her Sarah or Mehetabel; but when I saw Sarah's standing in the Scripture, viz: Peter, Galatians, Hebrews, Romans, I resolv'd on that side. Also Mother Sewall had a sister Sarah; and none of my sisters of that name.

Dec. 4, 1694. Lieut. Governour calls at 's entrance into the Town; I told him I had spoken to Mr. Willard to pray; tells me of his intended Treat at Mr. Coopers, and enquires whom He had best to invite. Between 2. and 3. P.M. we meet at Mr. Secretaries, from thence go to the Townhouse; viz. Lieut. Governour, Mr. Danforth, Gedney, Russel, Cook, Phillips, Brown, Hathorne, Addington, Sewall, Lynde, Hook, Sergeant. Mr. Willard prayed. Then Lieut. Governour made a brave Speech upon the occasion of the Government's being fallen on Him. After this, Col. Hutchinson came in and made 13.

After twas debated, and several Acts of Parliament view'd, gave the Lieut. Governour an Oath for his due Execution of the Acts referring to Navigation, so far as they concern the Plantations. Voted a Letter to be sent to the Government of Rode-Island that they would discountenance Capt. Tu's proceedings. Voted Capt. Hamond, of Kittery, Register and Clerk in the room of Capt. Wincoll, deceased; at the Instance of Major Hook. Lieut. Governour invites, and we go to Mr. Cooper's, where a Splendid Treat is provided, most cold meat. Councillors, Ministers, Justices there, and Col. Shrimpton, Mr. E^{m} Hutchinson, &c. Mr. Increase Mather Crav'd a Blessing; Mr. Willard return'd Thanks.

I mov'd Mr. Willard and Mr. Cotton Mather, that, seeing the Old and South Church fell short in their singing on the Thanksgiving-day, might make it up now, if they saw meet: Mr. Willard said would sing what He intended then, prevented by the night: Ask'd Lieut. Governour and read the 47. Ps. Clap hands.—Spake to me and I set it. Lieut. Govr. Usher was invited, but not there; He is gon to Prison this afternoon, as tis said, upon Mr. Shrimpton's Execution.

Feb. 9, 169$\frac{4}{5}$. Jacob Mason, the Instrument-maker, died last night very suddenly, as he sat in a chair at the widow Hanah Cowell's, where he was instructing a young man in the Mariner's Art. This day there is a very extraordinary Storm of Snow. It seems Jacob Mason was in Drink.

Feb. 12, 169$\frac{4}{5}$. Mrs. Moodey is stricken with the Palsie in her right side, and is made speechless. Mr. Moodey is sent for. The last night and this day, Feb. 12, the wether is extream Cold which Mrs. Moodey always hardly bears.

Feb. 15. Bastian fetches Sam's Chest from Mr. Perry's. It falls out so that neither he nor Mrs. Perry are at home. I gave the maid 12[d] and Robin a Real.

Third-Day, Feb. 19, 169$\frac{4}{5}$. Salem-Chamber [Prayer], Samuel to be disposed to such a Master and Calling, as wherein he may abide with God. Jane, and Fathers family.

Assembly that is to sit next week, that may be directed and succeeded by God, to doe for the Salvation of the Province. That a Man after God's own heart may be chosen for a Judge. Fronteers from Albany and Kinderhook, to Pemaquid. Spring. England.

Fourth-day, March 6, 169$\frac{4}{5}$. I had got a printed List of all the Councillors names except the Judges, that might serve for a Nomination, and indented them with Scissers, and so every one took as it pleas'd him, and put into Mr. Secretaries Hat. Elisha Cooke, Esqr. had Twenty Votes. Barthol. Gedney, John Hathorne, Elisha Hutchinson, John Foster, and Nathanael Thomas Esqrs. had One Vote apiece; which made up the whole number of Electors: for the Lieut. Governour voted not, sustaining the place of Governour; Col. Pynchon was not here, and Major Hook dead. So there remained 25. This day Joseph Belknaps little Son of about 4 years old, falls into scalding Wort and is kill'd. On the Sabbath a Roxbury Woman fell off her Horse and is since dead: On the day before, one Trusedal, of Newton, was pulling Hay from an undermined Mow in the Barn, which fell upon him and kill'd him. Mr. Wheelwright is chosen to succeed Major Hook as to the Probat of Wills, and Mr. Peperill as a Justice of the Inferiour Court. Mr. Elatson buryed his wife this day. Bearers had Scarfs and Rings; was buryed from Mr. Colemans.

March 18, 169$\frac{4}{5}$. Last night I dream'd that all my Children were dead except Sarah; which did distress me sorely with

Reflexions on my Omission of Duty towards them, as well as Breaking oft the Hopes I had of them. The Lord help me thankfully and fruitfully to enjoy them, and let that be a means to awaken me. This day Tim. Clark is buried, a great Funeral. He never spake after his Fall. Great Snow on the Ground.

March 29, 1695. Went to the Meeting at Mr. Olivers: Major Walley sat next me, and presently after the Exercise, ask'd me if I heard the sad News from England, and then told me the Queen was dead, which was the first I heard of it. It seems Capt. Allen arriv'd yesterday at Marblehead, who brought the News, and fill'd the Town with it this day. It seems the Queen died on the 27th of December, having been sick four days of the Small Pocks. C. Allen was at Coruna about the Groin, when the Packuet came thether that brought the News of it: Whereupon the Fleet performed their usual Ceremonies, and the Merchants went into Mourning. Mr. Willard preached from Jn° 21—21, 22. to prepare men to acquiesce in the Soveraign Disposal of God as to mens honouring of Him in Doing, or Suffering, or both.

April 1, 1695. Joseph speaking about my sending two Frenchmen to prison upon the Act relating to them, said, If this Country stand when I am a Man, I'll drive them all out.

April 3, 1695. I planted Two Locusts, two Elms at Wheelers pond, and one in Elm-Pasture near the Line over against the Middle-Elm. The middle Locust-Tree at Wheelers pond was set there the last year.

Apr. 5. There is pretty much Thunder and Lightening about break of day. Thunder seem'd to me like Great Guns at first.

Tuesday, Apr. 9, 1695. Piam Blower and others from Virginia and Barbados bring a Confirmation of the Queens death: and Report that the French King is dead; and his Genl Luxemburg; that two other duelled for the honour of his place, one fell, and the other went over to the Confederats. Ketch arrived that came from Plimouth the Tenth of February. This day father Daws makes my little Bridge.

Apr. 10. When I rise in the morn I find the Ground and houses covered with Snow. Be it that Lewis the 14th be indeed dead &c. yet we may have a sharp, though short winter in New England still. God defend.

Apr. 24. We are told from Madera, that one of the Mast-Ships is Taken and that Lewis 14 is yet alive. Very wet and Rainy Wether.

Monday, April 29, 1695. The morning is very warm and Sunshiny; in the Afternoon there is Thunder and Lightening, and about 2. P.M. a very extraordinary Storm of Hail, so that the ground was made white with it, as with the blossoms when fallen; 'twas as bigg as pistoll and Musquet Bullets; It broke of the Glass of the new House about 480 Quarrels [Squares] of the Front; of Mr. Sergeant's about as much; Col. Shrimpton, Major General, Govr Bradstreet, New Meetinghouse, Mr. Willard, &c. Mr. Cotton Mather dined with us, and was with me in the new Kitchen when this was; He had just been mentioning that more Ministers Houses than others proportionably had been smitten with Lightening; enquiring what the meaning of God should be in it. Many Hail-Stones broke throw the Glass and flew to the middle of the Room, or farther: People afterward Gazed upon the House to see its Ruins. I got Mr. Mather to pray with us after this awfull Providence; He told God He had broken the brittle part of our house, and prayd that we might be ready for the time when our Clay-Tabernacles should be broken. Twas a sorrowfull thing to me to see the house so far undon again before twas finish'd. It seems at Milton on the one hand, and at Lewis's on the other, there was no Hail.

I mentioned to Mr. Mather that Monmouth made his discent into England about the time of the Hail in '85, Sumer, that much cracked our South-west windows. Col. Archdell

Governour of Carolina comes to Town from Portsmouth this night.

May 5, 1695. About 3 hours News comes to Town of the death of Sir William Phips, Feb. 18th at which people are generally sad. Lay sick about a week of the new Fever as 'tis called. Cous. Hull says the talk is Mr. Dudley will be Governour. Tis said the King goes over Sea again, and Seven persons are to have the Regency in his absence.

May 6. The mourning Guns are fired at the Castle and Town for the Death of our Governour. Representatives the same as before, chosen this day.

May 8, 1695. I visit my Lady, who takes on heavily for the death of Sir William. Thinks the Lieutenant and Council were not so kind to him as they should have been. Was buried out of Salters Hall. This day, May 8, we have News of the Taking of Seven Vessels by a small French Pickeroon. One is a Briganteen, Mr. Greenwood, Master, out of which had 1000£ Money. Neither of the Frigats is yet got out.

Friday, June 21. My dear Mother Hull tells me of Capt. Daviss Invitation, and bids me to remember to be at the Meeting. Mr. Willard preaches excellently. At home, at prayer, we read the 16. of the Revelation; I spake somthing to the Sixth Vial, but little thought how presently those awfull Words, Behold I come as a Thief! did concern me and my whole family: And then, and at prayer with my Wife in the Chamber, was wofully drowsy and stupid. About one at night, Jane comes up with an unusual Gate, and gives us an account of Mothers Illness, not being able to speak of a considerable time. I went to Capt. Daviss and fetched some Trecle Water and Syrup of Saffron; Dame Ellis made a Cake of Herbs to try to strengthen Mothers Stomach. In the morn Roger Judd is sent to Cambridge for Dr. Oliver, mother chusing to speak with him and no other. When he comes he advises to a Plaister for the Stomach, which is aplied; and a Potion made of Bezar [Bezoar] to be taken in Syrup of Saffron and Treacle water; of which took once or twice. About 8. or 9. I call'd Mr. Willard at her desire, who prays with her. Finding the room free once, and observing her very great weakness; I took the oportunity to thank her for all her Labours of Love to me and mine, and ask'd her pardon of our undutifullness; She, after a while, said, God Pity 'Em; which was the last prayer I heard her make. About six I ask'd if I should call Mr. Willard, (for had said to him that he should come again if he could). As far as I could perceive, she said, Not so soon. But I called, or sent; yet could not discern any attention to the prayer, her disease had prevail'd so far, and a little before Sunset she expired, to our very surprising Grief and Sorrow. Roger Judd was here about noon, and said, that when some in the next room spake about who should Watch, my dear Mother answer'd, She should need no Watchers, she should be above at Rest.

June 24. About Seven aclock, my dear Mother is entombed. Bearers, Mr. Danforth, Russell, Cooke, Elisha Hutchinson, Addington, Sergeant.

July 7. Govr. Bradstreet is seised again with his old pains.

July 15. I discourse Capt. Saml. Checkly about his taking Sam. to be his Prentice. He seems to incline to it; and in a maner all I mention it to encourage me. The good Lord direct and prosper.

July 12, 1695. Kept a Day of Prayer in secret Respecting my dear Mother's death; and Sam's being to be placed out, &c.

July 26, 1695. Poor little Mary falls down into the Cellar of Matthias Smith's house, and cuts her head against the Stones, making a large orifice of more than two inches long; 'twas about 6 post meridiem. The Lord sanctify to me this bloody Accident.

Augt. 6, 1695. Mr. Obinson's wife comes to me and complains of her Husband's ill usage of her; kick'd her out of bed last night; lets her have nothing but water to drink, won't let her have Cloths or victuals. This was 2 post meridiem.

Fifth-day, Augt. 8, 1695. About 9. M. little Sarah has a Convulsion Fit; I and Mr. Torrey were sent for to see it. It lasted not long. When all quiet, Mr. Torrey went to Prayer. A little after Lecture, Sarah has another sore Fit. My wife and I take her to bed with us.

Augt. 8, 1695. About six in the Morn. Sarah has another sore Fit in her Mother's arms presently after she was brought down.

Third-day, Augt. 13, 1695. We have a Fast kept in our new Chamber. Mr. Willard begins with Prayer, and preaches from 2 Chron. 34. 27. Mr. Allen prays. P.M. Mr. Bayly begins with prayer, preaches from Luke 1. 50, and then concludes with prayer. Sung the 27 Ps. 7—10. I set Windsor Tune and burst so into Tears that I could scarce continue singing. Mr. Thornton was here, but went away when Mr. Allen was at Prayer. Mr. Cook, and Mr. Addington here, Mr. Sergeant was diverted. Note. Had better have invited all the Council in Town, at least. I apointed this day to ask God's Blessing after the death of my dear Mother, and in particular to bless Sam. with a Master and Calling and bless us in our new house. The Lord pardon and doe for us beyond our hopes, contrary to our Deserts.

Augt. 25. Robt. Williams the Bell-Ringer, Publisher [Crier] and Grave-digger died this morn. He was suddenly stricken the fifth-day before, just after his ringing the five-a-clock Bell; fell down as essayed to go up his own stairs, and I think so continued speechless till death. Mr. Baily took notice of the Suddeness of it in his prayer.

Second day, September 9, 1695. Set out for Bristow, with Mr. Danforth and Mr. Cook. Baited at Neponset, din'd at Billenges, where were also Mr. Newton and Mr. Cary; went to Woodcock's, refresh'd there, so to Rehoboth; lodgd at the Bear, Sheriff was there to meet us; Major Generall also lodged there in his way home from New-London.

Third-day, Sept. 10. To Bristow by the Bridge. Had two

Actions concerning Land. Sup at Mr. Saffin's. I lodgd at Mr. Wilkins's. Major Church is sick, I visit him; came with Mr. Danforth to Taunton, there din'd; from thence to Bridgewater, visited Mr. Keith. Lodg'd at our Landlord Hayward's, who, by Mr. Danforth's procurement, pray'd with us very well in the evening. Mr. Cook was sick and scarce slept all night.

In the morn, Sept. 12, set out about Sunrise; din'd at Mr. Pain's at Braintrey, got home a little after one of the Clock, and find all well, blessed be God.

Sept. 17, 1695. Govr. Bradstreet has the remainder of his Goods put on board Mr. Graften; The house being empty, I prevail with him and his Lady to walk to our house, and wish us joy of it. They sat there near an hour with Mrs. Corwin and Wharton. Govr. Bradstreet drank a glass or two of wine, eat some fruit, took a pipe of Tabacco in the new Hall, and wish'd me joy of the house, and desired our prayers; came to us over the little Stonebridge; went away between 12. and 1. in Madam Richard's new Coach and horses. About three, the Lieut. Governour, Mr. Secretary, Sergeant and Sewall waited on them at Madam Richards's, to take leave; in the way the Letter met us giving an account of ten men shot at Pemaquid, out of 24. going to get wood: four of whom are dead. Hugh March, George's Son, was killed at the first shot. This was Monday was Senight. This day, Sept. 17, was a great Training at Boston: many Gentlemen and Gentlewomen dine in Tents on the Common. Colonel had a Standard: Great firing most of the day. I should have remembered that Govr. Bradstreet this day sent the Halberts, Copies of the Records, and a Loadstone belonging to the Publick, to the Secretary, who caus'd them to be lodg'd at present in the Town-house Chamber; where I saw them when went to write Letters to Capt March.

Sept. 18. Govr Bradstreet sets sail for Salem about Six aclock in the morning.

This day Mr. Torrey and his wife, Mr. Willard and his wife, and Cous. Quinsey dine with us; 'tis the first time has been at our house with his new wife; was much pleas'd with our painted shutters; in pleasancy said he thought he had been got into Paradise. This day, Sept. 18, Mr. Cook enters the Lists with Col. Paige, and sues for Capt. Keyn's Farm again. Govr. Bradstreet arriv'd at Salem about 3 P.M.

Sixth-day, Sept. 20. Mr. Borland's Briganteen arrives, 6 weeks from Falmouth, in whom comes Mr. Edward Brattle, Mr. Governeur, &c. The Lord Bellamont is made our Governour. Hardly will come over before the Spring.

Oct. 12. Jno Cunable finishes the Stairs out of the wooden house to the top of the Brick house. Little Mary grows a little better after very sore illness.

Oct. 7th. Jno Brown's family, of Turkey hill, are led captive. All are brought back save one boy that was kill'd; knock'd the rest on the head, save an infant.

Oct. 14, 1695. I visit Mrs. Saunderson and pray God to grant her Mercy and Grace to help in time of need. Oct. 15. She dies. Oct. 17. Buried, so that house is emptied of its ancient Inhabitants. Sewall, Dumer, Frary, Butler, Hill, Maryon, bearers. Lord teach me to abide in, and to go out of the world. Mr. Moodey at the Funeral.

Seventh day, Oct. 19, 1695. Pray'd for God's Favour towards Sam. That might duely wait on Christ at his Table to morrow &c., with fasting.

Oct. 26. Mr. Banistar watches, and calls me about break of day to see the Comet, which seems to point from East to West.

Dec. 19. Thomas Maule, Shopkeeper of Salem, is brought before the Council to answere for his printing and publishing a pamphlet quarto, 260. pages, entituled Truth held forth and maintained, owns the book, but will not own all till sees his Copy which is at N. York with——Bradford who printed it. Saith he writt to the Governour of New York before he could get it printed. Book is order'd to be burnt, being stuff'd with notorious Lyes and Scandals, and he Recognises to answer at next Court of Assize and General Goal Delivery to be held for the County of Essex. He acknowledg'd that what was written concerning the circumstance of Major General Athertons death, was a mistake: p. 112, 113. was chiefly insisted on against him; which believe was a surprize to him, he expecting to be examined in some point of Religion, as should seem by his bringing his Bible under his Arm.

I was with Dame Walker, and Sam. came to call me to take T. Maule's Recognisance; I told her Sam. was there: she pray'd God to bless him, and to bless all my posterity.

Dec. 20. Dame Walker is very restless; said she was past all food now, had quite lost her Appetite. Said, why doe living man complain, man for the punishment of his Sin? Justified God, and pray'd Him to help her, and enable her to bear what He laid on her; spoke how hard twas to comply with that Text, Thy will be done; we would fain have our own Wills; but God could of unwilling make us willing. Last night she pray'd that God would take her to Himself. When I took leave this morn, she Thank'd me for all my Visits, and acknowledged the kindness of me and my family. After I was gon, in the Afternoon, Dec. 20. Mehetabel sais she heard her Grandmother say, How long Lord, how long? Come Lord Jesus! Mehetabel asked what she said to her, she reply'd, How good is God.

Seventh day, Dec. 21. Between 8. and 9. I went to see Dame Walker, and found her very weak and much alter'd Mehetabel told her I was there, she said with a low voice, thank him. Afterward Mehetabel ask'd her if should pray she said, I stand in need. Twas the last day of the Week, and so I went to prayer, insisting on God's being a present help in time of need, and pray'd that God would strengthen her Faith that so she might enter into his Rest. I ask'd her if she heard her Answer was, I thank God, I did. I went home to Prayer

Intending after that to go to Mr. Willard to pray him to give her one Lift more heaven-ward. But before I could get away, a Girl came runing to call me. And by that time I could get thether, the Good woman had expired, or was just expiring, being about Ten of the clock in the morning. God fulfilled his good Word in her and kept her Leaf from withering.

She had an odd Conceipt all the last night of her life, that she was in Travail; and though she ceas'd groaning and gave attention to me when at prayer; yet one of the last words I heard her say, was, My child is dead within me; which were indeed some of the very last.

Secund day, Jan. 6th 169$\frac{5}{6}$. Kept a Day of Fasting with Prayer for the Conversion of my Son, and his settlement in a Trade that might be good for Soul and body. *Uxor praegnans est.* Governour's expected Arrival, which will bring great changes. Suply for the South-Church. Three Courts sit to morrow. Lord's Supper the next Sabbath-day. Mr. Moodey's Entanglements, Watertown. Church of England. New England. My Hair. Read Epistles to Timothy, Titus, Philemon, Hebrews. Sung the 143, 51, and 130. Psalms. I had hope that seeing God pardon'd all Israel's Iniquities, He would pardon mine, as being part of Israel.

Jan. 11. 169$\frac{5}{6}$. I write a Letter to Mr. Zech. Walker acquainting him with his Mother's death and Funeral; that some Recompence ought to be made to Mehetabel and Mary for their faithfull and Laborious Attendance on their Grandmother. Altho' I reckon my self abundantly satisfied for any little Service I did or could doe for our dear friend, by her desireable Company and harty Thanks; yet I earnestly desire your Prayers, that my aged Father and Mother may live and die with such like Faith and frame of Spirit as this our Sarah did. I delivered this Letter to be given to the Post on Second day morning, Jan. 13, 169$\frac{5}{6}$.

About 10. aclock Jan. 13, 169$\frac{5}{6}$. Cous. Dumer came to invite me to goe along with him to Cambridge to visit Mr. Danforth. About Noon we set out, and at Mr. Danforth's Gate, meet with Mr. N. Hobart and Trowbridge; Mr. Danforth made us dine there; then after awhile, Mr. Hobart was called in to Pray, which he did excellently, Mr. Morton being by, who came with us from the Colledge. Note. When were there at first, Mr. Danforth bad me look on the Cup-board's head for a book; I told him I saw there a Law-book, Wingate on the Common Law. He said he would lend it me, I should speak to Amsden to call for it; and if he died, he would give it me. Again when took leave after prayer, He said he lent me that Book not to wrap up but to read, and if misliked it, should tell him of it. By that time Cous. and I could get to the Ferry twas quite dark. Capt. Hunting told us the River was full of Ice and no getting over. But I went to Sheaf and he hallowed over Jn° Russell again. Boat came to Ballard's Wharf below the lodg'd Ice, from whence had a very comfortable Passage over with Madam Foxcroft.

When I came in, past 7. at night, my wife met me in the Entry and told me Betty had surprised them. I was surprised with the abruptness of the Relation. It seems Betty Sewall had given some signs of dejection and sorrow; but a little after diner she burst out into an amazing cry, which caus'd all the family to cry too; Her Mother ask'd the reason; she gave none; at last said she was afraid she should goe to Hell, her Sins were not pardon'd. She was first wounded by my reading a Sermon of Mr. Norton's, about the 5th of Jan. Text Jn° 7. 34. Ye shall seek me and shall not find me. And those words in the Sermon, Jn° 8. 21. Ye shall seek me and shall die in your sins, ran in her mind, and terrified her greatly. And staying at home Jan. 12. she read out of Mr. Cotton Mather—Why hath Satan filled thy heart, which increas'd her Fear. Her Mother ask'd her whether she pray'd. She answer'd, Yes; but feared her prayers were not heard because her Sins not pardon'd. Mr. Willard though sent for timelyer, yet not being told of the message, till bruised Dinsdals [?] was given him; He came not till after I came home. He discoursed with Betty who could not give a distinct account, but was confused as his phrase was, and as had experienced in himself. Mr. Willard pray'd excellently. The Lord bring Light and Comfort out of this dark and dreadful Cloud, and Grant that Christ's being formed in my dear child, may be the issue of these painfull pangs.

Feb. 1. 169⅚. Sam. Haugh came to speak about Frank's burial: I sent Atherton away before and spake to Sam as to his Mistress' Maid being with child, and that she Laid it to him, and told him if she were with child by him, it concerned him seriously to consider what were best to be done; and that a Father was obliged to look after Mother and child. Christ would one day call him to an account and demand of him what was become of the child: and if [he] married not the woman, he would always keep at a distance from those whose temporal and spiritual good he was bound to promote to the uttermost of his power. Could not discern that any impression was made on him. I remark'd to him the unsuitableness of his frame under a business of so great and solemn Concern.

Sixth-day, Feb. 7th. Capt. Frary was pass'd by, though there, which several took notice of. Note. Last night Sam. could not sleep because of my Brother's speaking to him of removing to some other place, mentioning Mr. Usher's. I put him to get up a little wood, and he even fainted, at which Brother was much startled, and advis'd to remove him forthwith and place him somewhere else, or send him to Salem and he would doe the best he could for him. Since, I have express'd doubtfullness to Sam. as to his staying there.

He mention'd to me Mr. Wadsworth's Sermon against Idleness, which was an Affliction to him. He said his was an idle Calling, and that he did more at home than there, take one day with another. And he mention'd Mr. Stoddard's words to me, that should place him with a good Master, and where had fullness of Imployment. It seems Sam. overheard him, and now alleged these words against his being where he was because of his idleness. Mention'd also the difficulty of the imployment by reason of the numerousness of Goods and hard to distinguish them, many not being marked; whereas Books, the price of them was set down, and so could sell them readily. I spake to Capt. Checkly again and again, and he gave me no encouragement that his being there would be to Sam's profit; and Mrs. Checkly always discouraging.

Mr. Willard's Sermon from those Words, What doest thou here Elijah? was an Occasion to hasten the Removal.

Feb. 10. Secund-day. I went to Mr. Willard to ask whether had best keep him at home to day. He said, No: but tell Capt. Checkly first; but when I came back, Sam was weeping and much discompos'd, and loth to goe because it was a little later than usual, so I thought twas hardly fit for him to go in that Case, and went to Capt. Checkly and told him how it was, and thank'd him for his kindness to Sam. Capt. Checkly desired Sam. might come to their house and not be strange there, for which I thank'd him very kindly. He presented his Service to my wife, and I to his who was in her Chamber. Capt. Checkly gave me Sam's Copy-book that lay in a drawer.

Just before I got thether, I met Mr. Grafford who told me that Mumford said I was a knave. The good Lord give me Truth in the inward parts, and finally give Rest unto my dear Son, and put him into some Calling wherein He will accept of him to Serve Him.

Sabbath, Feb. 16. 169⁵⁄₆. Mr. Emmerson preaches twice in the new Meetinghouse at Watertown, which is the first time. Capt. Checkly's Son Samuel is baptized with us. I was very sorrowfull by reason of the unsettledness of my Samuel.

Feb. 22. 169⁵⁄₆. Betty comes into me almost as soon as I was up and tells me the disquiet she had when waked; told me was afraid should go to Hell, was like Spira, not Elected. Ask'd her what I should pray for, she said, that God would pardon her Sin and give her a new heart. I answer'd her Fears as well as I could, and pray'd with many Tears on either part; hope God heard us. I gave her solemnly to God.

Feb. 26. 169⅚. I pray'd with Sam. alone, that God would direct our way as to a Calling for him.

It seems John Cornish essay'd yesterday to goe to carry Cloth to the fulling-mill, and perished in the Storm; this day was brought frozen to Town, a very sad spectacle.

Sabbath, May 3, 1696. Betty can hardly read her chapter for weeping; tells me she is afraid she is gon back, does not taste that sweetness in reading the Word which once she did; fears that what was once upon her is worn off. I said what I could to her, and in the evening pray'd with her alone.

Fifth-day, May 7, 1696. Col. Shrimpton marries his Son to his wive's Sisters daughter, Elisabeth Richardson. All of the Council in Town were invited to the Wedding, and many others. Only I was not spoken to. As I was glad not to be there because the lawfullness of the intermarrying of Cousin-Germans is doubted; so it grieves me to be taken up in the Lips of Talkers, and to be in such a Condition that Col. Shrimpton shall be under a temptation in defence of Himself, to wound me; if any should hapen to say, Why was not such a one here? The Lord help me not to do, or neglect any thing that should prevent the dwelling of brethren together in unity.

May 18. By reason of the Major Generall's illness, I am forced to go to Ipswich Court; and being to go, my wife desir'd me to go on to Newbury; I went with Brother on Wednesday night. Visited Father, Mother, Friends, return'd to Salem, got thether about Nine. Supp'd well with the Fish bought out of Wenham Pond. Between eleven and noon, Tho. Messenger comes in, and brings me the amazing news of my Wive's hard Time and my Son's being Still-born. We get up our Horses from the Ship, and set out by Starlight about 12, yet the Bells rung for five before we got over the Ferry.

Found my wife as well as usually; but I was grievously stung to find a sweet desirable Son dead, who had none of my help to succour him and save his Life. The Lord pardon all my Sin, and Wandering and Neglect, and sanctify to me this singular Affliction.

27th At the Council the Lt. Govr. reads the Letters that give notice from the Lords of a French Squadron intending for America: they will afford us what Assistance they can under the present Circumstance of Affairs. Reads also Mr. Blathwayts Letter recomending the subscribing the Association by all in publick place and Trust, with one drawn for that purpose. This day also receiv'd an Express from Col. Pynchon, of Count Frontenac's coming ag^t^ the 5 Nations, or Albany, or N. E., or all, with 2000 French and 1000 Indians: Casteen with 4 or 500 to hold us in play the mean while. The wind coming North last night ships arrive at Nantasket this morn. Mr. Myles and Bullivant come to Town.

Fourth day Augt. 5th. Mr. Melyen, upon a slight occasion, spoke to me very smartly about the Salem Witchcraft: in discourse he said, if a man should take Beacon hill on 's back, carry it away; and then bring it and set it in its place again, he should not make any thing of that.

Seventh-day, Augt. 15th. Bro^r^. St. Sewall comes to Town; Gets an order to Col. Hathorne for erecting a Beacon on Pigeon hill on Cape-Anne, and for pressing 20. men at Marblehead. This day vessels arrive from Barbados, bring news of 10. great ships at Petit Quavers, of between 60 and 90 Guns. Mr. Williams, the physician, and his wife are both dead. Mrs. Hatch and her children in Tears for the death of her husband, which was brought to her about an hour by Sun. We are in pain for Saco fort. Guns were heard thrice on fifth day all day long. One Peters and Hoyt scalp'd at Andover this week; were not shot, but knock'd on the head.

Septr. 10. Letter. Mrs. Martha Oakes. Not finding oportunity to speak with you at your house, nor at my own, I write, to persuade you to be sensible that your striking your daughter-in-law before me, in my house, is not justifiable: though twas but a small blow, twas not a small fault: especially considering your promise to refrain from speech it self; or at least any that might give disturbance. As for New England, It is a cleaner Country than ever you were in before, and, therefore, with disdain to term it *filthy,* is a sort of Blasphemie, which, by proceeding out of your mouth, hath defiled you. I write not this to upbraid, but to admonish you, with whom I sympathize under your extraordinary provocations and pressures; and pray God comand you freedom from them. S. S.

S^{r}. 16. Keep a day of Prayer in the East end of the Town-House, Govr., Council and Assembly. Mr. Morton begun with Prayer, Mr. Allin pray'd, Mr. Willard preached—If God be with us who can be against us?—Spake smartly at last about the Salem Witchcrafts, and that no order had been suffer'd to come forth by Authority to ask Gods pardon.

Octr. 3, 1696. Mr. Joseph Baxter lodges here, being to preach for Mr. Willard on the Sabbath: Deacon Frary came to me on Friday; told me Mr. Willard put him upon getting help on the fifth day at even, because disapointed of Mr. Sparhawk. He sent that even to Braintrey; but for fear of failing rode thether himself on Sixth-day morn and secured Him: After the Meeting at Bro^{r}. Wheelers, came and told me of it, and earnestly proposed to me that He might lodge at my house; which I thought I could not avoid except I would shut my doors against one of Christ's servants; which I also inclin'd to, only was afraid lest som should take offence. And my Library was convenient for Him.

Fifth day Octr 22. Capt. Byfield Marries his daughter Debora to James Lyde, before Mr. Willard. Mr. Sparhawk would have had her. Octr. 29th Clouds hinder our sight of the eclipsed Moon; though tis aparently dark by means of it.

Octr 30. Mr. Wigglesworth tells me that one John Bucknam of Malden, above 50 years old, has been perfectly dumb near 18 years, and now within about 3 weeks has his understanding and speech restored. He is much affected with the Goodness of God to him herein.

2[d] day, Nov[r] 2. Mary goes to Mrs. Thair's to learn to Read and Knit.

Second-day, Nov[r]. 30. Many Scholars go in the After noon to Scate on Fresh-pond; William Maxwell, and John Eyre fall in and are drown'd. Just about Candle-lighting the news of it is brought to Town, which affects persons exceedingly. Mr. Eyre the father cryes out bitterly. Decr. 1. The body of Jn[o] Eyre is brought to Town. Dec[r]. 3. is buried. Ministers of Boston had Gloves and Rings, Counsellors Gloves, of Boston. Bearers, Hutchinson, Dudley, Sim. Bradstreet, Dumer Jer., Jn[o] Winthrop, Belchar. Maxwell was buried at Cambridge. Paul Miller, his 2 sons, and about 4 more drowned last week; vessel and corn lost coming from Barstable.

Dec[r]. 2. 1696. Now about Capt. Byfield brings in a long Bill from the deputys for a Fast and Reformation, written by Mr. Cotton Mather, to which a Streamer was added expressing that Partiality in Courts of Justice was obvious; with a Vote on it that 500 should be printed, should be read; and sent up for Concurrence: 'twas deny'd; and our Bill for a Fast was sent down; Dept[s] deny'd; and our Bill for a Fast was sent down; Dept[s] deny'd that. Gov[r]. told them the way was unusual, they had taken, sending out a Comittee, calling the Ministers, voting all, and never letting the Council know: that it pertain'd principally to the Gov[r]. and Council to set forth such orders with a motion from them. A while after Capt. Byfield came in, and said 'twas no new thing, and they had taken no wrong step. Little was said to him. It seems this message is enter'd in their Booke. The Council were exceedingly grieved to be thus roughly treated. About Dec[r]. 18, Mr. Mather, Allen, Willard, C. Mather give in a paper subscribed by them, shewing their dislike of our draught for the Colledge

Charter, and desiring that their Names might not be entered therein. One chief reason was their apointing the Gov[r]. and Council for Visitor.

Dec[r]. 21. A very great Snow is on the Ground. I go in the morn to Mr. Willard, to entreat him to chuse his own time to come and pray with little Sarah: He comes a little before night, and prays very fully and well. Mr. Mather, the President, had pray[d] with her in the time of the Courts sitting. Dec[r]. 22. being Catechising day, I give Mr. Willard a note to pray for my daughter publickly, which he did. Note, this morn Madam Elisa Bellingham came to our house and upbraided me with setting my hand to pass Mr. Wharton's acc[o] to the Court, where he obtain'd a Judgm[t] for Eustace's farm. I was wheadled and hector'd into that business, and have all along been uneasy in the remembrance of it: and now there is one come who will not spare to lay load. The Lord take away my filthy garments, and give me change of Rayment. This day I remove poor little Sarah into my Bed-chamber, where about Break of Day Dec[r]. 23. she gives up the Ghost in Nurse Cowell's Arms. Born, Nov. 21. 1694. Neither I nor my wife were by: Nurse not expecting so sudden a change, and having promis'd to call us. I thought of Christ's Words, could you not watch with me one hour! and would fain have sat up with her: but fear of my wives illness, who is very valetudinarious, made me to lodge with her in the new Hall, where was call'd by Jane's Cry, to take notice of my dead daughter. Nurse did long and pathetically ask our pardon that she had not call'd us, and said she was surpriz[d]. Thus this very fair day is rendered fowl to us by reason of the general Sorrow and Tears in the family. Master Chiever was here the evening before, I desir'd him to pray for my daughter. The Chapt[r] read in course on Dec[r]. 23. m. was Deut. 22. which made me sadly reflect that I had not been so thorowly tender of my daughter; nor so effectually carefull of her Defence and preservation as I should have been. The good Lord pity and pardon and help for the future as to those God has still left me.

Dec[r] 24. Sam. recites to me in Latin, Mat. 12. from the 6th to the end of the 12th v. The 7th verse did awfully bring to mind the Salem Tragedie.

6th day, Dec[r]. 25, 1696. We bury our little daughter. In the chamber, Joseph in course reads Ecclesiastes 3[d]. a time to be born and a time to die—Elisabeth, Rev. 22. Hanah, the 38th Psalm. I speak to each, as God helped, to our mutual comfort I hope. I order'd Sam. to read the 102. Psalm. Elisha Cooke, Edw. Hutchinson, John Baily, and Josia Willard bear my little daughter to the Tomb.

Note. Twas wholly dry, and I went at noon to see in what order things were set; and there I was entertain'd with a view of, and converse with, the Coffins of my dear Father Hull, Mother Hull, Cousin Quinsey, and my Six Children: for the little posthumous was now took up and set in upon that that stands on John's: so are three, one upon another twice, on the bench at the end. My Mother ly's on a lower bench, at the end, with head to her Husband's head: and I order'd little Sarah to be set on her Grandmother's feet. 'Twas an awfull yet pleasing Treat; Having said, The Lord knows who shall be brought hether next, I came away.

Mr. Willard pray'd with us the night before; I gave him a Ring worth about 20[s]. Sent the President one, who is sick of the Gout. He pray[d] with my little daughter. Mr. Oakes, the Physician, Major Townsend, Speaker, of whoes wife I was a Bearer, and was join'd with me in going to Albany and has been Civil and treated me several times. Left a Ring at Madam Cooper's for the Governour. Gave not one pair of Gloves save to the Bearers. Many went to the Church this day, I met them coming home, as went to the Tomb. 7th day Dec[r] 26. Roger Judd tells me of a ship arriv'd at Rode Island from England, and after, that Mr. Ive has written that most judged the King of France was dead, or dying. Ship comes from New Castle, several weeks after the Falkland. Jany 1. 6th day 169$\frac{6}{7}$. One with a Trumpet sounds a Levet [Blast] at our window just about break of day, bids me good morrow and wishes health and hapiness to attend me. I was awake before, and my wife, so we heard him: but went not to the window, nor spake a word. The Lord fit me for his coming in whatsoever way it be. Mr. Willard had the Meeting at his house to day, but We had no Invitation to be there as is usual.

On the 22th of May I buried my abortive son; so neither of us were then admitted of God to be there, and now the Owners of the family admit us not: It may be I must never more hear a Sermon there. The Lord pardon all my Sins of Omission and Commission: and by his Almighty power make me meet to be partaker of the Inheritance with the S^ts in Light. Second-day Jany 11, 169$\frac{6}{7}$ God helped me to pray more than ordinarily, that He would make up our Loss in the burial of our little daughter and other children, and that would give us a Child to Serve Him, pleading with Him as the Institutor of Marriage, and the Author of every good work. Jany 15. Gridley's wife dies in child-bed.

[Petition put up by Mr. Sewall on the Fast Day.]

Copy of the Bill I put up on the Fast day; giving it to Mr. Willard as he pass'd by, and standing up at the reading of it, and bowing when finished; in the Afternoon.

Samuel Sewall, sensible of the reiterated strokes of God upon himself and family; and being sensible, that as to the Guilt contracted upon the opening of the late Comission of Oyer and Terminer at Salem (to which the order for this Day relates) he is, upon many accounts, more concerned than any that he knows of, Desires to take the Blame and shame of it, Asking pardon of men, And especially desiring prayers that God, who has an Unlimited Authority, would pardon that sin and all other his sins; personal and Relative: And according to his infinite Benignity, and Sovereignty, Not Visit the sin of him, or of any other, upon himself or any of his, nor upon the Land: But that He would powerfully defend him against all Temptations to Sin, for the future; and vouchsafe him the efficacious, saving Conduct of his Word and Spirit.

Jany 26. 169$^{6}/_{7}$ I lodged at Charlestown, at Mrs. Shepards, who tells me Mr. Harvard built that house. I lay in the chamber next the street. As I lay awake past midnight, In my Meditation, I was affected to consider how long agoe God had made provision for my comfortable Lodging that night; seeing that was Mr. Harvards house: And that led me to think of Heaven the House not made with hands, which God for many Thousands of years has been storing with the richest furniture (saints that are from time to time placed there), and that I had some hopes of being entertain'd in that Magnificent Convenient Palace, every way fitted and furnished. These thoughts were very refreshing to me.

Jany 28. 169$^{6}/_{7}$ Mr. Palmer marries Mrs. Abigail Hutchinson. Febr. 4 Bro^{r} Hawkins and his wife, the Thurtons, Sam. and Atherton Haugh, Joseph Gerrish and W^{m}. Longfellow dine with us. Febr. 5. extream cold, which discern not when Joseph went away. This evening Mr. Willard, Bromfield, Eyre, Sergeant, Frary, Hill, Williams, Oliver, Checkly, Davis, Wally, Stoddard, met at my house. Mr. Willard pray'd. Then discours^{d} what was best to be done relating to the desires of some for a meeting; whether twere best to call one, or no. Mr. Willard shew^{d} his resentments of the disorderly carriage in striving to bring in Mr. Bradstreet, after only thrice preaching [as a candidate for the South Church], and that in that way, he should not be settled with us till he Mr. W. was in his Grave. That he had a Negative, and was not only a Moderator. Shew'd his dislike of the Person and his Preaching, inferiour to the ministerial Gifts of others. Before the Meeting broke up, I said his Preaching was very agreeable to me, I thought not of him, had no hand in bringing him to preach, had prejudices against him, was ready to start at first when any spake of fixing on him; yet as often as he preached, he came nearer and nearer to me. Spake this chiefly because all that Mr. Willard had said of Mr. Bradstreet, had been exceedingly undervaluing: and because Mr. Willard said no body had been with him to speak to him about Mr. Bradstreet but Mr. Stoddard. Mr. Oliver said if Mr. Willard were so averse, had rather let it rest. Sometimes said were now ready for a new Meetinghouse. Some, Let us call Mr. Bailey. At last agreed to mention the matter to the church after the Afternoon Exercise. Febr. 7. Mr. Willard recapitulats how long he had been our Pastor; near 20. years; and near 18. years alone, had to his measure served God faithfully, was desirous of Help, lay not in him, yet had none; if what he propounded more than a year ago had been attended, might have made for the Glory of God. Ask'd if now were ready to pitch on any; if were, then must have a Fast. None speake; at last Capt. Ephr. Savage desired might meet in sons dwelling house, many were there present which were not of us. Mr. Willard assented, and on Mr. Sergeants motion, apointed to meet at his house, 15. Inst[t] at 2 p.m. When at our house, some said Charlestown being before us, to call a Fast after they had call'd Mr. Bradstreet would be evil spoken of: the person of their desires being gon. Some said that Fasting now at Charlestown and here was but a Trick; not just so: but tending that way. Mr. Willard said Charlestown would be before us, do what we could; and if they call'd him 'twas not fit for us to meddle till he had given his Answer: som look'd at this as Artifice in the Ministers to prevent the South Church. For when Mr. Willard propounded Mr. Pemberton by name, 1695, No Fast preceded. If Mr. Willard had not so propounded, believe the thing had been issued at that time: but many look'd on it as an Imposition and tending to infringe their Liberty of choice. I had been with Mr. Willard the day before, and told him some scruples that I was not just ready to act till had enquired further.

Feb. 8. Mr. Bromfield and Eyre call me, and we visit Mr. H. Usher, who is now brought to Town about a week ago; Lay at Malden some time by reason of a fall from 's horse last 4th day five weeks. Febr. 9. I visit Mr. Willard: spake with him after he began, about our conference last 6th day, told him the reason of my speaking as I did; because had heard he should say, I forc'd the Church Meeting: whereas I intended not so; but as we had engaged silence, I told him my heart; as I said I always did when he confer'd with me and enquired of me in such cases. He said was sorry he propounded Mr. Pemberton as he did. Seem'd to resent my saying: That the Negative was a high point, and better not to talk of it then (which at the conference) term'd it a check, I think parted good friends. Much vilified Mr. Bradstreet; hardly allowed him any thing but a Memory, and the Greek Tongue, with a Little poesy. I said what shall Charlestown doe? Answer was, Let them do as they please. Mr. Willard is to assist on the Fast Day, which proves very cold, 4th day Feb. 10.

Febr. 10. 4th day 169 6/7 Goodw. Duen putting on a Rugg and going into our house much scares the children; so that come running to me throw the old Hall, with a very amazing Cry. I was sawing wood; and much surpris'd. Wife came and all. The Lord save me and his people from astonishing, suddain, desolating Judgmts; pardon all my folly and perverting my way, and help me to walk with a right foot. This was between 10 and 11. aclock. m. Deacon Maryon went from hence but a little before.

March 27, 1697. About 10. at night Govr Bradstreet dyes; which we are told of March, 29th at Cambridge, where we were upon the account of Mrs. Danforth's Funeral. Madam Leverett, Madam Cook, and my wife and I rode together in the Coach.

Sixth-day, Apr. 2. 1697. Lieut-Governour, Mr. Secretary, Col. Shrimpton, and Sewall ride to Salem. It rain'd most of the way, and yet, a little beyond the Butts, Col. Gedney met the Govr. with a small Troop; and in the Rain led us along through the Town to the Fort, to view it and see what condition 'twas in; and also the Brest-Work: From thence went back to Col. Gedney's. Governour, Mr. Secretary, Col. Phillips and Sewall dined there: From about two *post meridiem,* the wether clear'd and was warm. About 3 was the Funeral; Bearers, Mr. Danforth, Major Gen. Winthrop, Mr. Cook, Col. Hutchinson, Sewall, Mr. Secretary: Col. Gedney and Major Brown led the Widow; I bore the Feet of the Corps into the Tomb, which is new, in the Old Burying place.

April 29. 5th day is signalised by the Atchievment of Hanah Dustin, Mary Neff, and Samuel Lenerson; who, kill'd Two men [Indians], their Masters, and two women and 6. others, and have brought in Ten Scalps.

May 1. 1697. The first Sheet of *Phænomena Apocalyptica* is wrought off. 3^{d} day May 11. Elisabeth Sewall, and Joana Gerrish set sail for Newbury in Edward Poor, between 10. and 11. a-clock, fair wind. Sent my Father a cheese and Barrel of Flower by him. Aunt Quinsey, and Cousin Edmund here. Fourth-day, May 12., very brisk Southerly wind; so that hope Betty is got well to Newbury. This day wrought off the first half-sheet of the *Phænomena;* which I corrected my self. Hanah Dustan came to see us; I gave her part of Conecticut Flax. She saith her Master, whom she kill'd, did formerly live with Mr. Roulandson at Lancaster: He told her, that when he pray'd the English way, he thought that was good: but now he found the French way was better. The single man shewed the night before, to Saml. Lenarson, how he used to knock Englishmen on the head and take off their Scalps; little thinking that the Captives would make some of their first experiment upon himself. Sam. Lenarson kill'd him.

Fourth-day; Septr. 8. 1697. The Governour and Council

first meet in the Council-Chamber, as it is now fitted with cieling, Glazing, Painting, new Floor that brings it to a Level; New Hearth even with it. Deputies sent for in; Lt Governour made a Speech, that as they saw by the many Prorogations, He hoped my Lord should have now receiv'd them. I presented his Honour with the view of a half-sheet, which begins *In quatuor angulis terræ.* Col. Pierce gave an account of the Body of Lime-Stone discover'd at Newbury, and the order of the Selectmen published by James Brown, Dept. Sheriff, to prohibit any persons from carrying any more away under the penalty of 20^{s}. It seems they began to come with Teams by 30. in a day: The Town will have a Meeting, and bring it to some Regulation. Our Momford saith tis good Marble. Ens. James Noyes found it out.

Septr 14. Went to Bristow over the Ferry, Bridge being down. Lodge at Mr. Wilkins; were met by sundry of Bristow Gentlemen. Issued our Business to good Satisfaction to our selves; Fourth-day was a storm, else might have husbanded it so as to have come to Rehoboth that night: But are glad of the Rain after so sore a Drought.

Septr 16. fifth-day, Mr. Danforth and I and our men, set out to come home, Not one creature accompanying us to the Ferry. Had a very comfortable Journey No Dust moving. Visited Mr. Greenwood Din'd at Woodcocks with boil'd venison. Discours'd with a Lin Quaker removing to Philadelphia, one Burrel; Advis'd him to read the 35th of Jeremiah: The Contents in that Bible mentioned Pride, which he was guilty of. Go by Wrentham; visit Mr. Mann, who hath 11. children. From thence to Medfield, Lodge at Capt. Barbers, visit Mrs. Wilson in the even; give her 4 p^{s} 8/8 [pieces of eight, Spanish dollars].

Septr 17. I view Mr. Baxters House and the Orchard Capt Frary hath given to the Ministry, which lies very convenient; A living Brook runing by it; and throw Mr. Baxters. Visit Capt. Thurston, who was glad to see me. When at Dedham visit Mr. Belchar; Mr. Whitman is there, are going to Connecticut. Go home a little before one *post meridiem.* Is a Rumor at Rehoboth that Col. Gibson is gon into Canada. One Jamison brought on the news of our Armys Engagement. Blessed be God who hath carried us out and brought us home safely and that preserves so many of our Towns like Flocks of Sheep in a howling Wilderness, naked and defenceless.

Sixth-day, Octr 1. 1697. Jer. Balchar's sons came for us to go to the Island. My Wife, through Indisposition, could not goe: But I carried Sam. Hanah, Elisa, Joseph, Mary and Jane Tapan: I prevail'd with Mr. Willard to goe, He carried Simon, Elisabeth, William, Margaret, and Elisa Tyng: Had a very comfortable Passage thither and home again; though against Tide: Had first Butter, Honey, Curds and Cream. For Diner, very good Rost Lamb, Turkey, Fowls, Aplepy. After Diner sung the 121 Psalm. Note. A Glass of spirits my Wife sent stood upon a Joint-Stool which, Simon W. jogging, it fell down and broke all to shivers: I said twas a lively Emblem of our Fragility and Mortality. When came home met Capt Scottow led between two: He came to visit me and fell down and hurt himself; bruis'd his Nose, within a little of our House.

Upon the fourth day of the Week Septr 29, 1697, A Council met at Plimouth:

Septr 30. fifth day, They published their Advice, that Mr. Cotton should make an orderly secession from the Church. Advis'd the Church to dismiss him with as much Charity as the Rule would admit of; and provide for themselvs. "This was for his Notorious Breaches of the Seventh Comandmt, and Undue Carriage in Chusing Elders. Thus Christs words are fulfilled, Unsavoury Salt is cast to the Dunghill. A most awfull Instance! "

Fifth-day, Novr 4th Guns fired with respect to the King's Birth-day. At night great Illumination made in the Townhouse; Governour and Council and many Gentlemen there.

About 8. Mr. Brattle and Newman let fly their Fireworks from Cotton-Hill; Governour and Council went thither with a Trumpet sounding. Note. Governour, Mr. Secretary and I went to see Mr. Morton; before these works began, Had the Epistle to his Honour, a proof of it, in my pocket: but had not oportunity to shew it: was taken this day. I went and visited Mr. Baily, who discoursed pretty cheerily.

Fourth-day Novr 10th. Lt Governour and Council met at the Council Chamber, were warn'd by Maxwell the day before. I took that oportunity to present the Lt Governour with seven *Phænomena!* I said the Records and References were laid before his Hon^{r} as it were in open Court; and pray'd that his Honour would judge of the Cause according to its own Merits, and not according to the deficiency of the Attorney, who had fallen short as to the duely urging of many proper pleas. His Honour said it should be favourably Judged of. In the evening, not having a Thanksgiving sermon at hand, I resolv'd to read in course, not thinking what the Chapter might be, and it prov'd to be Luke, 1. I aplied Marys question to the business of the Natives; Though means fail'd, God could easily convert them: Sung the song of Zecharra and Simeon.

In the morn. Novr 12th Sung in course the 24th Ps., which was not aware of till my Son named it. Much Rain fell this day and night following; which was extreamly needed, for the Wells, for Cattell to drink, and for the Mills.

Sixth-day, Novr. 19. Mr. Higginson comes as far as Brothers to see me; which I wonder'd at. Mr. Hale and I lodg'd together: He discours'd me about writing a History of the Witchcraft; I fear lest he go into the other extream. Came home with the Maj^{r} General, din'd at Madam Paiges; there found Hancock, Allen, and Sam. Haugh. Found all well, *Laus Deo.*

Jany 23, 169⅞ Very Cold. Mr. Fitch preacheth with us and pronounceth the Blessing, Mr. Willard not being there, by reason of illness: Text was, The Lord is my shepherd &c.

Mr. Willard comes abroad in the Afternoon, and preacheth excellently; baptiseth a child and a woman. Very thin Assemblies this Sabbath, and last; and great Coughing: very few women there. Mr. Willard pray'd for mitigation of the wether; and the south Wind begins to blow with some vigor. My clock stood still this morning, and yesterday morn, which has not done many years.

Fourth-day, Febr. 9. Last night, about nine of the clock, Col. Shrimpton dyes of an Apoplexy. Capt. Ichabod Plaisted told me of it. He was seen at his door the last Sixth Day. I gave my Letters to Capt. Plaisted to carry to Newbury. Second-day, Febr. 14, 169$\frac{7}{8}$ Col. Saml. Shrimpton was buried with Arms; Ten Companies, 8, Muddy River and Sconce: No Horse nor Trumpet: but a Horse led—Mr. Dyers, the Colonel's, would not endure the cloathing: Mourning Coach also and Horses in Mourning: Scutcheon on their sides and Deaths heads on their foreheads: Coach stood by the way here and there and mov'd solitarily. Bearers Maj^{r} Genl Winthrop, Mr. Cook, L^{t}. Col. Hutchinson, Mr. Addington, Capt. Foster, Maj^{r} Walley. Mr. E^{m} Hutchinson and Mr. Allen led the widow, Capt. Clark fired twelve great guns at the Sconce, began as march'd to the New-burying place where the Corps was set int [*sic*] to the two wives. Very fair and large Paths were shovel'd by great pains and cost, three in the Burying place, one direct to the Tomb, the other compassing by the sides in which the souldiers stood Drawn up. Wm Scovel being well and having on his new Coat, I fitted him with my Musket, Rapier, mourning, Amunition, and he serv'd in the South-Company.

Febr. 15. Remarkable Sun-dogs and a Rainbow were seen. Febr. 16. Mr. Chr. Tapan comes hether. Sam. reads the 2^{d} Habakkuk out of course at evening prayer; next morn reads the 90th Psalm in course. Secret sins in the light of thy countenance, pained me. Feb. 19. I go over the Ice and visit Mr, Morton, who keeps his bed.

Second-day, March 7. Set out for Plimouth about 10. *mane.* Get to Barkers and lodge there. Maj^r General set out about Noon and came to us at Barkers in the night.

March, 8. Get to Plimouth about Noon, Are entertain'd at Cole's. Send two mile for Mr. Little, who prays at the opening of the Court: invite him to Diner: Speak not to Mr. Cotton. I lodge at Cole's, the house was built by Govr Winslow and is the oldest in Plimouth. March, 9. Word is brought us that our Horses are broke out of themselves, or else are taken out of the stable; viz. four, Maj^r Generals, Mr. Cooks, mine, and Mingo's Sent presently to their flat-house, but hear nothing of them. Court rises. Capt. Byfield goes home. Mr. Cook and I linger hoping to hear of our horses and trying to get more. Fifth-day, March 10. I walk out in the morn. to see the Mill, then turn up to the Graves, come down by the Meetinghouse, and seeing the door partly open, went in and found a very convenient Oportunity to pray, the wind being cold; for my self and family, for Plimouth, Bp Stoke, the Province, &c. Maj^r General, Mr. Sherriffe, Mr. Ward, Master of a Connecticut Sloop, and I Dine together at Coles. I pay for Ward because invited him, and Maj^r General for the Sheriffe. Had large discourse in the even with Mrs. Cotton, Mr. Cotton, Mr. Rowland. I told Mr. Coton, a free confession was the best way; spake of Davids roaring all the day long and bones waxing old whilest he kept silence. I spake with Deacon Fance today, sent for him to Mr. Cotton's: It seems upon the 5th of October, The Church, by speaking one by one, declared their Mind was to Release Mr. Cotton from his office-bond as Pastor; sent to Mr. Cotton to meet them (they were at Shirtly's, 25 in number, some that could not come sent their minds to the same effect: and New Society ready to do it). Mr. Cotton to come to the Meeting-house, thither they goe, and there Deacon Fance declares what the church had done. Mr. Cotton was at Cole's: when ready to come away March, 11. I said his danger was lest catching at shadows, he should neglect the cords thrown out to him by Christ and so be drown'd. Some of my last words to him was, Kisse the Son, lest he be angry! This was in the house between him and me alone. Just as was mounting, He desired me to pray for him till I heard he was dead.

As came along, went a little out of our way and came to Duxbury houses; so then resolv'd to visit Mr. Wiswall, who had been long sick of the Gout, and was very glad to see us. Gave us a very good Goose to Diner. It rained, and got but to Barkers that night. My horse flounder'd in a bank of Snow, and threw me off; but had no hurt. *Laus Deo.* Dine at Cushings, Get home a little before Sunset and find all well, blessed be God.

Fourth-day, March 16. 169⅞. I sent to the college Library my *Phænomena,* well bound in calvs Leather, with Mr. Oakee's election sermon, and Mr. Willard's Tract about Swearing; by Josiah Cotton.

Thorsday Apr. 7th. 1698. I acquainted Mr. Brenton that I had sold my 600. Acre Lot at Narraganset, as suposing he had no mind to hire it, but was cold in the matter, going away to Rode-Island and not perfecting the Lease, nor offering me any to sign, nor desiring me to stay till he should come back, that I remember. Bro^{r} St. Sewall visits us this day; lodges here Thorsday night and Friday night.

Sixth-day, April 8. I visited Mr. Morton. I was told he was asleep, but went in, and when I drew nigh his Beds side, he earnestly streach'd out his flaming hand to me, and strove to speak, but could not. I think the first I heard him say was, Sir, I asked him how he did in such long illness. He at first said, *That which can't be cur'd must be endur'd.* But seem'd presently after to correct himself and say, I *desire patiently to submit to the hand of God.* A while after I said, you canot speak to me, but you can speak to God, which is a thousand times better; I pray that God would help you to speak to him, and that he would graciously hear you when you doe speak.

He seem'd to ly still in a listening posture, and made a little pause, and said, *Excellent things! If I could receive them and live up to them!* Before this He said something about his man Tiler, that he heard he was become a new man. When I took leave, He said, *I wish you well and all your family.* I told him I doubted not but that I should fare the better for his Blessing. Second-day, Apr. 11. Mr. Willard and I having apointed it before, went to see Mr. Morton. He was in his Agonies, but Mr. Willard pray'd with him, and he seemed to be sensible by the motion of his eye. He died between two and three of the clock. Fowl, that us'd to tend him, clos'd his eyes; and Mr. Willard spake to them to close his under Jaw, which they did. Deacons desired us to go and see Mr. Bradstreet, which we did: but he was not at home, was gon to Cambridge.

May, 10. Mr. John Brown has home his Bride to Salem, Mrs. Sarah Burroughs. Very cold blustering day after the pleasant warm Rain yesterday, and Rainbow near night, south E and by East. Fourth-day, May, 11th. As I lay in my bed in the morn, this verse came into my mind,

> To Horses, Swine, Net-Cattell, Sheep and Deer,
> Ninety and Seven prov'd a Mortal year.

Tuesday, June, 28. 1698. Court at Salem, Major Brown praesident; were remov'd to the Ship Tavern and candles lighted; a cry of Fire was made. A Girl drawing Rum in a litle Warehouse of Mr. Lyndon's, or looking after a cask that leak'd, the candle fired it, which took the cask and broke it up with a Report, so catch'd Cotton and fired Mr. Willoughbys house in the Garret of which was a Barrel of Powder, that taking fire blew off the Roof and very much dispersed the flaming partickles; much of which was thrown on Major Brown's house over the way, the wind carrying it thither so that and his warehouse were quickly burnt down, and much Money and Goods lost with the Buildings. Five houses in all burnt, Mr.

Hirst's for one. This is the first considerable Fire that ever was in Salem. It seems the stroke makes a deep impression on Maj^r Brown. Has lost 3 or four Thousand pounds.

July, 15. 1698. Mr. Edward Taylor comes to our house from Westfield. Monday July 18. I walk'd with Mr. Edward Taylor upon Cotton Hill, thence to Becon Hill, the Pasture, along the Stone-wall: As came back, we sat down on the great Rock, and Mr. Taylor told me his courting his first wife, and Mr. Fitch his story of Mr. Dod's prayer to God to bring his Affection to close with a person pious, but hard-favoured. Has God answered me in finding out one Godly and fit for me, and shall I part for fancy? When came home, my wife gave me Mr. Tapan's Letter concerning Eliza, which caus'd me to reflect on Mr. Taylor's Discourse. And his Prayer was for pardon of error in our ways—which made me think whether it were not best to overlook all, and go on. This day John Ive, fishing in great Spie-pond, is arrested with mortal sickness which renders him in a maner speechless and senseless; dies next day; buried at Charlestown on the Wednesday. Was a very debauched, atheistical man. I was not at his Funeral. Had Gloves sent me, but the knowledge of his notoriously wicked life made me sick of going; and Mr. Mather, the president, came in just as I was ready to step out, and so I staid at home, and by that means lost a Ring: but hope had no loss. Follow thou Me, was I supose more complied with, than if had left Mr. Mather's company to go to such a Funeral.

Seventh-day; Octob^r 29. 1698. Thomas Savage jun^r, shopkeeper, and Sarah Threeneedles were brought face to face in a very great Audience: She vehemently accused him, and he asserted his innocency with vehement Asservations. She said he had ruin'd her; if he would have promis'd her any thing, it had not come to this. Said She forgave him, Judgment of God hung over him if did not repent.

Fifth-day, Novr. 10. Mr. Green is ordained at Salem Village, and likelihood of a stability of Peace and settlement there. Fifth-day, Novr 17th. Very fair serene wether; Mr. Cotton Mather preaches at the South-Meetinghouse: Sarah Threeneedles is an Auditor; is a very vast Assembly, and the street full of such as could not get in; 51. Psalm 2^{d} verse sung, 9—15 verses. Mr. Willard read the whole, and I set the Tune. After Lecture Sarah Threeneedles is executed. Mr. Woodbridge went to the place of execution and pray'd with her there.

Sabbath, December 4. 1698. Last night lying awake, but with my eyes fast shut, Lightening flash'd in my face, I could not certainly tell what Light it should be; but presently heard a loud clap of Thunder. This day between the ringing of the morning Bells, it Thundered several times, but with a more confused and rumbling noise. Much Rain, Mist.

Decr 24. 1698. Read and sung in course in the Family the 3^{d} part of the 77th Ps., which I hop'd was going to be partly fullfill'd by the company of Scotland. Decr 29th After Lecture I invite Major Vaughan and Mr. Partridge to Dinner, such as it was. At the Town-House with Mr. Justice Danforth, Winthrop, Cooke, took the New Oath made last sessions. And took an oath relating to the Special Court to try Jacob Smith; Mr. Danforth gave the comission to Mr. Cook. Voted some Money for Major Walley. Went to Vaughan and Partridge at Dering's, as told them I would, while in the chamber. Had only a piece of rost Beef, Minct pye and Tarts to Diner. It seems the Lt Govr invites the Council to Diner to morrow at his house. After Diner, Major Winthrop, Mr. Cook, Col. Hutchinson, Capt. Foster, Mr. Sergeant, Mr. Hutchinson came in to discourse with Mr. Partridge and Vaughan, and staid till about 6 aclock, or past. Mr. Cook ask'd me whether I was bidden. I told him I knew nothing of it. Major Genl looked upon me in good earnest, and almost angrily, at going away, and told me I must goe; but I heard nothing of it since, and tis now Decr 30th. past 3 *tempore pomeridiano*.

The Grievousness of this prœtermission is, that by this means

I shall be taken up into the lips of Talkers, and shall be obnoxious to the Governour at his coming, as a person deserted and fit to be hunted down, if occasion be; and in the mean time, shall goe feebly up and down my Business, as one who is quite out of the L[t] Govr[s] favour. The Lord pardon my share in the abounding of Iniquity by reason whereof the Love of many waxes cold.

Friday, Jan[y] 20. Capt. Brown and Turner breakfast here: Betty came in afterward, and serv'd Almonds and Raisins, and fill'd a Glass of Wine to us; and it fell to her to drink to Capt. Turner. She went out of the way at first, after I had spoke to her to fill wine: which surpris'd me: and I contrived that of the Raisins on purpose to mend the matter. Sabbath-day Jan[y] 22, Bro[r] Roger Judd is cast out of the Church for his contumacy in refusing to hear the Church, and his contemptuous behaviour against the same, and Mr. Willard the Pastor. Refus'd to be there.

Second-day, Jan[y] 23. 169⁸⁄₉ I carry my two sons and three daughters in the Coach to Danford, the Turks head at Dorchester: eat sage Cheese, drunk Beer and Cider and came homeward. Call'd at Madam Dudley's, then visited Mr. Walter; told him there was all my stock, desired his Blessing of them; which he did.

Wednesday, June 21. A Pack of Cards are found strawed over my fore-yard, which, tis suposed, some might throw there to mock me, in spite of what I did at the Exchange Tavern last Satterday night.

Third-Day, July, 11. 1699. I went with Mr. Willard to Pulling-Point to Mr. Dean Winthrop's, (77) *añorum.* Between one and two, Mr. Willard married Atherton Haugh and Mercy Winthrop: Said, Mr. Atherton Haugh, Mrs. Mercy Winthrop; forbad all unlawful comunion with other Women and *vice versa.* Gave very good Advice and Exhortation; especially most solemnly charged them never to neglect family Prayer. Between 3 and four Major Gen[l] and Mr.

Adam Winthrop came and many with them, when we had almost din'd. Sang a Psalm together, I set St. David's Tune: Sung part of two Psalms, concluded with the 4 last verses of the 115.

When Mr. Willard ask'd Mr. Winthrop's consent, he also complemented me respecting Atherton Haugh: I said I was glad that had found so good a Family and so good a wife. And after, when saw the Bridegroom and Bride together after the Wedding: I praid God to bless them, and give them such an Offspring wherein the Name of Haugh and Winthrop might flourish.

Mr. Dean Winthrop liv'd there in his fathers days, and was wont to set up a Bush when he saw a ship coming in; He is now 77 years old. In his Fathers time, his house stood more toward Dear Island. Wind was against us coming home; so that twas nine aclock before landed. Were four hours in the passage. Maj^{r} Genl &c bid there all night, and pass'd it but uncomfortably.

Octr 27. Lt Govr Treats the Governour and his Lady and many more: Two tables. Capt. Crow breaks a Glass Bottle of Madera as it stood on the floor, so that it run about with its Sanguin Colour; Capt. Crow mention'd its not being able to be gathered up again. Mr. Danforth crav'd a Blessing; Mr. Bridge return'd Thanks. Before Diner rid with the Governour to the end of Dorchester Neck. This day news comes to Town of Mr. Man's House being burnt last night. Capt. Foxcroft informs us at Dorchester of his Father Danforth's Sickness. Mr. Hirst and Sam. come home from Braintry where they lay the night before.

Seventh-day, Novr 11th about the middle of the night following, my dear Sister Hanah Tappan dies of a Fever. Mr. Addington told me of it first upon Novr 13 in the Council-Chamber, from Mr. Gerrish of Wenham. At 7, at night I received a Letter from Bro^{r} Sewall of it, and that the Funeral is to be the 14. Our notice is so lame and late, that I persuade Jane to stay at home, it being almost impossible to get thither time enough. Besides all this, the Court at Salem keeps me there, and Bro^{r} Sewall also. We had liv'd eight of us together Thirty years; and were wont to speak of it (it may be too vainly). But now God begins to part us apace. Two are taken away in about a quarter of a year's time; And me thinks now my dear Bro^{r} and Sister are laid in the Grave, I am, as it were laid there in Proxy—The Lord help me to carry it more suitably, more fruitfully, toward the Five remaining; and put me in a preparedness for my own Dissolution. And help me to live upon Him alone.

Fifth-day, Novr the last. 1699. The Rain freezes upon the branches of the Trees to that thickness and weight, that great havock is thereby made of the Wood and Timber. Many young and strong Trees are broken off in the midst; and multitudes of Boughs rent off. Considerable hurt is done in Orchards. Two of our Apple-trees are broken down, Unkles Tree, two thirds of it, are broken down. Peach Trees at Mrs. Moodeys are almost all spoil'd. And my little Cedar almost quite mortified. Some think the Spoil that is made amounts to Thousands of pounds. How suddenly and with surprise can God destroy!

Tuesday, Febr. 6, 1699-1700. A Council is held at my Lord's. The Advice of Councillors asked about sending the Pirats on Board. I motioned that by that time the Prisoners could be got from N. York, Conecticut, Rode-Island: the Assembly might sit if his L^{d}ship saw meet, and they would willingly rid themselves of them. Govr seem'd displeas'd. I had ask'd before, What Pirats, and the Govr said them and their Associates. Govr mention'd Kid, Gillam, Bradish, Witherly, to be sent aboard presently for better security. Council voted to leave it to the Govrs. Discretion whom to send aboard: only the Govr had said to some that enquired, He intended not [to let] them out upon Bail. I think only I, Col. Townsend and Capt. Byfield were in the Negative. I said I was not clear in it. The grounds I went upon were because I knew of no power I had to send Men out of the Province. Capt. Byfield said, He was for their going aboard: but reckon'd twas not so safe to send them presently as to keep them in Goal. Voted also the Treasure to be deliver'd to such as the Govr should apoint.

Friday, Febr. 9th. Will, formerly Capt. Prentices Negro, now living with Maylem, a Horse run away with him, threw him upon the hard frozen Ground, or Timber, near Houchins's corner, and kill'd him; died in a little while. I saw him panting as came from visiting Capt. Foxcroft. He was much delighted in Horses, and now dies by a Horse. About 1664. he sav'd his Master Prentice from a Bear. Went with Col. Townsend and me to Albany. Rid Post one while.

Capt. Belchar was at the Meeting, come home from burying his daughter Vaughan, who died in child bed. Child died first. Wast the most beautifull of all his Daughters. I wonder'd to see him at Mr. Bromfield's, the wether had been so excessive cold. Said, I was sorry for the croping of his desirable Flower.

Febr. 22. I had thoughts of sitting up to see the eclipse: but the cloudy thick sky discouraged me: yet kept a candle burning, and went to the Window at two of the clock; the wether was still thick with clouds, that I could see nothing: only seem'd very dark for a full Moon.

In the evening I visited Mrs. Williams in her Languishing. Am invited to a Fast there on Friday.

Wednesday, Febr. 28. We ship off the Iron chest of Gold, Pearls &c., 40 Bails of East-India Goods, 13 hogsheads, chests and case, one Negro Man, and Venturo Resail, an East-Indian born at Ceilon. Wether was doubtfull in the morning, which made us irresolute: but at last we set about it, and accomplish'd it very hapily. I look upon it as a great Mercy of God, that the Storehouse has not been broken up, no fire has hapend. Agreed in the Weight of the Gold with our former Weight, and had so comfortable a day at last to finish our work. Mr. Bradstreet, and Capt. Winn's Clerk took an account at the Crane; but Capt. Winn would not give a Rec^{t} till had them on board the sloop Antonio, which ridd off just without the Outward Wharf. Gave a Rec^{t} for the Gold at Capt Belchar's as soon as it was weighed.

Tuesday, March 26. The wind is very bleak that it was ready to put me into an Ague, having rid late the night before. Had a noble Treat at Maj^{r} Thomas's. Mr. Sheriff and his Gentlemen were so wearied that they were afraid of some Miscarriage at the Ferry. Began the Court about five. Wednesday and Thorsday were extravagantly stormy. On Friday Mr. Cooke comes home but the wind was strong in my face, and cold that I durst not venture. Satterday was also very cold and chose rather to keep the Sabbath at Plimouth than by the way. Staid at Plimouth. At Noon was a Contribution for one that had his house burnt. Mr. Little invited me to sup with him, which I did.

Monday, April, 1. I was in a great quandary whether I had best to avoid the wind, come home by water and leave my Horse, or no. At last I went on board Elisha Hedge's decked sloop laden with Oyle. He put in there in the storm from Yarmouth and lay till now for a wind. Came aboard about 2 hours by Sun, and landed at Mrs. Butlers Wharf before 3 p. m. Having had a very speedy and pleasant Passage, wherein I have experienced much of God's parental pity towards me, and care over me. I could not have got home to day by Land: and I fear my health would have been much impair'd, if I had come but part of the way. Jonathan Wheeler ridd in the Rain from Milton. I have now kept one Sabbath with those who first kept Sabbaths in New England.

May, 17th. Benj Moss jun^{r} is sent to me to acquaint me that my dear Father died the evening before. It rains hard. Holds up about 5 p.m. I ride to Hampton, lodge at Mr. Cottons, where am very kindly entertained.

May 24th set out for Salem about an hour by sun, Mr.

Joseph Woodbridge with me, Got to Brothers a little before Nine, met there Mrs. Ane Woodbridge. Proved my Fathers Will. May 25. 1700 went homeward in company Mrs. Anne as far as Col. Paiges. Got home about 3 aclock, found all well, Blessed be God. My Wife provided Mourning upon my Letter by Severs, All went in mourning save Joseph, who staid at home because his Mother lik'd not his cloaths. Sister Short here, came from Newbury the morn father died, and so miss'd being at the funeral. It seems about a 14night before, upon discourse of going to Meeting, my Father said, He could not goe, but hop'd to go shortly to a Greater Assembly. The Lord pardon all my sin of omission and commission towards him, and help me to prepare to Dye. Accept of any little Labour of Love towards my dear Parents. I had just sent four pounds of Raisins, which with the Canary were very refreshing to him.

Fourth-day, June, 19. 1700. Mr. Jn° Eyre is entomed in the new burying place. Nine of his children are laid there to handsel the new Tomb: Bearers, Sewall, Addington, Townsend, Byfield, Dumer, Davis: Scarvs and Rings. Lt Govr and many of the Council there. Mr. Thomas Brattle led his mourning widowed Sister. When I parted, I pray'd God to be favourably present with her, and comfort her in the absence of so near and dear a Relation. Having been long and much dissatisfied with the Trade of fetching Negros from Guinea; at last I had a strong Inclination to Write something about it; but it wore off. At last reading Bayne, Ephes. about servants, who mentions Blackamoors; I began to be uneasy that I had so long neglected doing any thing. When I was thus thinking, in came Bro^r^ Belknap to shew me a Petition he intended to present to the Genl Court for the freeing a Negro and his wife, who were unjustly held in Bondage. And there is a Motion by a Boston Committee to get a Law that all Importers of Negros shall pay 40^s^ p head, to discourage the bringing of them. And Mr. C. Mather resolves to publish a sheet to exhort Masters to labour their Conversion. Which makes me hope that I was call'd of God to Write this Apology for them; Let his Blessing accompany the same.

Thorsday Sept[r] 26th 1700. Mr. John Wait and Eunice his wife, and Mrs. Debora Thair come to Speak to me about the Marriage of Sebastian, Negro serv[t] of said Wait, with Jane, Negro servant of said Thair. Mr. Wait desired they might be published in order to marriage. Mrs. Thair insisted that Sebastian might have one day in six allow'd him for the suport of Jane, his intended wife and her children, if it should please God to give her any. Mr. Wait now wholly declin'd that, but freely offer'd to allow Bastian Five pounds, in Money p añum towards the suport of his children p said Jane (besides Sebastians cloathing and Diet). I persuaded Jane and Mrs. Thair to agree to it, and so it was concluded; and Mrs. Thair gave up the Note of Publication to Mr. Wait for him to carry it to Wm Griggs, the Town Clerk, and to Williams in order to have them published according to Law.

Oct[r] 17th 1700. Mr. Grove Hirst and Elizabeth Sewall are married by Mr. Cotton Mather. Present, I and my wife, Mr. Hirst and his wife, Bro[r] St. Sewall of Salem and his son Sam, Brothers and Sisters of Bridegroom and Bride. Madam Usher, Capt. Ephra Savage, Capt. Dumar and wife, Capt. Ballentine, Mrs. Mary Clark, Esther Wyllye, Margaret Stewart &c. Sung the 128. Psal. I set York Tune, not intending it. In the New Parlor.

Jan[y]. 14th. Having been certified last night about 10. oclock of the death of my dear Mother at Newbury, Sam. and I set out with John Sewall, the Messenger, for that place. Hired Horses at Charlestown: set out about 10. aclock in a great Fogg. Din'd at Lewis's with Mr. Cushing of Salisbury. Sam. and I kept on in Ipswich Rode, John went to accompany Bro[r] from Salem. About Mr. Hubbard's in Ipswich farms, they overtook us. Sam. and I lodg'd at Cromptons in Ipswich. Bro[r] and John stood on for Newbury by Moon-shine. Jan[y]

15th Sam. and I set forward. Brother Northend meets us. Visit Aunt Northend, Mr. Payson. With Bro^{r} and sister we set forward for Newbury: where we find that day apointed for the Funeral: twas a very pleasant Comfortable day.

Bearers, Jno Kent of the Island, Lt Cuting Noyes, Deacon William Noyes, Mr. Peter Tappan, Capt. Henry Somersby, Mr. Joseph Woodbridge. I follow'd the Bier single. Then Bro^{r} Sewall and sister Jane, Bro^{r} Short and his wife, Bro^{r} Moodey and his wife, Bro^{r} Northend and his wife, Bro^{r} Tapan and sister Sewall, Sam. and cous. Hanah Tapan. Mr. Payson of Rowley, Mr. Clark, Minister of Excester, were there. Col. Pierce, Major Noyes &c. Cous. John, Richard and Betty Dumer. Went ab^{t} 4. p.m. Nathan^{l} Bricket taking in hand to fill the Grave, I said, Forbear a little, and suffer me to say That amidst our bereaving sorrows We have the Comfort of beholding this Saint put into the rightfull possession of that Happiness of Living desir'd and dying Lamented. She liv'd commendably Four and Fifty years with her dear Husband, and my dear Father: And she could not well brook the being divided from him at her death; which is the cause of our taking leave of her in this place. She was a true and constant Lover of Gods Word, Worship, and Saints: And she always, with a patient cheerfullness, submitted to the divine Decree of providing Bread for her self and others in the sweat of her Brows. And now her infinitely Gracious and Bountiful Master has promoted her to the Honor of higher Employments, fully and absolutely discharged from all maner of Toil, and Sweat. My honoured and beloved Friends and Neighbours! My dear Mother never thought much of doing the most frequent and homely offices of Love for me; and lavish'd away many Thousands of Words upon me, before I could return one word in Answer: And therefore I ask and hope that none will be offended that I have now ventured to speak one word in her behalf; when shee her self is become speechless. Made a Motion with my hand for the filling of the Grave. Note, I could hardly speak for passion and Tears. Mr. Tappan pray'd with us in the evening. I lodg'd at sister Gerrishes with Joseph. Bro^{r} and Sam. at Br. Tapans. Jany. 16th. The two Brothers and four sisters being together, we took Leave by singing of the 90th Psalm, from the 8th to the 15th verse inclusively. Mr. Brown, the Scholar, was present. Set out ab^{t} 11. for Ipswich, got time enough to hear Mr. Rogers preach the Lecture from Luke 1. 76. about ministerial preparation for Christ. Sung the nine first verses of the 132. Psalm. Mr. Rogers prai'd for the prisoner of death, the Newbury woman who was there in her chains. This is the last Sermon preached in the old Meeting-house. Eat Roost Fowl at Crompton's. Delivered a Letter to the Widow Hale; got very comfortably over the Ferry to Brothers, whether Mr. Hirst quickly came to welcome us and invite us to dine or breakfast next day, which we did, the morning being cold: Visited Madam Bradstreet and Major Brown, and told them of the death of their fellow-passenger. Rec'd me very courteously. Took horse about one p.m. Baited at Lewis's; Stop'd at Govr Usher's to pay him a visit. He and his Lady being from home, we pass'd on, and got to Charlestown about Sun-set, very comfortably. Found all well at home through the Goodness of God.

Monday, June. 2 — 1701. Mr. Pemberton preaches the Artillery Sermon, from Luke. 3—14. Dine at Monk's. Because of the Rain and Mist, this day, the election is made upon the Town-house, Sewall, Capt.; Tho. Hutchinson Lieut.; Tho. Savage Junr, Ensign.; Tho. Fitch, 1 Sergt.: Oliver Noyes 2: Hab. Savage 3: Charles Chauncey 4. Call'd down the Council out of the Chamber, set their chairs below; Col. Pynchon gave the Staves and Ensign. I said was surpris'd to see they had mistaken a sorry pruning Hook for a Military Spear; but paid such a deference to the Company that would rather run the venture of exposing my own inability, than give any occasion to suspect I slighted their call.

Tuesday, June, 10th. Having last night heard that Josiah

Willard had cut off his hair (a very full head of hair) and put on a Wigg, I went to him this morning. Told his Mother what I came about, and she call'd him. I enquired of him what Extremity had forced him to put off his own hair, and put on a Wigg? He answered, none at all. But said that his Hair was straight, and that it parted behinde. Seem'd to argue that men might as well shave their hair off their head, as off their face. I answered men were men before they had hair on their faces, (half of mankind have never any). God seems to have ordain'd our Hair as a Test, to see whether we can bring our minds to be content to be at his finding: or whether we would be our own Carvers, Lords, and come no more at Him. If disliked our Skin, or Nails; 'tis no Thanks to us, that for all that, we cut them not off: Pain and danger restrain us. Your Calling is to teach men self Denial. Twill be displeasing and burdensom to good men: And they that care not what men think of them care not what God thinks of them. Father, Bro^{r} Simon, Mr. Pemberton, Mr. Wigglesworth, Oakes, Noyes (Oliver), Brattle of Cambridge their example. Allow me to be so far a *Censor Morum* for this end of the Town. Pray'd him to read the Tenth Chapter of the Third book of Calvins Institutions. I read it this morning in course, not of choice. Told him that it was condemn'd by a Meeting of Ministers at Northampton in Mr. Stoddards house, when the said Josiah was there. Told him of the Solemnity of the Covenant which he and I had lately enterd into, which put me upon discoursing to him. He seem'd to say would leave off his Wigg when his hair was grown. I spake to his Father of it a day or two after: He thank'd me that had discoursed his Son, and told me that when his hair was grown to cover his ears, he promis'd to leave off his Wigg. If he had known of it, would have forbidden him. His Mother heard him talk of it; but was afraid positively to forbid him; lest he should do it, and so be more faulty.

July, 15th. Funeral-day of L^{t}. Govr. To Ipswich; Try

Esther Rogers. Jury next morn ask'd advice, then after, brought her in Guilty of murdering her Bastard daughter. July, 17. Mr. Cooke pronounc'd the sentence. She hardly said a word. I told her God had put two Children to her to nurse: Her Mother did not serve her so. Esther was a great saviour; she, a great destroyer. Said did not do this to insult over her, but to make her sensible.

Monday, Oct[r] 6. 1701. Very pleasant fair Wether; Artillery trains in the Afternoon [Sewall in command]. March with the Company to the Elms; Go to prayer, March down and Shoot at a Mark. Mr. Cushing I think was the first that hit it, Mr. Gerrish twice, Mr. Fitch, Chauncy, and the Ensign of the Officers. By far the most missed, as I did for the first. Were much contented with the exercise. Led them to the Trees agen, perform'd some facings and Doublings. Drew them together; propounded the question about the Colours; twas voted very freely and fully. I inform'd the Company I was told the Company's Halberds &c. were borrowed; I understood the Leading staff was so, and therefore ask'd their Acceptance of a Half-Pike, which they very kindly did; I deliver'd it to Mr. Gibbs for their Use.

They would needs give me a Volley, in token of their Respect on this occasion. The Pike will, I supose, stand me in fourty shillings, being headed and shod with Silver: Has this Motto fairly engraven:

Agmen Massachusettense

est in tutelam Sponsæ

AGNI Uxoris.

1701.

Octr 20. Mr. Cotton Mather came to Mr. Wilkins's shop, and there talked very sharply against me as if I had used his father worse than a Neger; spake so loud that people in the street might hear him. Then went and told Sam, That one pleaded much for Negroes, and he had used his father worse than a Negro, and told him that was his Father. I had read in the morn Mr. Dod's saying; Sanctified Afflictions are good Promotions. I found it now a cordial. And this caus'd me the rather to set under my Father and Mother's Epitaph,—Psal. 27. 10.

Octr 9. I sent Mr. Increase Mather a Hanch of very good Venison; I hope in that I did not treat him as a Negro.

Octob^{r} 22. 1701. I, with Major Walley and Capt. Saml Checkly, speak with Mr. Cotton Mather at Mr. Wilkins's. I expostulated with him from 1 Tim. 5.1. Rebuke not an elder. He said he had consider'd that: I told him of his book of the Law of Kindness for the Tongue, whether this were correspondent with that. Whether correspondent with Christ's Rule: He said, having spoken to me before there was no need to speak to me again; and so justified his reviling me behind my back. Charg'd the Council with Lying, Hypocrisy, Tricks, and I know not what all. I ask'd him if it were done with that Meekness as it should; answer'd, yes. Charg'd the Council in general, and then shew'd my share, which was my speech in Council; viz. If Mr. Mather should goe to Cambridge again to reside there with a Resolution not to read the Scriptures, and expound in the Hall: I fear the example of it will do more hurt than his going thither will doe good. This speech I owned. Said Mr. Corwin at Reading, upbraided him, saying, This is the man you dedicat your books to! I ask'd him If I should supose he had done somthing amiss in his Church as an Officer; whether it would be well for me to exclaim against him in the street for it. (Mr. Wilkin would fain have had him gon into the iner room, but he would not.) I told him I conceiv'd he had done much unbecoming a Minister of the Gospel, and being call'd by Maxwell to the Council, Major Wally and I went thither, leaving Capt. Checkly there. 2 Tim. 2. 24. 25. Went to the Council, Sign'd Mr.

Mather's order for £25. Hamer'd out an Order for a Day of Thanksgiving.

Thorsday, Oct[r] 23. Mr. Increase Mather said at Mr. Wilkins's, If I am a Servant of Jesus Christ, some great Judgment will fall on Capt. Sewall, or his family.

Oct[r] 24. Rainy Day, yet Judge Atwood comes from Rehoboth to Boston. 25. Visits several, and me among the rest. This day in the morn. I got Mr. Moody to copy out my Speech, and gave it to Mr. Wilkins that all might see what was the ground of Mr. Mather's Anger.

Writ out another and gave it to Joshua Gee. I perceive Mr. Wilkins carried his to Mr. Mathers; They seem to grow calm.

Sabbath, Nov[r]. 30. Pray'd, sung — Contribution. Gave the Blessing. I spent this Sabbath at Mr. Colman's, partly out of dislike to Mr. Josiah Willard's cutting off his Hair, and wearing a Wigg.

Jan[y]. 2. 170½. My Wife had some thoughts the Time of her Travail might be come, before she went to bed: But it went over. Between 4 and 5 m. I go to prayer, Rise, make a Fire, call Mrs. Ellis, Hawkins, Mary Hawkins calls Midwife Greenlef. I go to Mr. Willard and desire him to call God. The Women call me into chamber, and I pray there. Jn[o] Barnard comes to me for Money: I desire him to acquaint Mr. Cotton Mather, and Father.

Jan[y]. 2. 170½. My Wife is well brought to Bed of a Daughter just about two p.m., a very cold day: Was got into Bed without a fainting Fit.

Sabbath-day night my wife is very ill and something delirious. Pulse swift and high. I call Mr. Oakes about Two aclock or before. Grows a little better.

Jan[y]. 6. 170½ Nurse Hill watch'd last night. Wife had a comfortable night.

What through my wives many Illnesses, more than ordinary, her fall upon the stairs about 5 weeks before; from which time she kept her chamber; her thoughtfullness between whiles whether she were with child or no; her Fears what the issue would be, and the misgiving of our Unbelieving hearts, GOD hath been wonderfully Mercifull to us in her comfortable Delivery; which I desire to have Recorded.

Note. This is the Thirteenth Child that I have offered up to God in Baptisme; my wife having born me Seven Sons and Seven Daughters. I have named this little Daughter Judith, in Remembrance of her honoured and beloved Grandmother Mrs. *Judith Hull*. And it may be my dear wife may now leave off bearing.

Thorsday, Febr. 19. Mr. I. Mather preached from Rev. 22. 16 — bright and morning Star. Mention'd Sign in the Heaven, and in the Evening following I saw a large Cometical Blaze, something fine and dim, pointing from the Westward, a little below Orion.

Febr. 21. Capt. Tim°. Clark tells me that a Line drawn to the Comet strikes just upon Mexico, spake of a Revolution there, how great a Thing it would be. Said one Whitehead told him of the magnificence of the City, that there were in it 1500 Coaches drawn with Mules. This Blaze had much put me in mind of Mexico; because we must look toward Mexico to view it. Capt. Clark drew a Line on his Globe. Our Thoughts being thus confer'd, and found to jump, makes it to me remarkable. I have long pray'd for Mexico, and of late in those Words, that God would open the Mexican Fountain.

June 10. 1702. Comittee Tryes Powder, and firing so much and long distempered me; that partly by that, and partly by my Wives intolerable pains, I had a most restless night. June, 11. Thorsday, before I was dress'd, Sam. Gave the Word that Govr [Joseph Dudley] was come. Quickly after I got down, Maxwell sumoned me to Council, told me the Secretary had a Letter of the Governours Arrival yesterday, at Marblehead. Mr. Addington, Eliakim Hutchinson, Byfield and Sewall, sent per the Council, go with Capt Crofts in his Pinace to meet the

Governour, and Congratulat his Arrival; We get aboard a little before got within Point Alderton; Capt Heron introduced us; After had all saluted the Govr. I said,

Her Majesty's Council of this Province have comanded us to meet your Excellency, and congratulate your safe Arrival in the Massachusetts Bay, in quality of our Governour: Which we do very heartily; not only out of Obedience to our Masters who sent us; but also of our own accord. The Cloaths your Excellency sees us wear, are a true Indication of our inward Grief for the Departure of K. William. Yet we desire to remember with Thankfullness the Goodness of God, who has at this time peacably placed Queen Anne upon the Throne. And as Her Majestys Name imports Grace, so we trust God will shew Her Majesty Favour; and Her Majesty us. And we look upon your Excellency's being sent to us, as a very fair First-Fruit of it, for which we bless God and Queen Anne.

June 12. as Governour came to Town, he alighted and call'd at my House, Thank'd me for my Kindness to his family. I was much indispos'd by my Throat being sore, and I feverish.

Satterday, Augt. 15. p.m. Govr brings home Sam., then takes me into the Calash to the Townhouse. Col. Hathorne and Townsend chosen: Govr delivers him his Comission, then me and Maj^{r} Walley. Said would never insert himself any way to influence any proceeding before; which has many times done with great Vehemency; exhorting us to doe Justice. Addington, Hathorne, Sewall, Walley sent for Mr. Elisha Cooke jun^{r}: constituted him our Clerk, and gave him the Oaths. So now the Superior Court and Inferior Court Suffolk are both open'd this day; which is a considerable celebration of my son Joseph's Birth-day. The Lord cause his face to shine on us!

7^{r} 11th. Went to Billinges in the Cart-way; Had a very good Diner, Venison &c. Got home in good time. Capt. Williams with his Red-Coats met us betwen Dedham and the Turning to Fowl-Meadow. Capt. Belchar and sundry Boston Gentlemen met us at Dedham. Note. Wednesday, at Osburn's, about Break-a-day, I heard one riding as I lay awake. (Mrs. Sparhawk having miscarried, I lodg'd there.) Thought I, I fear there may be some bad News from Boston. The man knock'd, and when he could make any hear, he ask'd if Capt. ——were there: I took it he said me. They answer'd yes. He said must come away presently: for his daughter was very bad. Then I said to my self, I must undertake a sorrowful Journey, as from Salem to Boston, upon the advice of my Still-born son: But God dismiss'd me from the burden of that sorrowfull Surprise, having laid it on Capt Brown of Swansey. We saw the Funeral as went over the Ferry on Thorsday.

Monday, Octr 26. 1702. Waited on the Govr to Wooburn, dined there: From thence to Billericay, Visited languishing Mr. Saml Whiting, I gave him 2 Balls of Chockalett and a pound Figgs, which very kindly accepted. Saw the Company in Arms led by Capt. Tomson. Went to Chelmsford, by that time got there twas almost dark. Saw Capt. Bowles and his Company; Gave a Volley and Huzza's. Sup'd at Mr. Clark's; I and Col. Pierce in his study. Some went on to Dunstable by Moonshine. Octr 27. Went to Dunstable in the Rain, Din'd and lodg'd at Col. Tyng's. Saw and drunk of Merrimack. No Indians come in. Octr. 28. Went to Groton, saw Capt. Prescot and his company in Arms. (Govr had sent to them from Dunstable that would visit them). Lancaster is about 12 Miles Southward from Groton. Concord is 16 Miles ¾ and Ten-Rod from Groton. Got thither about 2. Horses and Men almost tired by our very hard riding. Dine at Capt. Prescot's. Lodge at Mr. Estabrooks with Col. Foxcroft. Their Foot Company, and Troop, in Arms, Seem'd to be numerous and well apointed.

Octr 29. Breakfast at Capt. Minott's, Set out for Cambridge. In Company Col. Pierce, Thomas, Partrigge, Foxcroft, Capt. Cutler, son Sewall, young Mr. Tyng. At Mr. Hancocks Mr. Secretary, Leverett met us. Mr. Dyer, Col. Byfield; at Russel's Mr. Dudley. There the Calash met the

Govr. and weary Major Brenton rid in it with the Govr. to the Town: Col. Hobbey rid his Horse. Dined with the Govr at Mr. Leveretts, Madam Leverett the Grandmother. Went home with Col. Hutchinson, Walley, Foster. Col. Foster invited us to drink at his house. Found all well, and David Sinclair rocking Judith; he came to our house after I was gon my Journey.

Novr 10. Mr. Leverett comes from Cambridge; open the Court in the Meetinghouse, because the Townhouse is very near a house that has the Small Pocks; so that people are afraid to goe there; and Sharp is not willing to let us have his chamber. Sat in the Deacon's seat, Col. Hathorne on my Right Hand, and Mr. Leverett on my Left. After the Reading of the Queen's Proclamation, I spake to the Grand-Jury, having written it down before hand in my Daughters chamber.

Novr 30. Rid to Salem to visit my Daughter Hirst, who was brought to bed of a dead child Novr 28.

From Lewis's in company of Mr. Lyde. Got thither about 2 hours by Sun. Daughter very glad to see me. xr. 1. My Daughter being threatened with the headache, I send Chapman to Cambridge to Dr. Oliver for a Plaister: He follow'd the Dr. to Boston, and brought word of Mrs. Mathers death. Laid on a Plaister; Daughter grows better: but then again had an ill turn; yet grew fine and well agen by Satterday and cheerfully dismiss'd me. Had a very comfortable Journey home. Son Hirst brought me going to the Butts. At Lewis's fell in with Maj^r Epes, Major Wainright and Mr. Fitch, going to Ipswich. Maj^r Wainwright tells me of the death of Mr. Brakenbury.

xr. 16. Heard the church [Kings Chapel] Bell ring for Capt. Crofts. He dyed last night.

xr. 19. Is buried in the New burying place in Capt. Hamilton's Tomb. Corps was first had into the church and a Funeral Sermon preach'd. For Debauchery and Irreligion he was one of the vilest Men that has set foot in Boston. Tis said he refused to have any Minister call'd to pray with him during his Sickness, which was above a fortnight.

Dec[r] 30. 1702. I was weigh'd in Col. Byfield's Scales: weight One Hundred One Half One Quarter wanting 3 pounds, i. e. 193 pounds Net. Col. Byfield weighed Sixty three pounds more than I: had only my close coat on. The Lord add, or take away from this our corporeal weight, so as shall be most advantagious for our Spiritual Growth. July 31. 1721 [in Margin]. I weighed 228 £ p cous. Sam[l] Sewall's Scales.

Febr. 22. Mrs. Willard and several of her children had like to have been cast away coming from Cambridge by Water, wind was so very high; put ashore at last on Muddy-River Marsh: Got to the Gov[rs] by that time twas dark. This morning as I was praying alone, I was much affected to think how concern'd and inquisitive I was in my Journeying about my Way; whether I was in the right or no; and yet not so constantly and effectually inquisitive about my Way to Heaven, although I was equally hastening to my Journey's End; whether in the right or wrong way. May He who is the Way, the Truth, and the Life, bring me into and always keep me in the right Way!

March, 16. 170⅔ Though all things look horribly winterly by reason of a great storm of Snow, hardly yet over, and much on the Ground: yet the Robbins cheerfully utter their Notes this morn. So should we patiently and cheerfully sing the Praises of God, and hope in his Mercys, though Storm'd by the last efforts of Antichrist.

Second-day of the Week July 5th 1703. I had my son to Cambridge again in Austin's Calash. Paid Andrew Bordman his Cautionary Three pounds, in order to my Son Joseph's being Admitted. Went to Mr. Flynt's Chamber, where Col. Wainright's Son and others were upon Examination. When that was doing, and over, Mr. Willard call'd for Joseph's Theme. Read it, gave to Mr. Flynt, Then in Mr. Flynt's Study, The President and Fellows sign'd his Laws; President said, your Son is now one of us, and he is wellcom. I thanked him; and took Leave. Coming home I order'd Mr. Sheriff to take up a Scurvy post out of the middle of the High way, that had been a Nusance for many years. Gave his Son a shilling for his pains. Got home well. *Laus Deo.* Was pretty much Rain at Charlestown; yet we went almost quite dry, being but a small Sprinkling where we were.

Aug[t] 23. 1703. I went to Cambridge to see Joseph settled in his study, help'd to open his Chest. Joseph was at home the Sabbath, and went up on foot by Charlestown. This day several very unusual Circles were seen about the sun. Mr. Leverett first told me of them, but I saw them not.

Dec[r] 11. Poor little Hull Sewall dies in Mr. Phips's house at Muddy-River about 6. in the evening, of Convulsions. About 8. at night the Gov[r] sends us word of it. Dec[r] 14th. Corps is brought to Town in the Governours Slay. Dec[r] 15. is born to our Tomb, and set upon a Box that his great Grandfathers Bones now put into it at William's desire, some being wash'd out. On the Box is made with Nails, 1683.

Second-Day; Jan[y] 24. 170¾ I paid Capt. Belchar £8—15—0. Took 24[s] in my pocket, and gave my Wife the rest of my cash £4.3—8, and tell her she shall now keep the Cash; if I want I will borrow of her. She has a better faculty than I at managing Affairs: I will assist her; and will endeavour to live upon my Salary; will see what it will doe. The Lord give his Blessing.

Jan[y] 31. Second day of the week, about four hours before day, my Daughter Hirst was delivered of a Living lively Daughter. Her mother went to her after the forenoon exercise Jan[y] 30. Mother Hirst came the evening before. We have an Answer of Peace to our many Prayers. *Laus Deo.* Mrs. Wakefield was Midwife. Madam Usher, Pemberton, Hubbard, Welsteed, Nurse Johnson assisted. Nurse is from Salem.

Febr. 5. Seventh-day of the week; I fasted and pray'd to

God that Satan might not be commissioned any longer to buffet me and my wife; for my self and family in the advancing year: and Province &c. for Daughter Hirst, and little Mary to be dedicated to Him the next day.

March 5. The dismal News of the Slaughter made at Deerfield is certainly and generally known, Mr. Secretary came to me in the morning, and told me of it: I told Mr. Willard; by which means our Congregation was made a Bochim. [Judges, II. 1—5.] Tis to be observ'd that the great slaughters have been on the Third day of the week; our Court day. This was Febr. 29th 170¾ My Tenant Kibbee was arrested this day.

April, 10. 1704. The Seven and Thirty French privateers are brought to Town, who were put a-Shore at Marshfield last Friday in the vehemency of the Storm. *Feria quarta,* Apr. 12. In the morning I saw and heard three Swallows playing over my head. I think I never observ'd them so soon in the year before. *Feria Secunda,* April, 17th. 1704, I go to Salem to see my Bror Hirst; Speak with Mr. Noyes, who conceives that the Witnesses were slain at the conclusion of the Peace of Ryswick, 1697. Passing away of the 2d Wo. at the conclusion of the Peace of Carlowitz with the Turk. [1699.] Resurrection of the Witnesses by the Convulsions following the death of Charles 2d K—of Spain; The 1260 days Expire, and then the Witnesses Rise; namely the 1260 Days of the Ten-horn'd Beast, his power to make war. Antichrist's Reign begins at the Time of the great Whore's mounting the Beast, the 10 horned beast, viz. Año 1073. Hildebrand papa. At the death of Valentinian, the Ten-horn'd Beast set up; viz. anno, 458. Taken from Mr. Noyes's mouth at Bror Sewall's.

April, 27, 1704. Little Judith is carried on Horseback, Jane Green attending her, unto the house of Mr. Robert Avery of Dedham, for to be healed of her Rupture. Had Mrs. Wigglesworth's advice. In the morning, not thinking of her departure, I first got her to say after me, Create in me a clean heart, O

God; and renew a right spirit within me. It was near sun-set, when they went away, which made us uneasy: But Mrs. Avery was in a readiness with Horses and Company; and the spring advancing apace made us consent. I intended 4. p.m. to be the latest for their setting out.

May, 13. I visit little Judith; find her well: visit Mr. Belchar.

Wednesday, June 7th. 1704. Col. Nathan[l] Byfield, Mr. Palmer and my self have rec'd an Order from the Gov[r] to search for and seize Pirats and their Treasure, and to hold a court of Enquiry for this end at Marblehead; because Capt. Quelch in the Charles Galley arrived there: we set forward this day for Salem, having James Noyes and Joseph Gerrish to wait on us. We got to Salem about 8 aclock. There Sam. Wakefield, the Water Baily, inform'd Col. Byfield of a Rumor there was that Capt. Larrimore was now with the Larramore Gally at Cape-Anne; and that two of Quelch's company designed to go off in her. Upon this we made out a Warrant to the said Wakefield to goe and see into this matter and seize the Men if true. Despatch'd him about midnight.

Thorsday, June 8. We went to Marblehead in the Rain, and held our Court at Capt. Brown's by the Fireside; took Major Sewall with us, who return'd to Salem the same night.

Friday, June, 9th about 6. m. An Express from Cape-Anne, gives an Account of 9. or 11. Pirats, double arm'd, seen in a Lone-house there. This Express found us a-bed. We rose imediately, Sent for Col. Legg, and directed him to send warrants to the Northward Companies within his Regiment; to send such parties as they could raise, to Cape-Anne upon this Extraordinary occasion. And writt to Col. Wainright to do the Like in his Regiment, intimating that we were moving thither our selves to be witness of their forwardness for Her Majesties Service. Sent this by James Noyes to shew it to Capt. Fisk of Wenham, as he went along. Col. Byfield and I rode to Salem; there met Dr. Gatchman, took his Affidavit for some better foundation for our Actions. Sent him post to the Govr. Bro^r^ got a shallop, the Trial, and his Pinace, and about a score of his Comp^a^ to go by water. Mr. Dudley went by water from Marblehead with Col. Legg. Col. Byfield and I proceeded with Sheriff Gedney and Capt. Turner and part of his Troop by Land: call'd on Lt Brisco at Beverly; that Troop resolv'd to go by Jabacko [Chebacco]. Manchester Company was mustering upon the top of a Rock; shook hand with Mr. Webster. When drew nigh the Town of Glocester a Letter from Mr. Dudley and Legg met us, to acquaint us that Larramore Sail'd in the morning and took in the Pirates at the head of the Cape. Messenger seem'd to discourage our going forward. However, we sent back the Sheriff to post their Letter to the Govr, and as many of Salem Troops as would go back, persuading them to return. Mr. Dudley had sent to stay Ipswich Regiment and direct their Return. When came to Capt. Davis's, waited Brother's arrival with his Shallop Trial, and Pinace: When they were come and had Din'd, Resolv'd to send after Larramore. Abbot was first pitch'd on as Captain. But matters went on heavily, 'twas difficult to get Men. Capt. Herrick pleaded earnestly his Troopers might be excus'd. At last Brother offer'd to goe himself: then Capt. Turner offer'd to goe, Lieut Brisco, and many good Men; so that quickly made up Fourty two; though we knew not the exact number till came home, the hurry was so great, and vessel so small for 43. Men gave us three very handsom cheers; Row'd out of the Harbour after sun-set, for want of wind. Mr. Dudley return'd to Salem with Beverly Troop. Col. Byfield and I lodg'd at Cape-Ann all night; Mr. White pray'd very well for the Expedition Evening and morning; as Mr. Chiever had done at Marblehead, whom we sent for to pray with us before we set out for Glocester. We rose early, got to Salem quickly after Nine. Din'd with Sister, who was very thoughtfull what would become of her Husband. The Wickedness and despair of the company they pursued, their Great Guns and other warlike Preparations, were a terror to her and to most of the Town; concluded they would not be Taken without Blood. Comforted our selves and them as well as we could. Call'd at Lewis's. Col. Byfield went to Cambridge; Mr. Dudley and I to Boston, Joseph Gerrish waiting on us. June 12th Joseph Gerrish comes to my Bed-Chamber-door and Tells of Brother's good success. He dispatched Chapman in the night to the Govr. He came to the Isles Sholes about 7. m. June 10, kept his men rank'd with their Arms on both sides the shallop in covert; only the four Fishermen were in view: as drew near saw the Boat goe ashoar with six Hands, which was a singular good Providence of God. Wormwall and three of the Pirats were of the six. When were so near that were descryd, Larramores Men began to run to and fro and pull off the Aprons from the Guns, draw out the Tomkins [Tompions], Brother shew'd his men. Ask'd Larramore to come aboard. He said he could not, his Boat was gon ashore. Bror told him he would come to him: imediately man'd the Pinace, and did it as soon almost as said it, He, Capt. Turner, Abbot step'd aboard. Brisco attempted; but one swore no more armed Men should come there. Bror got the Capt ashore to discourse him, got him there to sign two orders; one to send the Lt and one of the Pirats ashore; the other for Abbot to comand the Galley till they return'd; and so quickly finish'd his business thorowly without striking a stroke, or firing a Gun. See the News-Letter. Twas all order'd and Tim'd and effected by the Singular all-powerful gracious Providence of God.

Feria Sexta, Junij, 30, 1704. After Diner, about 3. p.m. I went to see the Execution. By the way (cous. Ephr. Savage with me) James Hawkins certifies us of Madam Paiges death; he was to make a Tomb. Many were the people that saw upon Broughton's Hill. But when I came to see how the River was cover'd with People, I was amazed: Some say there were 100 Boats. 150 Boats and Canoes, saith Cousin Moody of York. He told them. Mr. Cotton Mather came with Capt. Quelch and six others for Execution from the Prison to Scarlet's Wharf, and from thence in the Boat to the place of Execution about the midway between Hanson's point and Broughton's Warehouse. Mr. Bridge was there also. When the scaffold was hoisted to a due height, the seven Malefactors went up; Mr. Mather pray'd for them standing upon the Boat. Ropes were all fasten'd to the Gallows (save King, who was Repriev'd). When the Scaffold was let to sink, there was such a Screech of the Women that my wife heard it sitting in our Entry next the Orchard, and was much surprised at it; yet the wind was sou-west. Our house is a full mile from the place.

July, 12. *feria quarta,* went to Dedham in company of Mr. Gray, and David Jeffries; find Judith well, carried her a little Basket and some Cakes. Mr. Belcher preach'd from Lam. 3. Why doth living man complain. Din'd at Mr. Avery's with Judith. Harvest begun.

Jany. 6. Begins to be some heat between the Govr and the Deputies. At last the Govr sends in Mr. Secretary, Mr. E^m^ Hutchinson and Mr. Stoddard, to prorogue the Assembly to the 21. Febr. at 10. m. At first the Deputies seem'd to be against Prorogation; afterward sent in Capt. Checkly to say, That by reason of the thinness of their House, Shortness and Coldness of the days, inclined to a Prorogation. Speaker intimated their Desire of a Fast.

Tuesday, Feb^r^. 13th. Last night I had a very sad Dream that held me a great while. As I remember, I was condemn'd and to be executed. Before I went out I read Dr. Arrowsmith's Prayer p 274 —— which was a comfort to me. A Council was warn'd to meet at Noon. I was there one of the first: Governour came in and quickly put Capt. Lawson's Petition into my hand; and upon my speaking somthing to it, He fell to a vehement chiding about Philip Morse's business, and then with great Loudness and passion spake to the affair of Capt. Lason's; several times said He would dy if ever any such thing was done in England except in case of Felony or Treason, or the like. I objected against that ridiculous part of the Petition of his being forc'd by Mr. Clark or me to retire into the neighbouring Province; as being a great Reproach to the whole Governm^{t}. No body apeared, I expected my Accuser face to face. Govr mov'd that a day might be set for a Hearing: but the Council being but 7, besides my self, declared they did not understand what was contain'd in the Petition belong'd to them to deal in, i. e. settling a Maintenance. Govr said, then it must be left to another time.

Febr. 24. Singing of Birds is come.

March, 2. Deputies present the Govr with Two Hundred pounds. Towards night the Govr called upon the Council to consider George Lason's Petition; If he might have a Protection, he was ready to come. Council excepted against their meddling with settling estates of Maintenance; knew not that it was his Petition. Spoke pretty much to it.

March, 3. Govr said he would now take their vote whether they would hear Lason: Twas carried in the Negative, not one that I observ'd, speaking for it. I read a Clause out of Dalton shewing when an officer might break open a House. Mention'd the Act of Parliam^{t} about cutting Poles where the Fine is but Ten shillings; yet a suspected person's house might be entred. In presence of 2 Justices Peers house might be broken up and yet peer must not be attach'd or imprison'd. Because the Govr had said, Must be Treason or Felony. And upbraided me, because had broken up the house, and then taken his parol till morning. Should have sent him to Prison with 20 Halberts. No Law for a man to live with his wife. I said Govr [Thomas] Dudley's saying was, A bargain's a Bargain and must be made Good; If we look'd to the Form of Marriage should find twas a great deal Lason had promis'd. Govr seem'd to reject it with disdain, and ask'd Col. Hutchinson when he lay with his wife? Col. Hutchinson answer'd, The Question should not have been when he lay with his wife; but when he lay with another woman. I said, The people were ready to pull down Lason's house, high time for the Government to interpose. Mr. Henchman had not complain'd of the Watch for knocking him up the other night. Lason's house was on fire, and he was not aware of it; high time for the Government to awaken him. Last night mention'd the Queen's Proclamation, and Governours to do to the utmost to supress Imorality and profaneness: None had yet shew'd me any Law I had broken. Govr mention'd Dalton.

April, 12, 1705. Thanksgiving Day. The Night was so cold that was a very great Frost, thick Ice, and the street frozen like winter. Remain'd frozen at Noon in the shady places of the street. Mr. Melyen had a great Tub of water frozen so hard, that it bore two men standing upon it in his sight.

Monday, April, 23. Sam. Robinson sets four Poplars in the Foreyard, to shade the windows from the Western sun in Sumer. Remov'd the little Peach-Trees. As were setting the Trees, heard and saw several Swallows; which are the first I remember to have seen this year. Widow Holland visits us. Guns fired about Noon: Flags, and Ships Colours flying.

Lord's Day, June, 10. 1705. The Learned and pious Mr. Michael Wigglesworth dies at Malden about 9. m. Had been sick about 10. days of a Fever; 73 years and 8 moneths old. He was the Author of the Poem entituled The Day of Doom, which has been so often printed: and was very useful as a Physician.

July, 19. Govr had a New Comission read relating to Pirats, and Queens Pleasure read for pardoning the surviving Pirats; and they in prison were sent for, and their Pardon declared in open Court, Chains knock'd off; but must go into the Queens service.

Augt. 24. 1705. Mr. Samuel Myles comes with his Bro^r before me; I bid him, Sam., sit down: but he quickly fell upon Nichols [the constable], the complainant against his Bro^r, and said by his Looks one might see the Gallows groan'd for him; I check'd him, and said it did not become a Minister so to speak. The constable ask'd me what weight the Money must be, 15. or 17. I answered there was no Money but 17^{d} w^{t}: but if Capt. Myles offer'd Bills of Credit he must take them. Mr. Saml Myles told me he complain'd of Nichols, but withall told me he was not ready to pursue it.

Novr 24th. Snow falls and covers the Ground. Has been very cold wether this week.

The College at Quebec was burnt the third time when they were there; that set a small chapel at a distance, on fire; the chapel fired a high Cross with a Crucifix on it, so that it bowed and fell down. [Judges V. 27.]

Novr. 25. Mrs. Allen dies, 28, buried, 29. Snow. This day hear of Capt. Samuel Clark's death very suddenly at Sea, about 3 weeks ago: Sail'd from St. Thomas 2 or 3 days before. Was a good man, liv'd in our house more than Ten years, left one Son. The Lord fit me for my change. Decr. 1. made this Distich on the burning of the Quebeck Cross:

Crux atrox tandem flammam sentire jubetur:
Ipso Salus fallax igne probata perit.

The bawdy bloudy Cross, at length
Was forc'd to taste the flame:
The cheating Saviour, to the fire
Savoury food became.

Decr. 1. Deputies send in a Bill against fornication, or Marriage of White men with Negros or Indians; with extraordinary penalties; directing the Secretary to draw a Bill accordingly. If it be pass'd, I fear twill be an Opression provoking to God, and that which will promote Murders and other Abominations. I have got the Indians out of the Bill, and some mitigation for them [the Negroes] left in it, and the clause about their Masters not denying their Marriage.

Decr 7. Went to Brooklin, set out about Noon, saw the Govr at his Fence, who invited me in to Diner, stood with his Son W^{m}. But I fear'd should lose visiting Mr. Bayley, and so pass'd on. After Diner met the Govr upon the Plain near Sol. Phip's; told me of what hapend on the Road, being in a great passion; threaten'd to send those that affronted him to England. As I went back, Jno Bartlet, the middlemost Carter, shew'd me the Ground where the three carts stood, which was a difficult place to turn; and the Govr had a fair way to have gon by them if he had pleas'd. Upon the Meetinghouse hill met Mr. P. Dudley: I ask'd him how he got the men along, he said he walk'd them along. Upon Satterday just at night Mr. Trowbridge and Winchester came to speak to me that their sons might be released out of Prison. It being so late, I refer'd them to second-day Morning Decr 10. to meet at the Secretary's office. Major Walley and I met there and Mr. Attorney, who desired Mr. Leverett might be sent for, being so near; and writt a Letter accordingly in our Names, which was given to Mr. White. Mr. Leverett came not till 3^{d} day xr. 11th. Then in the Afternoon, we agreed to grant a Habeas Corpus, and I sign'd it, but Mr. Cook being at Charlestown-Court twas not seal'd till Wednesday morning. The writt commanded them to be brought to the Court-Chamber in Boston on Friday morn, 9. aclock. Twas put off till then that might have Mr. Leverett's company, whose business allow'd him not to be here sooner: And that Mr. Attorney [Paul Dudley] who was attending Charlestown-Court, might have oportunity to be present.

Sixth-day, xr. 14. Mr. Leverett came, and Mr. Sheriff order'd the Prisoners to be brought: Mr. Attorney spoke against them: They had no counsil, could procure none. Justices withdrew into the Counsil Chamber, and agreed to Bail to the Super^{r} Court, 300£ Prisoners and 3 Sureties each 100£. Examin'd the first and put it in writing. And I sent Mr. Cook to Mr. Secretary to desire his Assistance, or presence, which he declin'd. Some would have had five Hundred pounds and more sureties. I urg'd the words of the Act, that saith regard is to be had to the quality of the person; These men were not worth so much. At last came to Three Hundred pound. I propounded Two Hundred, and Two sureties. Thomas Trowbridge 300£ James Trowbridge 100. Abraham Jackson 100. and Capt. Oliver Noyes 100. John Winchester 300£, John Winchester the Father 100£, Josiah Winchester, unkle, 100. Mr. John White £100. I could hardly be brought to their being bound to their Good Behaviour, because there was no Oath to justify the charge laid in the Mittimus; and the Prisoners pleaded their Inocence. No Complaint in writing. A little after Two aclock all was finish'd. I am glad that I have been instrumental to Open the Prison to these two young men, that they might repair to their wives and children and Occasions; and that might have Liberty to assemble with God's People on the Lord's Day. I writt earnestly to Col. Hathorne to desire him, an experienced Traveller, to help us to steer between Scylla and Charibdis: I mentiond it in Court. Mr. Willard sung 72 PS. from the 4th v. two Staves—Poor of the People.—While we were deliberating in the Council-Chamber, P. Dudley writt a Letter, that would not Bail them yet; that would be an error on the right hand; he would write to his father Mompresson, Mr. Secretary was not Settled in his opinion. Not one Gentleman present but thought they would not be Bail'd. Mr. Leverett shew'd me the Letter, writt an Answer and copied it on Mr. Dudley's. In publick I offer'd Coke's pleas of the Crown to be read, especially as to that clause of High Treason for killing the Chancellor &c. He declined having it read. I had the Statute Book there, Coke pleas Crown, and Reading on the Statutes, stuck to 31. Car. 2d, that Comands all to be Bail'd that are not Committed for Felony or Treason.

Feb. 27. My Neighbour Deming came to me, and ask'd of me the Agreement between himself and Joana Tiler; I told him I was to keep it for them both and could not deliver it; he said he was going to Cambridge to ask Mr. Leverett's Advice, he would bring it safe again. When he still urged and insisted, I told him I would not have him lose his time, I would not deliver it; I would give him a copy if he pleas'd. He said he was in haste and could not stay the writing of it. I said, You would not take it well that I should deliver it to Tiler; no more could I deliver it to him. He said some what sourly, I am sorry you have not more Charity for him. And going away, murmuring said, passing out of the Stove-Room into the Kitchen, I have desired a Copy, offered Money and am Deny'd: I was then more mov'd than before, and said with some earnestness, Will you speak false to my face? He went away, and came not again, but his son came, and I gave him a Copy of the Agreement, writen with my own hand. I thank God, I heartily desired and endeavoured a good Agreement between him and his Neighbour as to the Bounds of their Land although he be thus out of Tune, upon my denying to grant his Unjust Petition.

Tuesday, Apr. 23. Govr. comes to Town guarded by the Troops with their Swords drawn; dines at the Dragon, from thence proceeds to the Townhouse, Illuminations at night. Capt. Pelham tells me several wore crosses in their Hats; which makes me resolve to stay at home; (though Maxwell was at my House and spake to me to be at the Council-Chamber at 4. p. m.) Because to drinking Healths, now the Keeping of a Day to fictitious St. George, is plainly set on foot. It seems Capt. Dudley's Men wore Crosses. Somebody had fasten'd a cross to a Dog's head; Capt. Dudley's Boatswain seeing him, struck the Dog, and then went into the shop, next where the Dog was, and struck down a Carpenter, one Davis, as he was at work not thinking anything: Boatswain and the other with him were fined 10s each for breach of the peace, by Jer. Dumer Esqr: pretty much blood was shed by means of this bloody Cross, and the poor Dog a sufferer.

Friday, 8r 18. I visit Mr. Baily: as I enter, he saith, I am even gon, even gon! said he had a Fever; the night before and that day had subdued his Nature. In his Paroxism said, Cutting, Cutting, Cutting all to pieces: My Head, my Head; could not bear the Boys choping without door.

Tuesday, 8r 22. I go to Roxbury Lecture, Mr. Cotton Mather preach'd from 1 Jno 5. 13. Concerning Assurance, with much affecting Solidity and Fervor. Went to see Mr. Baily, whose Mouth and Tongue were so furr'd, he could hardly speak at first: said he had been a long time in a storm at the Harbours Mouth, hop'd he should not be swallow'd on Quicksands, or split on Rocks. God had not yet forsaken him, and he hop'd He never would. Said, Here I Wait!

Midweek, Decr 11th. I visited Mr. Bayley, find Mr. Walter with him; I moved that seeing Mr. Walter and I seldom met there together, Mr. Walter might go to prayer; which he did excellently; that Mr. Bayley and we our selves might be prepared to dye. Mr. Bayley is now, the night before last, taken with Pleuretick Pains, which go beyond those of the stone; New Pains: Cryes out, My Head! my Head! what shall I doe? Seems now to long, and pray for a Dismission. At parting I gave his Sister Cheyny a Ten-Shilling Bill for him, to help to buy some Necessaries; I could not help them to watch. Mr. Bayley said he thought he should dye of a Consumption of the Lungs; by's Cough he found they were touch'd. When he mention'd the pain in his side: I said, twas sad for a Man to be circumvented with his Enemies: He answered pretty readily, He hop'd there were more with him than against him. He desired me to write to his Brother Joseph to come and see him. Decr 13. I gave my Letter to J. Bayley to Mr. Simkins, who said he had one to send it by.

Decr 24. *Feria Tertia.* My wife and I execute a Lease to Mr. Seth Dwight, for 21. years, of the House he dwells in. Mr. Eliezer Moodey writt the Leases; and he and David Sinclair were Witnesses: Twas transacted in our Bedchamber.

Feria septima, Decr 28, 1706. A large fair Rainbow is seen in the Morning in the Norwest. Madam Walley call'd her Husband into the Shop to see it. The Govr being indispos'd with the Gout, call't a Council to meet at Roxbury; and by that means I gain'd an Oportunity to see my friend Bayley once again: He is now brought very low by his Stone, Fever, Sore Tongue and Mouth; could hardly speak a word to me. But he said, sit down. His wife ask'd him if he knew me? He answer'd, with some quickness, He should be distracted, if he should not know me. He Thank'd me when I came away. I said Christ would change his vile body, and make it like his glorious body. And when the Coachman call'd, saying the Company staid for me, I took leave, telling him God would abide with him; Those that Christ loves, he loves to the end. He bow'd with his head. His wife and sister weep over him.

Midweek, Jany 15th. A great Storm of Snow; yet Danl Bayley breaks through, and brings us a Load of Walnut Wood. I had transcribed some choice sentences out of Calvin's Exposit. Mat. 4. 1, 2, 3, 4. and sent them by Daniel; Letter was just seal'd before he came, written and dated today. The Storm prevail'd so, that not one of our Meeting ventured to come to our House where it was to be. Mrs. Deming, and her daughter-in-Law, and Mrs. Salter came over; waited till six-a-clock, and then sung the 2 last Staves of the 16. Ps. Eat some Bread and drank.

Saturday morn, Jany 18th. James Robinson, the Baker, coming from Roxbury, tells me Mr. Bayley dyed the last night 2 hours after midnight; one in Roxbury-street bid him tell me so.

Jany 26th. I dream'd last night that I was chosen Lord Maior of London; which much perplex'd me: a strange absurd Dream!

Febr. 9th Lord's Day; The latter part of the Night, and this morn, we had great Lightening, and Thunder, Rain and Hail.

Febr. 10. A pleasant, Serene, sun-shiny Day; sweet singing of Birds.

27th. Dr. Mather was not at Lecture. Mr. Cotton Mather preached, Sung 10——14th 27th Ps. Mr. Dwight is much troubled about digging his Cellar; I get Mr. Cook and Capt. Clark to go to him after Lecture, and view the work and speak to Mr. Gibbins; they seem'd to be offended at Mr. Dwight's smart Replyes to Mr. Gibbins and his wife; and spake a little coldly, and told me it were best to agree. I went again near night, and Dwight told me, Mrs. Gibbins intended next day to make another Gateway, and hinder'd the workmen from digging home at that corner: whereupon I order'd the Men to digg it down, which they quickly did, at which Gibbins storm'd and ask'd me why I did not bid him pull down his House, if I did, they would do it. And Mrs. Gibbins spake many opprobrious words: But the men went on vigorously. Febr. 28. Gibbins orders Mr. Bernard's men to cutt another Gate-way, and with the Boards cut out nail'd up her own former Gateway: then laid a Board, a door, over from the Cutt Gate-way over the Corner of the Cellar and pass that way, and the Negro said, This is our passage-way. I said little to it, but went in, and talk'd with Mr. Gibbins, his wife and son; and were ready to put it to Men to determin what should be; Mr. Dwight came in: and said he would not agree to put it to Men: I told Mr. Gibbins I would speak to him, and come again after Diner. I went accordingly, and when I return'd found they had been Pumping Tubs of Water, and throwing them into my new-dug Cellar, to soften the Workmen's Corns, as they said, so that the men were forc'd to leave off working. Several Tubs of water were thrown in while I sat in the House: I only call'd to Mrs. Gibbins and told her I saw she could not wait till I came. Durham came and dug through the Stone-wall into this little new Cellar, and I think that quell'd our antagonists: for our Cellar being a little higher than theirs, all the water would have run upon themselves.

And after, the Select-Men, several of them viewing it, countenanc'd my Tenant; Mr. Secretary also look'd in upon us: and the workmen went on peaceably.

Lord's Day, June, 15th. I felt my self dull and heavy and Listless as to Spiritual Good; Carnal, Lifeless; I sigh'd to God, that he would quicken me.

June 16. My House was broken open in two places, and about Twenty pounds worth of Plate stolen away, and some Linen; My Spoon, and Knife, and Neckcloth was taken: I said, Is not this an Answer of Prayer? Jane came up, and gave us the Alarm betime in the morn. I was helped to submit to Christ's stroke, and say, Wellcome CHRIST!

June, 19th. The measuring Bason is found with Margaret Barton just carrying of it to Sea, to Hingham; said she had it of James Hews, he gave it her to sell for him. Mr. Secretary sent her to Prison.

June, 21. Billy Cowell's shop is entered by the Chimney, and a considerable quantity of Plate stolen. I give him a Warrant to the Constable, they find James Hews hid in the Hay in Cabal's Barn, on the Back side of the Comon; while they was seising of him under the Hay, he strip'd off his Pocket, which was quickly after found, and Cowell's silver in it. At night I read out of Caryl on Job, 5. 2 . The humble submission to the *stroke* of God, turns into a *Kiss* — which I thank God, I have in this Instance experienced. *Laus Deo.*

7r 10th. Midweek, sentenced a woman that whip'd a Man, to be whip'd; said a woman that had lost her Modesty, was like Salt that had lost its savor; good for nothing but to cast to the Dunghill: 7 or 8 join'd together, call'd the Man out of his Bed, guilefully praying him to shew them the way; then by help of a Negro youth, tore off his Cloaths and whip'd him with Rods; to chastise him for carrying it harshly to his wife. Got out of Town to Rehoboth.

Tuesday, Octr 28. 1707. The Fellows of Harvard College meet, and chuse Mr. Leverett President: He had eight votes,

Dr. Increase Mather three, Mr. Cotton Mather, one, and Mr. Brattle of Cambridge, one. Mr. White did not vote, and Mr. Gibbs came when voting was over.

Novr. 25. 1707. The Govr read Mr. Cotton Mather's Letter to Sir Charles Hobby in Council, the Copey being sign'd by Mr. Povey, and animadverted on several paragraphs; When the Govr came to the *horrid Reign of Bribery:* His Excellency said, None but a Judge or Juror could be Brib'd, the Governour could not be bribed, sons of Belial brot him no Gifts. Mov'd that Col. Hutchinson, Mr. Secretary, Col. Townsend and Mr. Cushin go to Mr. Cotton Mather with the Copy of his Letter to Sir Charles Hobby, and his Letters to the Govr, and speak to him about them: this was agreed to. I shew'd some backwardness to it, fearing what the Issue might be; and hinting whether it might not be better for the Govr to go to him himself: That seem'd to be Christ's Rule, except the Govr would deal with him in a Civil way.

Novr. 26. Mr. Secretary reports the Discourse with Mr. Cotton Mather favourably; It seems they stay'd there more than two Hours; and Dr. Mather was present. Mr. Mather neither denys, nor owns the Letter: Think his Letters to the Govr, and that to Sir Charles Hobbey, not so inconsistent as they are represented. By Candle-Light before they went, It was debated whether Mr. Mather should be sent for before the Council; or whether the Gentlemen should go to him. Then I that had been backward to meddle in it before, plainly declar'd my mind that twas best for the Gentlemen to go to him; and so twas carried when put to the Vote. Mr. Secretary is well pleas'd that he went.

Friday, Novr. 28. 1707. The Govr puts forward to have the vote of July 9. 1706. of the Representatives, the vote of the Council of Novr 1., the vote of the Representatives Novr. 21., Printed, to prevent spreading false Reports: I said I could not vote to it because I had withdrawn my vote. The Govr said, I pray God judge between me and you! Col. Townsend told me I was a Temporiser; I hop'd Mr. Higginson would be Govr, and endeavour'd to procure his favor. Prayer. Lord, do not depart from me, but pardon my sin; and fly to me in a way of favourable Protection! Capt. Phips brings in Mr. Leverett Non-Concurr'd. Moves from the House that a suitable person be thought of to take care of the College till May Sessions. Col. Townsend tells me that my purpose to withdraw my Vote was known a week ago; Mr. Oaks mention'd it in the House; He was my Counsellor. Whereas he really knew nothing of it; and now tells me, he never mention'd my Name.

Decr. 5. Dine at Holm's. I supos'd the Council had Treated the Govr, But the Govr would pay. A Message is sent in to the Deputies about the College; whereupon they withdraw their Non-concurrence; rase out (Non) and turn it to Concur'd; And vote Mr. Leverett a Salary of One Hundred and Fifty pounds per añum out of the publick Treasury.

Decr. 6. Some desire that it may be put in the Bill that Mr. Leverett Lay down all his Civil offices; as Judge of Probate and judge of the Superiour Court. And entirely to attend that service, was inserted, and Mr. Secretary carried it in to the Deputies, and took their Consent. Govr has Two Hundred pounds given him. Col. Jno Appleton, Hunt and I are sent in to speak to the Deputies about their denying any Reward to the commissioners to Port-Royal; Told them, denying all Remuneration was in a maner to make them Criminals: Twas a burden God in his providence had laid on us, and to go about thus to shake it off, would be to his Dishonor. Spake also in behalf of Salem Fort and Marblehead. Upon this a Resolve was sent in to leave the consideration of it to another Sessions being now a very thin House. Deputies had sent in a long Roll of Grievances to be Reform'd, as their Advice: Govr would have had the Council advis'd the contrary in the whole: I oposed it, as inconvenient to vote against all together: and it was staid. And yet when the Deputies were come in, the Govr

took the paper and spoke to it; said he could not go according to it without having the Frontiers defenceless; said the Council were unanimously against it. Court is prorogued to the fourth of February.

Feria quinta, Decr 11th 1707. Thanks-giving-day, very serene, moderate, comfortable Wether. Mr. Pemberton preaches forenoon and afternoon. Yesterday I was told of a vast number of Pigeons in the Woods this Moneth. Capt. Mills at his Sister's Wedding says he saw an incredible Number at Woodstock last Friday.

Jany. 23, 170⅞. I go to the Funeral of Anne Needham, who died in Child-bed: her former Husband was Lawson: her first, Airs, to whom I married her Novr. 5. 1690. At first I walk'd next the women with Mr. Wentworth: when had gon a little way Mr. Cotton Mather came up and went with me. Funeral was from Coney's Lane, to the new Burying-place. There Mr. Mather ask'd me to go with him to Madam Usher's, where we staid till past six. Speaking of death, I said twas a Hapiness to be so Conform'd to Christ, And it was a pleasure to take part with God in executing a righteous Sentence upon one's self, to aplaud his Justice —— Mr. Mather said that was high-flying; he would have such High-flyers be at his Funeral. Had been mentioning Mr. Dod's Will. As went thence told me of his Letter to the Govr of the 20th Ins^t. and Lent me the Copy; intends to send another to Mr. Paul Dudley. Dr. Mather it seems has also sent a Letter to the Govr. I wait with Concern to see what the issue of this plain homedealing will be! I desir'd Mr. Mather to promote Col. Thomas's being brought into the Superior Court, if there was oportunity: the 12th Feb^r. is apointed for a Nomination.

Jany 30. 170⅞ John Neesnummin [Indian Preacher] comes to me with Mr. R. Cotton's Letters; I shew him to Dr. Mather. Bespeak a Lodging for him at Matthias Smith's: but after they sent me word they could not doe it. So I was fain to lodg him in my Study. Jany 31 p. m. I send him on his way towards Natick, with a Letter to John Trowbridge to take him in if there should be occasion. About half an hour by sun I went to the Funeral of my neighbour Sam Engs: I went first with Mr. Meers, and then with Mr. Pemberton, who talk'd to me very warmly about Mr. Cotton Mather's Letter to the Govr, sem'd to resent it, and expect the Govr should animadvert upon him. See Feb. 6. Said if he were as the Govr he would humble him though it cost him his head; Speaking with great vehemency just as I parted with him at his Gate. The Lord apear for the Help of his people.

Second-day, Feb^{r} 9. 170⅞. The Apointment of a Judge for the Super. Court being to be made upon next Fifth day, Febr. 12, I pray'd God to Accept me in keeping a private day of Prayer with Fasting for That and other Important Matters: I kept it upon the Third day Febr. 10. 170⅞ in the uper Chamber at the North-East end of the House, fastening the Shutters next the Street.——Perfect what is lacking in my Faith, and in the faith of my dear Yokefellow. Convert my children; especially Samuel and Hanah; Provide Rest and Settlement for Hanah: Recover Mary, Save Judith, Elisabeth and Joseph: Requite the Labour of Love of my Kinswoman Jane Tappin, Give her health, find out Rest for her. Make David a man after thy own heart, Let Susan live and be baptised with the Holy Ghost, and with fire. Relations. Steer the Government in this difficult time, when the Governour and many others are at so much Variance: Direct, incline, overrule on the Council-day fifth-day, Febr. 12. as to the special Work of it in filling the Super. Court with Justices; or any other thing of like nature; as Plim^{o} infer Court. Bless the Company for propagation of the Gospel, especiall Govr Ashurst &c. Revive the Business of Religion at Natick, and accept and bless John Neesnumin who went thither last week for that end. Mr Rawson at Nantucket. Bless the South Church in preserving and spiriting our Pastor; in directing unto suitable Supply, and making the Church unanimous: Save the Town, College

Province from Invasion of Enemies, open, Secret, and from false Brethren: Defend the Purity of Worship. Save Connecticut, bless their New Governour: Save the Reformation under N. York Governm^{t}. Reform all the European Plantations in America; Spanish, Portuguese, English, French, Dutch; Save this New World, that where Sin hath abounded, Grace may Superabound; that CHRIST who is stronger, would bind the strong man and spoil his house; and order the Word to be given, Babylon is fallen.——Save our Queen, lengthen out her Life and Reign. Save France, make the Proud helper stoop [Job. IX. 13], Save all Europe; Save Asia, Africa, Europe and America. These were gen^{l} heads of my Meditation and prayer; and through the bounteous Grace of GOD, I had a very Comfortable day of it.

Feria quinta, March, 25, 1708. Intending to set out for Plimouth the 27th. I went to the Major Gen^{ls} and to Mrs. Sergeant's to Receive their Bills if they pleas'd to pay them: found neither at home, and so went not in. Coming back, in the prison-Lane I met Mr. Sergeant. He ask'd me where I had been, I told him at his house: He said, What for, Money? I said Yes. At which he was angry, and said I was very hasty, I knew very little of that nature. He would enquire how others paid me &c. I told him I was going out of Town, this was the day, and I thought it convenient to offer the Bills; he said he should not break; and at last call'd out aloud, he should not break before I came back again! I know no reason for this Anger; the Lord sanctify it to me, and help me to seek more his Grace and favour. This day was very stormy with Rain, and then with Snow; a pretty deal of Thunder. Maj^{r} Cutler was with me in the morning.

Feria Sexta, April, 2. Last night I dream'd that I had my daughter Hirst in a little Closet to pray with her; and of a sudden she was gon, I could not tell how; although the Closet was so small, and not Cumber'd with Chairs or Shelves. I was much affected with it when I waked.

Feria septima, Apr. 3. I went to Cous. Dumer's to see hi News-Letter: while I was there Mr. Nathl Henchman cam in with his Flaxen Wig; I wish'd him Joy, i. e. of his Wed ding. I could not observe that he said a Word to me; and gen erally he turn'd his back upon me, when none were in th room but he and I. This is the Second time I have spoken t him, in vain, as to any Answer from him. First was upon th death of his Wife, I cross'd the way near our house, and ask' him how he did: He only shew'd his Teeth.

Feria secunda, Apr. 5. Great Rain, whereby I am pre vented meeting Major Thaxter at Milton to run a Line, as intended.

Feria secunda, Apr. 12, 1708. I went and met Majo Thaxter at Miller's at Milton to run the Lines of the 30 Acres bought of Mr. Stoughton; Cousin Quinsey, Mr. Swif Miller, White, Hunt, assisted us. Mr. William Rawson, hav ing Land adjoining, was with us all day; Billing a considerabl while. Capt. Culliver and others perambulating for Braintre and Milton, went with us from B. to C. which was measure whereby the place we set out from was ascertain'd to be th North Corner, of which there was some doubt before: At C the old white Oak mark with H., we drank a Bottle of Made together, read the Queens Speech to the first Parliament great Britain, and so took leave of the perambulators. Maj Thaxter, Cous. Quinsey, and White went quite through th Swamp, marking Trees: southward of the Swamp is a sma Chestnut White-Oak; a little after that the Line brushes a Ledge of Rocks, touches them. At D. the Oak upon th Rock is cut down injuriously, there it lyes and no use made it: by the Stump grows up a fine little Chestnut Oak, whi was prun'd; twas double and one is cut away to make the oth grow the better. In the Line from D to A found several Tre mark'd with H. At A. we enlarg'd the Heap of Stones up the Rock and from thence, as all along, run by Compass a the anciently marked Trees to C., where we begun; whi prov'd all the Work to be Right: There we made a large heap of Stones upon the Stump of a Tree burnt down.

Wednesday, 8[r] 27, 1708. My wife is taken very sick as she was last April; taken with Shaking and intolerable pain in her Brest. Maj[r] Gen[l] visits her and she takes some of his powder; but it cast up so soon, that it works little. Great Rain. Dr. Noyes visits and administers: on Friday grows better, *Laus Deo.*

Monday, Nov[r] 1. Gov[rs] best Horse dyes in his Pasture at Roxbury as goe to Dedham. Bouroughs, a worstedcomber, was at Mr. Colman's Meeting on the L. day p. m., went homeward towards Roxbury in the night; got beyond the Salt-ponds, and fell down a-cross the Cart path in the Mud, and there perished; was found dead on Monday morn, Nov[r] 1. And tho the Coroner did his Office in the Morning; yet the Corps lay as a sad spectacle, gazed on till late in the Afternoon.

Gov[r] calls and smokes a pipe with my wife at night 9[r] 1.

Jan[y] 31, 170$\frac{8}{9}$. Mr. Spensar calls here, and I enquire of him about Mr. Gerrish of Wenham, what he should say; He answer'd not directly; but said his Cousin would come if he might have admittance. I told him I heard he went to Mr. Coney's daughter. He said he knew nothing of that: I desired him to enquire, and tell me. I understood he undertook it; but he came no more.

Febr 4th Nurse Smith buried. Coming from the Grave I ask'd Mr. Pemberton whether S. Gerrish courted Mr. Coney's daughter; he said No; not now. Mr. Coney thought his daughter young.

Febr 5. Storm of Snow, and I goe not out.

Febr 6. is a Comfortable day. Febr 7th I deliver a Letter to S. Gerrish to inclose and send to his father, which he promises to doe.

Febr. 17. I receive Mr. Gerrishes Letter just at night. Febr. 18th. I leave Word at Mr. Gerrishes shop that I would speak with him after Mr. Bromfield's Meeting was over. He came and I bid him wellcom to my house as to what his father writt about. So late hardly fit then to see my daughter, apointed him to come on Tuesday, invited him to Super; I observ'd he drunk to Mary in the third place. Febr. 23. When I came from the Meeting at Mr. Stephens's I found him in the Chamber, Mr. Hirst and wife here. It seems he ask'd to speak with Mary below; her Mother was afraid because the fire was newly made: and Mr. Hirst brought him up. This I knew not of: He ask'd me below, whether it were best to frequent my House before his father came to Town: I said that were the best introduction: but he was wellcom to come before, and bid him come on Friday night. Febr. 24. Mr. Hirst tells me Mr. Gerrish courted Mr. Coney's daughter: I told him I knew it, and was uneasy. In the evening daughter Hirst came hether, I supose to tell that Mr. Gerrish had courted Mr. Coney's daughter: and if she should have Mr. Stoddard, she would mend her market. Friday, Febr. 25. Madam Winthrop, Oliver, and Mico visit my wife. In the evening S. Gerrish comes not; we expected him, Mary dress'd her self: it was a painfull disgracefull disapointment. Febr. 26. Satterday, Sam Gerrish goes to Wenham unknown to me, till Lords-day night Capt. Greenleaf told me of it. He was not seen by us till Wednesday March 2, David saw him.

March, 14. The Rever^d^ Mr. Joseph Gerrish comes to our house in the evening. Dines with us March 15th Tuesday. At night his Son comes, and Mary goes to him. Mr. Gerrish goes home on Wednesday. His son comes and is entertain'd then also.

Friday-night. S. Gerrish comes. Tells Mary except Satterday and Lord's-day nights intends to wait on her every night; unless some extraordinary thing hapen.

Satterday, March 19. I call at S. Gerishes shop; he was not within: but came in presently: I desired him to Bind me a Psalm-Book in Calv's Leather.

May, 2. Being Artillery day, and Mr. Higginson dead, I

put on my Mourning Rapier; and put a black Ribband into my little cane. When I enter'd the Council-Chamber, the Govr with an Air of displeasure said, You are Chidden! pretending my late coming; though I think I was there before eleven, and am, I think, the most constant attender of Councils.

I dined with the Artillery at Powells, whether Maxwell came and warn'd me to Council at 3. There I waited all alone, as many times I doe. At length the Govr came. When Col. Hathorne had his Quota 76. given him, he expostulated a little; upon which the Govr was very angry, and took him up with very smart words. I was on the same side of the board, and saw his Warrant. Then I went to my own, and seeing a number of Letters ly under the Secretaryes hand, I made a motion to see one which the Secretary declin'd: and the Govr taking notice of it with a very angry Air said to me, I will not be Govern'd by You!

Midweek, July, 13. 1709. N.B. Last night, between 2 or 3 hours after midnight, my wife complain'd of Smoak; I presently went out of Bed, and saw and felt the Chamber very full of Smoak to my great Consternation. I slipt on my Cloaths except Stockings, and run out of one Room into another above, and below Stairs, and still found all well but my own Bed-chamber. I went into Garret and rouz'd up David, who fetch'd me a Candle. My wife fear'd the Brick side was a-fire, and the children endangered. She fled thither, and call'd all up there. While she was doing this, I felt the partition of my Bed-Chamber Closet warm; which made me with fear to unlock it, and going in I found the Deal-Box of Wafers all afire, burning livelily; yet not blazing. I drew away the papers nearest to it, and call'd for a Bucket of Water. By that time it came, I had much adoe to recover the Closet agen: But I did, and threw my Water on it, and so more, and quench'd it thorowly. Thus with great Indulgence GOD saved our House and Substance, and the Company's Paper. This night, as I lay down in my Bed, I said to my Wife, that the Goodness of God apeared, in that we had a Chamber, a Bed, and Company. If my Wife had not waked me, we might have been consumed. And it seems admirable, that the opening the Closet-Door did not cause the Fire to burst forth into an Unquenchable Flame. The Box was 18 inches over, Closet full of loose papers, boxes, Cases, some Powder. The Window-Curtain was of Stubborn Woolen and refus'd to burn though the Iron-Bars were hot with the fire. Had that burnt it would have fired the pine-shelves and files of Papers and Flask and Bandaliers of powder. The Pine-Floor on which the Box stood, was burnt deep, but being well plaister'd between the Joysts, it was not burnt through. The Closet under it had Hundreds of Reams of the Company's Paper in it. The plaistered Wall is mark'd by the Fire so as to resemble a Chimney back. Although I forbad mine to cry Fire; yet quickly after I had quench'd it; the Chamber was full of Neighbours and Water. The smell of Fire pass'd on me very much; which lasted some days. We imagine a Mouse might take our lighted Candle out of the Candle-stick on the hearth and dragg it under my closet-door behind the Box of Wafers. The good Lord sanctify this Threatening; and his Parental Pity in improving our selves for the Discovery of the fire, and Quenching it. The Lord teach me what I know not; and wherein I have done amiss help me to doe so no more!

Midweek, Augt 24. In the evening Mr. Pemberton marrys Mr. Samuel Gerrish, and my daughter Mary: He begun with Prayer, and Mr. Gerrish the Bridegroom's father concluded: Mr. Mayhew was present.

Augt 25. Mr. Cotton Mather, Mr. Pemberton and wife, and others, dine with us after Lecture. In the even I invited the Govr and Council to drink a Glass of Wine with me; About 20 came; viz. Govr., Winthrop, Hathorne, Elisha Hutchinson, Addington, Brown, Foster, Sergeant, Walley, Phillips, Townsend, Bromfield, Eliakim Hutchinson, Corwin, Higginson, Jn° Apleton, Lynde, Hunt, Cushing, Nordon, Epes. Gave them variety of good Drink, and at going away a large piece of Cake Wrap'd in Paper. They very heartily wish'd me Joy of my daughter's Marriage.

8r 3. Govr calls a Council. I acquainted the Govr with the Condemnation of the two Indian Men at Bristol for Murder, and the time intended for their Execution. Col. Vetch mutter'd somthing as if there was no malice prepense: I told him of the man's kicking his wife into the fire. He said he heard not of that. Capt. Blackmore arrives this day and brings the Wellcom Orders for going on to point the Bible [Indian] and countermanding the selling any more of the Genoa Paper, with a considerable Remittance.

Octr 5. Midweek, Mr. Hirst and I take a Calash and meet Mr. Gerrish with John behind him. Son Gerrish, his wife and Hannah in a Calash. It was a little beyond Newhill's, who now keeps the Swan, that we met them. Din'd there, and there Mr. Gerrish would return, delivering up his Charge to me. As came homeward went over Charlestown Hill on the Neck of Land; and came into the Rode again by Mr. Emerson's. Got home very well, and I went to our Meeting at Mr. Thornton's. *Laus Deo.*

Novr 6th. Lord's day; Mr. Rowland Cotton preach'd in the forenoon; Mr. Corwin in the Afternoon. Mr. Pemberton had propounded Hanah Butler to renew her Baptismal Covenant; and now mention'd it, and said she had sin'd scandulously against the 7th Comandment; read her Confession imediatly, and by the silential vote restored her. I think it is inconvenient, when persons have so fallen, not to give the Church some previous notice of it; that the Brethren may have Oportunity to enquire into the Repentance. An ignorant Consent is no Consent. And I understood Mr. Pemberton that he would not go in that way again. Once before he did it, saying he knew not of it when the party was propounded.

Feb[r] 6, 170$\frac{9}{10}$. the Queen's Birth-day. The Council Treat the Gov[r] at the Green Dragon, with Col. Vetch and several others. Mr. Tho. Bridge, Mr. Wadsworth, and Mr. Colman were there. Cost us 5^s apiece. After our Return to the Council-Chamber, Burnt near Six Thousand pounds of decay'd Bills. When the Candles began to be lighted, I grew weary and uneasy, and even slip'd away without drinking. When I came home, it was a singular Refreshment to me to read 2 Cor. 6. especially from the 14th to the end. See Mr. Pemberton's Sermon, March, 5th &c.

March, 27. Am much disheartened by the Snow on the ground, and that which was falling, there being a dismal face of Winter. Yet the Sun breaking out, I stood along about 10. m. Every thing look'd so wild with Snow on the Ground and Trees; that was in pain lest I should Wander: But it pleas'd God graciously to direct, so that I got well to D. Jacobs, and then call'd his Tenant Riply to guid us over the Rocky Swamps to Curtis's. Din'd at Bairstow's; from thence had the under-Sheriff Briant. At Cook's the Sheriff met me. Mr. J. Cotton, Otis and others with him. Got to Rickard's about Sun-set. *Laus Deo.*

April 30. Last night the Rudder of Capt. Rose's Ship was cut; The reason was Capt. Belchar's sending of her away Laden with Wheat in this time when Wheat is so dear.

Second-day, May, 1, 1710. Fourty or fifty Men get together and seek some body to head them to hale Capt. Roses Ship ashoar: but they were dissuaded by several sober Men to desist, which they did. This was about 5. m. I heard of it as I was going to Hog-Island to see my Tenant's Loss of Sheep. Went off about Nine, and return'd between 2 and 3.

May, 2. Mr. Pemberton prays; 5 Judges there. First Lieut Sam. Johnson was made Foreman of the Jury. May, 3. He pray'd to be dismiss'd by reason of sickness, which was granted while I was withdrawn into the Council-Chamber, and writing to Mr. C. Mather to dine with us; and Mr.

Cumby was made Fore-man. At Noon Mr. Attorney objected against Cumby that he should say, Sure they cut the Rudder themselves, that is, Capt. Roses Men. Upon this Mr. Cumby was spoken to by the Court, and he in open Court desired dismission, or at least from being Fore-man. He was dismiss'd; and Mr. William Torrey was put in. Mr. Attorney and Capt. Belchar went to the Grand-Jury to forward the Bill against those that made the unlawfull Assembly. Just after Mr. Cumby was dismiss'd, Capt. Belchar made a motion that he might be sworn as a Witness. I look'd upon it as an indignity, he having been hardly enough dismiss'd from the Grand-jury: and nothing led to the calling him forth but his Situation. So I oposed it, and it was not done. I insisted it most convenient to proceed with a few and not seek to inflame the Reckoning by multiplying Articles. And Col. Foster complain'd that twas almost like an Inquisition; the manor of Capt. Belchars pursuing it in Council.

This Midweek morn, Mr. Pemberton stood in his Gate, and occasion'd my going in with him. He spake very warmly about the Unlawfull Assembly: I said such motions ought to be supress'd; the thing should be thorowly and effectually dealt in. I said twas an ill office in Capt. Belchar to send away so great a quantity of Wheat (about 6000 Bushels besides Bread) in this scarce time. Mr. Pemberton said I cherish'd those evil seditious Motions by saying so. I said he unjustly charged me. He that withholds Corn, the people will curse him, though I did not affirm that Scripture Justified the Rioters. I mention'd something of God's people, that though they brought themselves into Straits by their own fault; yet God pitied and help'd them. Mr. Pemberton said, with much fierceness, They were not God's people but the Devil's people that wanted Corn. There was Corn to be had; if they had not impoverish'd themselves by Rum, they might buy Corn. I was stricken with this furious Expression. Mr. Pemberton also spake very sharply and upbraidingly, that he was invited to Diner, and then not sent for at Dinertime; was sick with waiting; lost his own Diner; knew not where we din'd; 'twas indecent to ly lurking at the ordinary; wanted not a Diner.

Aug[t] 11. Sixth-day, I visited Mr. Tho. Brattle, who is very low and languishing; He express'd great respect to me: yet plainly told me, that frequent visits were prejudicial to him, it provok'd him to speak more than his strength would bear, would have me come seldom. He told me his Thigh was no bigger than my Wrist. I said I hop'd as the Wether grew Temperat, he might recruit which he seem'd to assent to.

Nov[r] 10. 1710. Daughter Gerrish is brought to bed of a daughter about 6. m. My wife being with her, I sat up late and lay alone. This day with much adoe twas voted that would Salem Middle precinct put to vote; and in the Afternoon twas carried clear in the Affirmative. Mr. Secretary stood firm for this. Though the Salem Gentlemen would not suffer Capt. Gardener and Company to voted in Salem Town Meting; they made no bones of voting against them in the Council.

Nov[r] 13. 1710. I visit Daughter Gerrish, and then ride alone to Lewis's. From thence had Company, and was met by the Sheriff.

Nov[r] 14. Finished the Business of the Court, sitting a little by Candle-light. Visited Madam Bradstreet, Bro[r] Hirst, Major W[m] Brown.

Nov[r] 15. Came home, fair Wether, and not very Cold. Enquired of Mr. Gerrish as I came along concerning his wife: He said she was something disorder'd; but I aprehended no danger, and being just come off my journey, went not to see her that night.

Nov[r] 16. Thanksgiving. My wife sent my daughter Gerrish part of our Diner, which as I understood she eat of pleasantly. But twas a Cold Day and she was remov'd off her Bed on the Palat Bed in the morning. After the Evening Exercise my wife and I rode up in the Coach: My daughter ask'd me to pray with her, which I did; pray'd that God would give her the Spirit of Adoption to call Him Father. Then I went away with Mr. Hirst to his House, leaving my wife with my daughter Gerrish, till she call'd to go home. After our coming home, the northern Chimney of the New house fell a-fire and blazed out extreamly; which made a great Uproar, as is usual. An hour or two after midnight Mr. Gerrish call'd me up acquainting us of the extream illness of his wife; All the family were alarm'd, and gather'd into our Bed-Chamber. When I came there, to my great Surprise my Daughter could not speak to me. They had try'd to call up Mr. Wadsworth; but could not make the family hear. I sent for Mr. Mayhew, who came and pray'd very well with her. (Joseph pray'd at home with the family). [Near] four a clock after Midnight my dear child expired, being but Nineteen years, and twenty days old. When this was over, I advis'd them to take Mrs. Hubbard's Assistance; left Mr. Mayhew there and went home. When I entred my wife's Bed-Chamber, a dolefull Cry was lifted up.

7th day, Novr 25th Dr. Increase Mather lays before me the first Libel, the Copy being of Sam. Sewall's writing; and mentions Mr. Bromfield, for me to consult with what to doe. When at Charlestown Lecture Novr 26th I writ a Letter to the president to invite him to Diner the 28. that night goe to the Commissioners Meeting together.

Novr 27. Mr. Bromfield and I grant a Warrant to bring John Banister before us at 9. m. 9^{r} 28.

Novr 28. I send my Son to invite Mr. Pemberton to dine with me and the President.

Novr 28. John Banister apears, sumond by Constable Kallender. I had desired Col. Townsend to be with us, who came. Mr. Tho. Bratle came of himself and pleaded much in favour of the Libellers (for Aaron was brought in too) and against the injured Doctors, which was the Cause I invited him not to Dinner. Fin'd Jno Banister 20^{s} for each Libel, Aaron Stuckey 20^{s} for publishing the 2^{d}. Bound them to their good Behaviour. Mr. Brattle argued hard to issue it, and not Bind them over to the Sessions: and had Dr. Cotton Mather's Letter in favour of Banister. But he offer'd no Acknowledgment of his Crime in writing; so we took this middle way.

Novr 28. p. m. When the President and Mr. Pemberton came to Diner, I was in my Apartment, Mr. Mayhew and my Son with me. The President and Mr. Pemberton being come to us; Mr. Pemberton quickly begun to say, What you have been holding a Court to day! Had it over again; I was a little amus'd at the word Court; however, I began to relate what had been done. Mr. Pemberton with extraordinary Vehemency said, (capering with his feet) If the Mathers order'd it, I would shoot him thorow. I told him he was in a passion. He said he was not in a Passion. I said, it was so much the worse. He said the Fire from the Altar was equal impartial. Upbraiding me, very plainly, as I understood it, with Partiality. The President said, The Governour was barbarously Treated (meaning Dr. Cotton Mather's Letter to his Excellency). I answered; That was put to the Council. Mr. Mayhew told me afterward, that I said his Carriage was neither becoming a Scholar nor Minister. The Truth is I was surpris'd to see my self insulted with such extraordinary Fierceness, by my Pastor, just when I had been vindicating two worthy Embassadors of Christ (his own usual Phrase) from most villanous Libels. And I dont know any syllable intimating that I had done Well. As for the Letter, the Govr was not in humor to trust me about it; because I just then Fil'd my Reasons for withdrawing my Vote. Mr. Pemberton speaks hard Words, and very reflecting. We went to Dinner, I sat next Mr. Pemberton and ask'd him to crave a Blessing; He also Return'd Thanks, the President declining it. Mr. Sergeant came into our Company. The President walked on his right hand to the Council-chamber; I and Mr. Pemberton went next. In the Way Mr. Pemberton charg'd me again, I was griev'd and said, What in the Street! He answer'd, No body hears. But Mr. Sergeant heard so much, that he turn'd back to still us. Mr. Pemberton told me that Capt. Martin, the Comadore, had abus'd him, yet I took no notice of it: I answer'd, you never laid it before me. He said, You knew it. I said, I knew it not. (For every Rumor is not ground sufficient for a Justice of Peace to proceed upon; and Mr. Pemberton never spake word of it to me before). He said Capt. Martin call'd him Rascal in the Street, and said had it not been for his coat, he would have can'd him. Mr. Pemberton said I excluded him, or he was excluded from Dining with the Superiour Court by the Invitation of Capt. Martin. I said 'twas with difficulty that his Company was obtain'd at our Diner. The matter of Fact was this: Upon Midweek Nov[r] 8., as I take it, twas nois'd that General Nicholson was going out of Town to Pascataqua, in order to his Voyage home: Hereupon the Justices agreed to wait upon his Honor at his Lodgings; to take Leave of him if going, to invite him to Diner if he staid in Town so long: (The Chief Justice was at New London), Sewall, Hathorne, Walley, Corwin went in the morning to the House of Mr. John Borland; When the Gen[l] came, and we had Saluted him, and understood his Honor staid in Town that day; We invited him to Diner to the Green Dragon; and Mr. Myles being there, I invited him; and enquired of the Gen[l] if there were any we should ask to Dine with him? He mention'd Capt. Martin, the Comadore. Accordingly we sent, and for Major Handy. When Mr. Pemberton had Pray'd, I desir'd him to Dine with the Court, the Gen[l] was invited. Mr. Pemberton ask'd whether Capt. Martin was to be there, I said yes; Then said Mr. Pemberton, you must Excuse me! I reply'd, His Invitation was not of my proposal. And yet this was now thus brought over again: Mr. Pemberton said the Council took so little notice of Capt. Martin's Abusing him (though it had been talk'd of in Council) that they invited him to their Treat at the Return from Annapolis Royal. This concerns the whole Council, and therefore

I have nam'd it last, as in which I am least concern'd. But this is to be said for the Council. The Fleet was a chief Mean of Taking Port Royal; Capt. Martin was Comadore of that Fleet, and therefore could not be separated from the Gen[l]. A personal Resentment of what had pass'd before the going to Port-Royal, ought not to make a Balk in a Publick Invitation after God's granting Success; which had been so much and Publickly pray'd for; and Thanks to God Return'd. And if the Justices had [not?] sent for Capt. Martin, I cant tell what could have been made of the Offence. Tis difficult medling with Captains of Frigats. Reasons of State require the over-looking many grievous Things. The Sons of Zerviah were too hard for David, his calling them to Account. He was fain to leave Joab to the Reign of Solomon.

These Things made me pray Earnestly and with great Concern, that God would vouchsafe to be my Shepherd, and perform for me what is mention'd in the 23. Psalm, that He would not leave me behind in my Straglings; but bring me safely to his Heavenly Fold.

In the Afternoon Mr. Pemberton order'd the 5 first verses of the 58th Psalm to be sung. I think if I had been in his place and had been kindly and tenderly affectioned, I should not have done it at this time. Another Psalm might have suited his Subject as well as the 5th verse of this. Tis certain, one may make Libels of David's Psalms; and if a person be abused, there is no Remedy: I desire to leave it to God who can and will Judge Righteously.

Dec[r] 12. I went to Mr. Pemberton and Expostulated about his Treatment of me.

Nov[r] 28. Ask'd him whether the Mathers were not Embassadors of Christ and therefore ought to be vindicated; I might have expected his Escape. As to Capt. Martin, the Comadore, when I had related the matter of Fact, he said he knew it not before. I visited Madam Pemberton, and gave the Nurse 3[s].

Mid-week, Jan[y] 31, 17$\frac{10}{11}$. Went and heard Mr. Bridge, and Dr. Cotton Mather pray and preach, at the said Dr's House. Mr. Bridge's Text was about God's lifting up a Standard, when Enemy breaks in as a Flood. Dr. Mathers, The whole world lyes in Wickedness. Had Cake and Butter and Cheese, with good Drinks, before parting. As I went home, I heard Col. Vetch was arriv'd from Anapolis.

Feb[r] 1. As I go to Lecture, I wait on Gov[r] Vetch and congratulat his Safety; He thanks me for my Respect to him and to his Spouse.

At 3. p. m. The Council meets according to Adjournment. Upon Conference with Col. Vetch, the Expedition is set forward by Water. Mr. Secretary reads a paper given him by Col. Vetch, Certifying that the Government of Anapolis Royal had not Traded with the Indians as they were aspers'd, but with all in a vile maner loading New-Engld with Calumnies; a spirit of Witchcraft, and now 7 fold a Spirit of Lying, haters of Monarchy, regretting Her Majesties success in Taking Port-Royal. I took it of the Secretary, and read it, and mov'd several of the Council that they would speak to it. I told them it would otherwise be taken as a tacit License to print it. When no body spake, and Col. Vetch was going away, I pray'd him to stay a little; and said I fear'd the reading that paper without being spoken to, would be taken as a tacit Licensing of it. I was for the Certificat so far as it vindicated their innocency; but was against the Reflections on New-England, they would be dishonorable to Nova Scotia, and New-England. I was against printing it with them. Col. Vetch said, if it could not be printed here, he would have it printed elsewhere; Copies of it were sent to England, I said it was Raillery unbecoming a Government. When Col. Vetch was gon, I pray'd the Gov[r] to forbid the printing it unless those Reflections were first taken out. The Gov[r] said, he could not hinder it; they might take their own way. And yet own'd twas Raillery. I don't know but Col. Vetch may reckon that he has a tacit License to print the Certificat just now read in Council. I am very free the Substance of the Certificat, relating to their own inocency, may be printed: But to print the bulky Reflections would be dishonorable to Anapolis, and Boston. And I can no way consent to it. I think it should be spoken to.

Febr. 9. Seventh-day, between 11 and 12m. Col. John Foster expires. His place at the Council Board and Court will hardly be filled up. I have lost a good Left-hand man. The Lord save New-England! Now just half the Counsellours mention'd in the Charter, are dead; The good Lord prepare the rest, and me especially to follow after.

Now about I dream'd of being at the Comencment and seeing Mr. Leverett in Scarlet.

Febr. 28. $17\frac{10}{11}$. Midweek: This being my Marriage-day, and having now liv'd in a married Estate Five and Thirty years, notwithstanding my many Sins and Temptations, I spent some time in Meditation and Prayer in the Castle-Chamber. I was much encouraged by reading in Course the 32[d] Psalm at family prayer without any foresight of mine. And when I came to pray I was much heartened to ask Forgiveness of God for my multiplied Transgressions, seeing He had directed Peter a sinfull Mortal to forgive to 70. times 7. I hope God will forgive and do as the matter may require.

March, 4. Lord's Day; To my aprehension God assists my Son remarkably in prayer and preaching I hope tis an Answer of my prayer last Midweek. Preaches again in the Evening.

April, 3. I dine with the Court at Pullin's. Mr. Attorney treats us at his house with excellent Pipins, Anchovas Olives, Nuts. I said I should be able to make no Judgment on the Pipins without a Review, which made the Company Laugh. Spake much of Negroes; I mention'd the problem whether should be white after the Resurrection: Mr. Bolt took it up as absurd, because the body should be void of all Colour pake as if it should be a Spirit. I objected what Christ said o his Disciples after the Resurrection. He said twas not so fter his Ascension.

7^{r} 18th Third-day, set out for Boston; Baited at Dedham. Refresh'd our selv's at Mr. Belcher's: Got well home a little fter Diner time: we recreated our selves with Mr. Watt's Poems, going and coming. *Laus Deo Servatori.* About 7 or 8 aclock of the night between the 2^{d} and 3^{d} of October, a Dreadful Fire hapens in Boston; broke out in a little House elonging to Capt. Ephraim Savage, by reason of the Drunkeness of —— Moss: Old Meeting House, and Town-House urnt. Old Meetinghouse had stood near 70. years. I had a ouse burnt, wherein Mr. Seth Dwight was Tenant, who paid ne Twenty pounds per añum. Oct. 3. The Lt. Govr Taylor rrives. He saw the Fire 20 Leagues off.

Octob^{r} 11. Fifth-day, Fast. A Collection was made for ufferers by the Fire; Two Hundred Sixty odd pounds athered at the South church, the oldest Meetinghouse in Town.

Friday, Febr. 8. A Duel is fought between Lt James Douglas, and Lt James Alexander, near the new Burying place.

Satterday, Febr. 16, 171½. Mr. Jonathan Belchar comes o me with Mr. Bromfield, and tells me the near approach of Lt James Alexander's Death; I think this was after Noon. I vent to the chief Justice who declar'd his opinion, that twas itter for other Justices to meddle with than the Judges. I vent to Dr. Clark as the next Justice and a Chirurgeon, whom found indispos'd and keeping house. Lt Alexander Douglass, he Dueller, lodg'd at Barnsdell's near Scarlet's Wharf. I all'd again at Mr. Bromfield's who inform'd me, Alexander, prehensive of death, was just going to receive the Sacrament. went home, (twas now Sun-set) and writ a Letter to Mr. Attorney, telling where I had been and what I had heard; and esir'd him to take some order about it. About 7 aclock he sent for me, I went to the chief Justice, and there sign'd Warrants to the sheriff &c., and Mr. Weaver, an Admiralty Warrant; Franklin made Constable Oliver his Deputy. Sent Mr. Deputy Dyer and him to Barnsdell's; and order'd him to go to Nantasket as soon as the Wether would admit (for the wind now was intolerable as to its height and cold). Came home, Benj. Larnell lighting me.

Monday, Febr. 18. 'Twas mention'd in Council, that Govr Vetch might be spoken to to send Douglass from Anapolis hither. It was reported he was gon thither in Capt. John Alden. Lt James Alexander dyed, on Satterday night about 10. aclock. The Govr's Answer was, Let Warrants be first granted out; and then 2 or 3 days after, Let a Motion be made to Govr Vetch from the Council-Board. A Warrant was drawn by Mr. Secretary to all the sheriffs and Constables in the Province, and given to Dept. Dyer. Mr. Joseph Gerrish comes to Town; I write to him to invite him to Diner to morrow. A Letter is written to the Govr to regulat the Funeral of Lt Alexander, and prevent its being Great.

Sixth-day, March 28. Court met: order'd Oyster-Island not to be sold; but the Attorney, Mr. Parker, to represent the state of it at the next Term. Upon reading Hittee's Indenture (which was now brought), Left her in Prison uncondemned; and order'd Col. Otis her first master, and Major Basset, to take Affidavits concerning her Birth. Adjourn'd *sine die*. Left my Statute Book with Capt. James Warren. Came homeward; Rain'd hard quickly after setting out, went by Mattakeese Meetinghouse, and forded over the North-River. My Horse stumbled, in the considerable body of water, but I made a shift, by GOD'S Help, to sit him, and he recover'd and carried me out. Rain'd very hard that went into a Barn awhile. Baited at Bairsto's. Din'd at Cushing's. Dryed my Coat and Hat at both places. By that time got to Braintry, the day and I were in a maner spent, and I turn'd in to Cousin Quinsey, where I had the pleasure to see GOD in his providence shining again upon the persons and Affairs of the Family after long distressing Sickness and Losses. Lodg'd in the chamber next the Brooke.

7th day March, 29. Rode home, Mr. Rawson overtook me and accompanied me on the Neck; Got well home about Noon; found all well. *Laus Deo.* Mr. Colman, the father, died last Thorsday night.

Midweek, April 9th. Capt. Paxton reviles Mr. Jonathan Bel-char upon the Parade, calls him Rascal, many times, strikes him with his Cane: Mr. Dudley upon his view fines him 5s. He carried it insolently, and said, He would doe so again. Twas about Noon.

Sixth-day, April, 11. I saw Six Swallows together flying and chipering very rapturously.

Augt. 24. Son sends Tom with a Letter to acquaint me that his daughter Mary died about 1 or 2 aclock last night; his wife sick. p. m. I send the Letter to Mr. Pemberton. Both Mr. Bridge and Pemberton pray very Expressly for my Son as call'd to the south-church. I goe to the Funeral of Capt. Oli-ver's child. Bearers, Mr. Jno Walley, Mr. David Jeffries. Mr. Pemberton deliver'd me my Son's Letter at the house of Mourning.

Second-day, Augt. 25. Between Roxbury, and Brooklin I met a youth of Newtown, who told me Mr. Hobart dyed about sun-rise this morning. Proceeded and waited on Madam Dud-ley in her Charret to Brooklin. So soon as I could get the Coffin, I had little Mary nail'd up in it, and brought my dear Grand-Child to Town in my son's Calash, leaving my Horse for him. The Rain overtook me near the Governour's, yet I proceeded, and got to my House, just about Two a-clock. About sun-set, or a little after, little Mary Sewall, born July, 10, 1711, was born to the Tomb by Mr. William Cooper, and Mr. Appleton, Mr. Danl Oliver's Aprentice. The Father fol-low'd alone, then the Govr and I. The Grandmothers rode in the Governour's Charret.

Midweek, Augt. 27. I went to Hog-Island with Latherby to see how the Workmen finished the Barn. Saw two Sloops go away with Hay; Turn'd down with them against the Wind. Visited Dr. Increase Mather. He is touch'd with the Gravel. Benj. Larnell kick'd Joshua Gee.

Octob^{r} 31. Order for Thanksgiving is past. The Secretary writ *Peace;* the Govr added *Happy;* which I objected against; because we saw but one side, we saw not what the French had reserved for themselves. Voted it not. I would have had it plentiful *later* Harvest; because the Wheat and Rye were much blasted; the Barly much diminished; but I prevail'd not. Sister Northend returns.

Tuesday, Febr. 10 $171\frac{2}{3}$. A vehement storm of Snow. Mr. Stoddard sent his Coach to fetch me to the Commissioners Meeting at his House. When return'd could scarce get in at my door for a great Drift of Snow blown up there; were fain to Shovel it away first.

Wednesday, Febr. 11. Mr. Aaron Porter is ordain'd pastor of the church at Meadford. Mr. Angier gave the charge; Mr. Hancock, the Right Hand of Fellowship. The storm foregoing hinder'd my Son from being there. And Mr. Jonathan Belchar made a Splendid Treat for Mr. Wainwright, to which my Son was invited on Tuesday; were many more people there than the Meetinghouse would hold.

Febr. 12. Sam. comes not to Town as he intended. In the Afternoon Devotion informs my wife of his very uncomfortable Circumstances, and of the Necessity of fetching him to Boston.

Friday, Febr. 13. Joseph and I ride in Mr. Stoddard's Coach to Brooklin, got thither at Eleven a. m., find Sam abed. In a little while got him up, din'd there, came away. I was somwhat afraid, by reason his [Joseph's] Pulse was disorder'd. But the Coach being close, Harry drove us home well about 4. p. m. At Brooklin I saw the Lambs, encourag'd Tom. to be faithfull in his Masters business, which he promis'd. Told him he could not obey his Master without obedience to his Mistress; and *vice versa;* bid him take that as a Rule. Gave him a Two-shilling Bill of Credit. When my daughter alone, I ask'd her what might be the cause of my Son's Indisposition, are you so kindly affectioned one towards another as you should be? She answer'd, I do my Duty. I said no more. At parting I pray'd God to be with us going, and with them staying. Son gave Hanah a piece of Silver.

Febr. 17. Great Snow. Tom comes for Meal. I give him half a Bushel of pease home with him, of our best. All well at Brooklin. I enquired of my daughter, Hanah, and the whole family.

Febr. 19. Lecture-day, son S. goes to Meeting, speaks to Mr. Walter. I also speak to him to dine. He could not; but said he would call before he went home. When he came he discours'd largly with my Son; I also spake to him: His advice was, that Ilsly should be put away; some Friends talk to them both and so come together again. My Son was very helpfull to me in copying out Dr. Mather's Circular Letter.

Febr. 21. Satterday, Daughter Sewall calls and gives us a visit; I went out to carry my Letters to Savil's, that were to be carried by Mr. Crocker to Barnstable. While I was absent, My Wife and Daughter Sewall had very sharp discourse; She wholly justified her self, and said, if it were not for her, no Maid could be able to dwell at their house. At last Daughter Sewall burst out with Tears, and call'd for the Calashe. My wife relented also, and said she did not design to grieve her; Son carried his daughter to the Calash, and desired her to send Tom with the Horse for him on Friday.

Febr. 27. Friday, A Council is held at the Governour's, who is now below Stairs. Saw my Son, but spake not to him. When the business of the Council was over, and pipes were call'd for, I slipt into Kitchen; but my Son was gon; sat with Madam Dudley alone a pretty while; She said nothing to me; I gave her my Silk-Hand-kerchief, which I bought last Satterday for my daughter, but was prevented giving it to her, she being just gon before I got home. Yet this occasion brought her not to speak; Ask'd kindly after my wife. Went to the Govr agen, Took leave, came home as went, with Capt. Belchar, Bromfield, Norden.

March 2. Note. James Peniman was buried last Lord's-day night; Bearers, Mr. Cutler, Creese; Benet, Brisco; Ellis, Steward. Mr. Bridge and Wadsworth were there, being I supose invited, and to comfort the Relations. He had been such a Drunkard and Idler that I went not to the Funeral, having no heart to it. My son preaches at Mr. Bridgham's Meeting Lord's day night.

Friday, Apr. 24. Mr. Pemberton calls at my house; Hanah went to the door, and suposing me at the Townmeeting said I was not within; whereas indeed I was, but in the Chamber. Mr. Pemberton said his business was with me, and declin'd coming in. When I understood it, I went to Mr. Pemberton's the same morning. He not within, I sat some time with Madam Pemberton: Ask'd her what people thought of my Son's Courtship; She spake well of it; Said Mr. Alford had done ungentlemanly by her, and she thought at the time of it, she would have a better Husband; comended Mrs. Betty. I told her I would call again about 3. p. m. I went again, she crav'd my pardon, said she had forgot to tell Mr. Pemberton what I had said of calling. He was gon out.

April, 25. Satterday, About 4 p. m. as soon as I could get my book finish'd, I went to Mr. Walley's. Neither of the Sisters within. At last Mrs. Lydia came in, and sat with me. I gave her Mr. Walter of CHRIST, very well bound in Calvs Leather, to give Mrs. Betty. I had written her Name in it. When had staid about half an hour or little more, I came away.

April, 27. The first Court was open'd in the New Townhouse. I was present. Mr. Colman pray'd Excellently. It was a damp to me that the first thing was done was the calling out the monstrously profane John Green. p. m. Waited on the Court at the Green Dragon, with Capt. Tim°. Clark, to inform against Richard Vince, who is more like a wild-Cat than a man. From thence went to Dr. Increase Mather. Thank'd him for the Perseverance of his Love to my Son Joseph: agreed to call a Meeting of the Commissioners at the Town House at 4. p. m. next Thorsday.

Tuesday, April 28. I waited on Mr. Pemberton. Mr. Wisewall was there. Mr. Marsh of Braintry came in. Mr. Pemberton spake very fiercely against the Govr and Council's meddling with suspension of Laws, respecting Church of England men not paying Taxes to the dissenting Ministers. Spake very fiercely in dislike of the overseers, that nothing had been done; would chuse others. I think this was before Mr. Marsh came in. At the Gate said what I did twould be reckon'd my Son did; intimating as I conceive, twere best for me to lay down my Overseers place. Post m went to Roxbury Lecture with Mr. Thair and Josiah Oakes. Mr. Walter preach'd excellently from Ps. 41. 4. I saw Samuel; It is yet dark wether at Brooklin. Came home with Thair and Oakes. Thair went off at his Brother's; Oakes and I visited the Bride Adams, they were married last Tuesday morn before Govr Saltonstall went out of Town.

May, 27. Din'd at the Green Dragon. Went late to the Election. 102 Voters at first: Mr. Addington had all but his own, 101. Col. Hutchinson and I had 97. each. But tis to be lamented that Maj^r Winthrop had but 46. and was left out. He was the great Stay and Ornament of the Council, a very pious, prudent, Couragious New-England Man. Some spread it among the Deputies, that he was out of the province, and not like to Return. (Has been absent ever since April, 1712. but through Sickness.) Lieut Govr said he was a Non-Resident. Staid the Election; but voted not, said 'twas against his principles; the Councillors ought not to vote. Said of voting by papers, It was a Silly way! I took no notice of it. Thus Mr. Winthrop is sent into Shade and Retirem't while I am left in the Whirling Dust, and Scorching Sun.

So falls that stately Cedar! whilest it stood
It was the truest Glory of the Wood.

Satterday, June 6. The Rain-water grievously runs into my son Joseph's Chamber from the Window above. As went out to the Barber's I observ'd the water to run trickling down a great pace from the Coving. I went on the Roof, and found the Spout next Salter's stop'd, but could not free it with my Stick. Boston went up, and found his pole too big, which I warn'd him of before; came down a Spit, and clear'd the Leaden-throat, by thrusting out a Trap-Ball that stuck there. Thus a small matter greatly incomodes us; and when God pleases, tis easily remov'd. The Rain that fell the two Nights and Lords-day following was in such Abundance, we had been almost Drown'd, if the Spout had not been cleared.

June, 7. Lord's Super, I could not discern that Mr. Pemberton pray'd for my son; observ'd not so much as the ordinary prayer for him that is to preach in the Afternoon. The Lord Help!

Tuesday, 7^r^ 22. I go to Roxbury, wait on the Govr with the Letter of Mr. Justice Corwin, and Lynde. Govr tells me a sad story of Sam, as if he were disguis'd with Drink in the Salt-Marsh; His wife comes in with little Hanah: I sit a little while, and go away to Brooklin, find Sam very hard at Work mowing up Stalks.

7^r^. 23. Sam. comes to our house, goes home late after the Rain that Tom might come to the Execution as tis promised him.

Octob^r^. 1. Fifth-day, Dr. C. Mather preaches Mrs. Rock's Funeral Sermon, from PS. 25. 13. His Soul shall dwell at ease. Sam was here, I invited him to come to us on the Lords

Day; The Lords Super being administred at both churches in Roxbury, and he under disadvantages to partake.

Octob^{r}. 4. Mr. Jno Barnard preaches a Sermon too much savoring of Arminianisme. p. m. Son preaches from ps. 37. 37. on occasion of Mrs. Rock's death. Samuel Eliot, son of Andrew Eliot, Baptis'd. Sam. here all day. Sup'd here. went home about 7.

Second-day, 8^{r}. 5th. I goe to Brooklin, meet my daughter Sewall going to Roxbury with Hanah, to dine with her Bro^{r} Winthrop. Sam. and I dined alone. Daughter return'd before I came away. I propounded to her that Mr. Walter might be desired to come to them and pray with them. She seem'd not to like the motion, said she knew not wherefore she should be call'd before a Minister! I urg'd him as the fittest moderator; the Govr or I might be thought partial. She pleaded her performance of Duty, and how much she had born. Mr. Hirst came in and smok'd a pipe and we came away together. I gave Sarah a Shilling. Hanah ditto and cake, the sick Indian Boy a cake, Tom. a Shilling.

Got home a little before 7.; visited Mr. Sergeant confin'd to his house: was not abroad on the Lords Day.

8^{r}. 6. Sam. comes to Town on account of his Sick Boy.

Octob^{r}. 16. 1713. I went to see the portentous Birth; it seems to be two fine Girls to whom an unhapy Union has been fatal. The Heads and Necks, as low as a Line drawn from the Arm-pits, are distinct. A little below the Navel, downward again distinct, with distinct Arms and Legs; Four of each. I measured across the perfect Union about the Hips and found it to hold about eight Inches. Oh the Mercies of my Birth, and of the Birth of Mine! *Laus Deo!* Dr. Cotton Mather introduc'd me and Mr. John Winthrop to this rare and awfull Sight.

Octob^{r}. 19. Mr. Winslow of Marshfield comes to Town; Set out so long before Sun-rise that he was here about 3. p. m. and in the Council-Chamber, in his own Hair.

Octob^r^. 20. He appears with a Flaxen Wigg, I was griev'd to see it, he had so comly a head of black Hair.

Octob^r^. 25. In the Night after 12. Susan comes, and knocks at our chamber door, said she could not sleep, was afraid she should dye. Which amaz'd my wife and me. We let her in, blew up the Fire, wrapt her warm, and went to bed again. She sat there till near day, and then return'd; and was well in the morning. *Laus Deo.* I was the more startled because I had spilt a whole Vinyard Can of water just before we went to Bed: and made that Reflection that our Lives would shortly be spilt.

Friday 8^r^. 30. Sam. and his Wife dine here, go home together in the Calash. William Ilsly rode and pass'd by them. My son warn'd him not to lodge at his house; Daughter said she had as much to doe with the house as he. Ilsly lodg'd there. Sam. grew so ill on Saturday, that instead of going to Roxbury he was fain between Meetings to take his Horse, and come hither; to the surprise of his Mother, who was at home. Lord save him and us! Mr. Jno Williams preached for my son in the morn, and went at Noon to preach for Mr. Walter. About 9. on Satterday night, Mr. Bridge was taken with another paralytick Fit, was in danger of falling into the fire.

Novr. 2. Sam. is somthing better, yet full of pain; He told me with Tears that these sorrows (arising from discord betwen him and his wife) would bring him to his Grave. I said he must endeavour to be able to say, O Death, where is thy sting? O Grave, where is thy victory? He is refresh'd by discoursing with Simon Gates of Marlborough, and Amos Gates.

Tuesday, 9^r^. 24. Joseph visits us after his sickness of the Measles; dines with us. David brings Susan's Mother from Braintrey to tend her.

26. Dr. Mather preaches. I could not discern that he return'd any Thanks for Joseph's Recovery, though he knew he was at Lecture. Return'd Thanks Expressly for Mr. Bridge.

Mr. Thacher of Milton, Son of Brooklin, and Cousin Quinsey din'd with us.

28. Sam. comes to Town from Brooklin, dines with us, comes to keep the Sabbath with us. I visit Mr. Pemberton. Very cold day. John Gerrish has the Measles at Mr. Lowder's.

Decr. 6. Sam. keeps Sabbath with us.

Decr. 6. 1713. Sun is Eclipsed just about the beginning of the Fore noon Exercise; when well enter'd many Guns are Fired by Capt. Brown Going down to Nantasket. Mr. Holyoke observes the Eclipse in the Town House Turret. Very clear day. I saw it plain as I came home at Noon.

Tuesday, Jan. 5, 171¾. I go to the Funeral of Capt. Benet's daughter Butler; is said to be the most desirable of his daughters, but about 25 or 6. years old. Cousin Moodey strikes in, and I go in the middle between him and Joseph S. Mr. Saml Moodey of York lodges here.

Jany 6. I visit Cousin Mrs. Anna Dumer. In the evening, Mr. Walter, Cousin Moodey and I had discourse about my son at Brooklin, his Circumstances. Yesterday after Mrs. Butler's Funeral, I visited Mr. Pemberton, who has Sore Eyes.

Fifth-day, Jany 7th, Son J. Sewall preaches the Lecture, which is the first Sermon he has preached in the old church. 1 Cor. 6, 19. 20. Was invited, and din'd with the Court at Holm's. Was a very great Fogg all day. Rain'd toward night.

Jany 29. Great Storm of Snow began about 3. p. m. yesterday: Last night, about Midnight, was a dreadfull Cry of Fire; was stop'd at Mr. Blunt's Work-house where it begun. *Laus Deo*. This day I sent Joseph my Pole's Synopsis Criticorum. I have enjoy'd them one and Thirty years; and now have the pleasure to bestow them on a worthy Minister, my Son. O the patience, Longe Suffering, and Goodness of GOD!

Seventh-Day, Feb^{r}. 6. I went to the Town-house on the

occasion of the Queen's Birthday; Mr. Bromfield and I sat a-while in one of the windows, Table being full; afterward sat in. A little before Sun-set I went away. Mr. Eliakim Hutchinson seeing me about to rise up, Said we would go and see Mr. Sergeant; I went with him. Mr. Sergeant took my Hand and held it with great Affection. My neighbour Colson knocks at our door about 9. or past to tell of the Disorders at the Tavern at the South-end in Mr. Addington's house, kept by John Wallis. He desired me that I would accompany Mr. Bromfield and Constable Howell thither. It was 35. Minutes past Nine at Night before Mr. Bromfield came; then we went. I took Aeneas Salter with me. Found much Company. They refus'd to go away. Said were there to drink the Queen's Health, and they had many other Healths to drink. Call'd for more Drink: drank to me, I took notice of the Affront to them. Said must and would stay upon that Solemn occasion. Mr. John Netmaker drank the Queen's Health to me. I told him I drank none; upon that he ceas'd. Mr. Brinley put on his Hat to affront me. I made him take it off. I threaten'd to send some of them to prison; that did not move them. They said they could but pay their Fine, and doing that they might stay. I told them if they had not a care, they would be guilty of a Riot. Mr. Bromfield spake of raising a number of Men to Quell them, and was in some heat, ready to run into Street. But I did not like that. Not having Pen and Ink, I went to take their Names with my Pensil, and not knowing how to Spell their Names, they themselves of their own accord writ them. Mr. Netmaker, reproaching the Province, said they had not made one good Law.

At last I address'd my self to Mr. Banister. I told him he had been longest an Inhabitant and Freeholder, I expected he should set a good Example in departing thence. Upon this he invited them to his own House, and away they went; and we, after them, went away. The Clock in the room struck a pretty while before they departed. I went directly home, and found it 25. Minutes past Ten at Night when I entred my own House. About 5. in the Morning there was a cry of Fire; Bells rung. Son J. Sewall came to our Chamber door and acquainted us. But quickly after our rising, the Bells left off ringing, and I saw no Light. Mr. Webb's Malt-house, near Mr. Bronsdon's, was burnt down. Twas a great Mercy that the Fire was not spread all over the North-End. Part of the house of Mr. Bronsdon, the Landlord, began to burn.

Monday, Feb^{r}. 8. Mr. Bromfield comes to me, and we give the Names of the Offenders at John Wallis's Tavern last Satterday night, to Henry Howell, Constable, with Direction to take the Fines of as many as would pay; and warn them that refus'd to pay, to apear before us at 3. p. m. that day. Many of them pay'd. The rest appear'd; and Andrew Simpson, Ensign, Alexander Gordon, Chirugeon, Francis Brinley, Gent. and John Netmaker, Gent., were sentenc'd to pay a Fine of 5^{s} each of them, for their Breach of the Law Entituled, An Act for the better Observation, and Keeping the Lord's Day. They all Appeal'd, and Mr. Thomas Banister was bound with each of them in a Bond of 20^{s} upon Condition that they should prosecute their Appeal to effect.

Capt. John Bromsal, and Mr. Thomas Clark were dismiss'd without being Fined. The first was Master of a Ship just ready to sail, Mr. Clark a stranger of New York, who had carried it very civilly, Mr. Jekyl's Brother-in-Law .

John Netmaker was fin'd 5^{s} for profane cursing; saying to ——Colson, the Constable's Assistant, God damn ye; because the said Colson refus'd to drink the Queen's Health. This he paid presently. Then Mr. Bromfield and I demanded of the said Netmaker to become bound in a Bond of Twenty pounds, with two Sureties in Ten pounds a-piece, to Answer at the next Genl Session of the Peace for Suffolk, his Contempt of Her Majesties Government of this Province and vilifying the same at the house of John Wallis, Innholder in Boston, last Satterday night. Mr. Banister declin'd being bound; and none else offer'd (To imbarrass the Affair as I conceiv'd). Upon this Mr. Netmaker was dismiss'd, giving his Word to apear on Tuesday. at 10. m. that he might have Time to provide Sureties.

Tuesday, March, 9th. Mr. Bromfield and I waited till past 11. and dismiss'd the Constables Howell and Feno, suposing No body would come. Constable met Mr. Netmaker at the door, and came back again with him: He came all alone. Mr. Bromfield and I spent much time with him to bring him to some Acknowledgment of his Error, but all in vain. Offer'd not so much as his own Bond: which constrain'd us to Write a Mittimus, and send him to Prison. Angry words had pass'd between him and Const. Howell; he Threatn'd Const. Howell what he would do to him; or his Servants for him. For this reason I dismiss'd Constable Howell; sent for Mr. John Winchcomb, and gave him the Mittimus, out of respect to Mr. Netmaker; and he took it kindly. This about ¼ past 12. at Noon by my Clock. Went into Town; Mr. Wm Pain spake with me near the Townhouse; express'd himself concern'd that Mr. Netmaker was in prison; he would pay his Fine that he might be releas'd. I told him there was no Fine. Went on, visited Hanah Parkman, saw the place, where the Malt-house was burnt down. As I return'd, went to the Funeral of Mrs. Green. There, Mr. Secretary (who was a Bearer), Told me, a Council was Warn'd to meet after the Funeral. Accordingly I went. Present, Govr, Lt Govr., Winthrop, Elisha Hutchinson, Sewall, Mr. Addington, Townsend, E^m^ Hutchinson, Belchar, Bromfield. It was late and Duskish, and Col. Elisha Hutchinson went away before any thing was Voted. Sat round a little Fire; I hapen'd to sit next Genl Nicholson. He aply'd himself to me and Mr. Bromfield, ask'd whether did not know that he was here with the Broad Seal of England? I answer'd, Yes! Ask'd whether did not know that Mr. Netmaker was his Secretary? I answer'd, Tis generally so receiv'd. Then with a Roaring Noise the Genl said, I demand

JUSTICE against Mr. Sewall and Bromfield for sending my Secretary to prison without acquainting me with it! And hastily rose up, and went down and walk'd the Exchange, where he was so furiously Loud, that the Noise was plainly heard in the Council-Chamber, the door being shut. The Governour vehemently urg'd the Discharge of Netmaker; argued that Gen[l] Nicholson was as an Embassador; his Servant ought to have been delivered to him. I said, Mr. Netmaker was upon his Parole from Monday to Tuesday; in which time he might have acquainted Gen[l] Nicholson with his Circumstances. The Gov[r] said, Mr. Bromfield and I ought to have acquainted him our selves. Would have had the Vote so Worded. Would have had us that committed Mr. Netmaker to have released him. I objected to that; saying, we had committed him: but I did not know that we had power to release him. Then the Keeper was sent for with the Mittimus, which Mr. Secretary read by Candle-Light, in these words:

MASSACHUSETTS,
SUFFOLK SS.

Seal.
Seal.

To the Keeper of Her Majesties Gaol in Boston,
Greeting,

We herewith send you the body of John Netmaker, Gent: who being Order'd by our selves, two of Her Majesties Justices for Suffolk, to give Bond with Sureties, to appear at the next General Sessions of the Peace to be held for the County of Suffolk, to make Answer for his Contempt of Her Maj' Government of this Province, and Vilifying the same at the house of John Wallis, Innholder, in Boston in the Night Between the Sixth and Seventh of this Instant February: Refus'd so to doe;

You are therefore in Her Majesties Name required to receive the said Netmaker, and him safely keep till he be discharged by due course of Law.

Given under our Hands and Seals in Boston, this Ninth day of February 17$\frac{13}{14}$. *Annoque Regni Annæ, Reginae Magnae Brittanicae* &c., Duodecimo,

SAMUEL SEWALL.
EDW. BROMFIELD.

Upon reading this, Mr. Secretary drew up an Order, importing that those general Words would not hold him, and order'd his Discharge. The Governour Ordered the Keeper to discharge Mr. Netmaker, and the Secretary should give him a Copy of the Council's Order. And order'd Mr. Secretary to Copy it out, and wait upon Genl Nicholson with it in the Morning. They that voted being hardly drawn to it. Some of them, were Lt Govr, Mr. Addington, Eliakim Hutchinson, Penn Townsend, Andrew Belchar; Mr. Winthrop was in the Negative; said he understood not how it belong'd to the Council to meddle with it. Sewall and Bromfield were the parties complain'd of. If they had withdrawn, there had been no Council left; but the Govr charg'd that none should withdraw. This was pretty hard, seeing a General Council was to meet the next day; and the Bond required, was but Twenty pounds the principal, and Ten pounds a piece two Sureties.

June, 1714. Just after I saw Mr. Pemberton, by Mr. Gerrishe's Shop: I told him the Court was prorogu'd. He and I after a little Space walk'd together, he was going, it seems, to Madam Saltonstall's: I went with him having Election-Sermons in my Pocket. When we came against Mr. Myles's he vehemently upbraided me with the uncivil Treatment he met with when he pray'd with the Council; as if were us'd like a Boy. They pointed to him. It put him in mind of what Mr. Belchar had told him of Hanover, their setting a youth to Crave a Blessing. I said We were of another mind or else would not take the pains to get the Divines of the Town. No body went with him to the door. I said I supos'd twas a meer accident. No body asked him whether he were out of breath. As to this last it behooved him to have step'd into Mr. Gerrishes Shop, or some other convenient place, till he had taken breath. As to the pointing, I aprehend it was thus; Just as he came in, there was a great Message from the Deputies; and the Lieut. Govr with his hand directed him to go into the Closet till that was over. Mr. Pemberton could not fairly complain of this, and not being enquired of whether he were out of Breath, at the same time. I am sure I endeavour'd with respect to desire Mr. Pemberton to take his Turn with the other Ministers. He at last consented. Only as the week began with Friday, he desired to be excus'd till the begining of the week following, by which means Friday and Satterday were suplied by my Son out of his Turn. And then the next week, one morning, Govr Saltonstall was with Mr. Pemberton; and he declined coming upon that score and sent the Messenger to my Son. Altho^{o}, Mr. Pemberton had been fill'd with G^{r} Saltonstall's company before.

July, 19. Began to rain about 11. at night; held all night, and this morning, *Laus Deo*. When it held up, I went to Mr. Pemberton's, desired him to come and pray with my Family before he went; he said he had a great deal of Business; yet I had some expectation of his coming, and forbore to ask my son to pray that might the more reserve our selves for him. He came not. In the Afternoon I went to have accompanied the Gentlemen to the Sloop, but they were gon a little before, before 4 o'clock.

July, 28. 1714. According to my Promise, I carried my Daughter Hanah to Meadford to visit Cousin Porter lyeing in; In her Mother's Name she presented her Cousin with a red Coat for her little Aaron, blew facing for the sleeves, Galoon. Cost about 12^{s}. 2^{d}. I carried her 3. oranges. Gave the Nurse 2^{s}; maid 1^{s} Hanah gave the Nurse 1^{s}; got thither about 1. Over the Ferry before dark: 5^{s} for the Calash.

7^{r}. 26. My son of Brooklin, who came hither on Tuesday, by reason of his Indisposition, goes not abroad. David fetched him in a Coach.

Midweek, Decr. 22. My Son Joseph and I visited my Son at Brooklin, sat with my Daughter in the chamber some considerable time, Drank Cider, eat Apples. Sarah Cumin sat in the same Room on the Bed with her sore Leg. Daughter said nothing to us of her Greivances, nor we to her. Mr. Josiah

Winchester, and Aspinwall were below with my Son upon Business.

Decr 23. Dr. C. Mather preaches excellently from Ps. 37. Trust in the Lord &c. only spake of the Sun being in the centre of our System. I think it inconvenient to assert such Problems.

Decr. 27. Very pleasant wether. My Son tells me that Thomas Sewall went to the Church of England last Satterday: He expostulated with him about it.

Tuesday, February 1, 171$\frac{4}{5}$. As I was busy in signing Bills, Mr. Bromfield came to me and desired me to go to the Major Genl at Ten a-clock; they had some discourse yesterday at the Sessions, Several would be there. I got thither about 11., was the first and were but 4. in all, as I remember; Sewall, E^m Hutchinson, Jos. Lynde Mr. Bromfield. Agreed to call as many as we could together at the Council-Chamber at 3. p. m. There met 12. viz. Mr. Winthrop, Tailer, Elisha Hutchinson, Sewall, Jos. Lynde, E^m Hutchinson, Bromfield, Winslow, Clark, Davenport, Hutchinson Thomas, Mr. Secretary. Col. Townsend was at Roxbury, to hear his son That preaches. Col. Phillips came not over; Mr. Comissary was indispos'd by the Gout. Col. Lynde sent his son Phillips with the Letters; we had Spoken of another. Mr. Bromfield had spoken to Flag to warn them. Lt Govr, as I hear, enquir'd what the Major Genl had to do to warn a Council? When were together in the Closet, I mollified a little by saying we were not a Council, but some Gentlemen of the Council met together upon an extraordinary occasion, which Mr. Tailor took up with, placidly; After a pretty deal of Talk, I motion'd that we might send to the Governour to enquire whether He had received any Orders; which was readily agreed to. At last, when I could shift it no longer, Sewall, Jo. Lynde, Davenport, Tho. Hutchinson went into the said Hutchinson's Coach. Got thither a little after Five, only the Governour's Lady was there; Mr. Wm Dudley received us, and call'd the Govr. After a-while I rose up, and began to do the Message, Govr would have me sit down. The Message was this; May it please your Excellency, whereas the Six Months given by the Parliament of Great Britain, for continuing persons in their Civil and Military Offices; do expire this day: These are humbly to enquire whether your Excellency has received Orders from our Soveraign Lord King George, enabling you to sustain the place of Governour of this Province longer? If you have receiv'd no such Orders, we are of opinion that Authority is devolv'd upon His Maj^{s} Council, by the direction of our charter; and that we are oblig'd in obedience thereunto, and for the welfare of His Majesties Subjects here, to exert our selvs accordingly.

We humbly thank your Excellency for your good Services done this people which are many; and for your Favour to our selves in particular, and take leave to subscribe our selves your Excellency's most humble and faithfull Servants.

I intended it as a Letter: But they would have it by word of Mouth. So I shew'd not the paper. The Governour's Answer was, I have received no Orders: and express'd an Aversion to enter into discourse. I said, If was out of the Province, this much more. Govr said that was a Jest; might be out of the Province at a great distance, at Virginia, and yet give Orders in writing. Twas more to be at Cascobay, than at New Hampshire. Drank to me, saying, Judge Sewall. 'Twas Candlelight, went to the door and crav'd Excuse for not going to the Gate. And sent no body with us.

Govr said there were Thirty Canada Indians at Piscataqua, he was listening after it.

When return'd, found our Company Waiting for us. When we had related the Governour's Answer, and they perceived by his declining to argue the matter, he design'd to hold his place, it put the Gentlemen to it. Col. Hutchinson said, There must be a Council Call'd, all seem'd to be of that mind; Mr. Winthrop would have had the Secretary write Letters; but he said, 'Twas no Council, he could not doe it. I said Let us write and all subscribe. Mr. Winthrop was so knockt that he said it could not be done, if the Secretary declin'd. The Lt Govr and Secretary left us. At last resolv'd to Write, and writ Five Letters; To Situate, Marble-head, Salem, Ipswich, Newbury. Gave the Northern Letters to Col. Lynde to send from Charlestown by an Express. Gave Capt. Cushin's to a Marshfield man whom Col. Winslow directed us to; he to pay him for how much he went out of his way. Time fix'd in the Letter sign'd by Ten, was two a-clock p. m. Febr. 3.

Thorsday, Feb^{r}. 3. Very great Congregation; Dr. Mather prays for them that had the Administration of the Government; mentions neither Govr nor Lieut. Govr. Lt Govr was present.

Thorsday, Feb^{r} 3. p. m. The Councillors met, whose Names are to the Proclamation. Had long debate, drew up votes to state the Question till I was weary. At last voted the Devolution; only 2 or 3 that did not vote. Then ordered 4. to acquaint the Govr what was done; viz, Elisha Hutchinson esqr. Eliakim Hutchinson esqr. Penn Townsend Esqr. and Josiah Winslow esqr. They went though the night was pretty well enter'd. Many of us stayed till they return'd: Govr said was not dead, nor out of the province. Adjourned to the morning.

Friday, Febr. 4. Drew up a Proclamation; at my going to Diner Col Hutchinson desired me to draw something, which I did, and 'twas agreed to with very little alteration.

Note. I had said King William and Queen Mary of Blessed Memory, I pleaded when spoken to, They were our Founders. Lt Govr spake hard against it, unless the same was said for Queen Anne, so twas struck out.

Mr. Secretary drew that in the English Letter: Mr. Secretary first drew, *till His Majesties Orders;* which Mr. B. Lynde and I opos'd, as that which bound up our hands, from doing anything: so twas struck out. Publish'd it by Beat of Drum. Paper was sullied with the Rain. Mr. Hiller read it, out of the Council-Chamber Gallery; Col. Checkley, Major Fitch, Capt. Abijah Savage &c. present. Dr. Cotton Mather could not be found, Sent for Mr. Pemberton, who was at Capt. Winslow's, and he pray'd with us. I should have noted, that Mr. Tailer Contested the precedency with Mr. Winthrop, seeing he had had the Honor to sit at the Board as Lieut Govr. and that the order of privy seal, a Copy of which he produc'd, was Dead. But the Council carried it for Mr. Winthrop *nemine Contradicente.*

Febr. 6. No Govr nor Lt Govr mentioned in our publick prayers.

Febr. 9. Council; Col. Phillips, and Capt. Norden take their Oaths, to the Devolution Government. I told Col. Phillips, we wanted him last week: He said his heart was with us; but he was not well.

Febr. 14. I wait on Dr. Incr. Mather to have a Comissioners Meeting appointed to morrow, at 3 aclock. But when I came to Dr. C. Mather, he said should be employ'd in the Afternoon; so appointed it in the Morning: Gave Flagg the List to warn, because Maxwell was Cast out of the Church yesterday, and is superanuated.

In the Afternoon, Col. Townsend, Mr. Bromfield, Mr. Addington, Davenport and I visited the Governour, who Treated us with good Drink and Apples. No body went with us to the Gate. Govr. Hunter's Proclamation comes to Town dated Jany. 29. ordering those of pernicious principles to be aprehended and punished, who assert that Commissions are void at the end of the Six Moneths.

18. Dr. Cotton Mather, Mr. Pemberton, Colman, come into Council and intimat what was discours'd last night at Mr. Winthrop's. Council order me and Mr. B. Lynde to give their Answer, viz, That 'tis agreeable to them, and they wish it may be gone forward with. We went imediately but can't find them, went to Mr. Pemberton's, Colman's. At last as were going to Dr. Mather's, Mr. Lynde call'd at his Brother's and

found the Dr. there. We went in, drank Tea, after we had done our Message. A comission was drawn and sign'd for Mr. Wm Dudley as Sheriff; he was sent for, to offer it to him, He said he had one already from the Govr and Council and saw no reason to take another, with a Little seeming Banter he said his had a Seal, This had none.

Monday, Febr. 21. Son Sewall intended to go home on the Horse Tom. brought, sent some of his Linen by him: but when I came to read his wive's Letter to me, his Mother was vehemently against his going: and I was for considering. I took the Horse and rode to Tim^{o} Harris of Brooklin. Staid there so long that twas almost dark before I got to Roxbury Meting house, yet call'd and saw Mrs. Mary Mighell. Visited Mr. Walter, staid long with him, read my daughters Letters to her Husband and me: yet he still advis'd to his going home. Went home in the dark between 7 and 8. My Wife can't yet agree to my Son's going home.

Midweek, March, 2. Mr. Secretary offers a Draught for a Fast. The President persuaded him to strike out words about *Establishment of the Government.* Mr. Tailer procured to have the *Prince* particularly mention'd. I prevail'd to have *Rain* Specially inserted, and gave the Words, which I prepar'd at Noon; carried it to the Press.

Midweek, March, 16. Lt Govr comes to me in the morning, shews me Mr. Dudley's case truly stated; 'twas laid at his Steps. Councillors were much surpris'd: p. m. sent for the Printers: before had done examining them, I went away to the Funeral of my Grandson, Billy Hirst, after I had acquainted the President.

March, 20. Lt Govr. comes to my house, shews me the printed Copy from the London Gazett in Govr Hunter's hand at New-York. It seems Mr. Paul Dudley bestirr'd himself to have his Father pray'd for as Govr, and that the Order for the Fast might not be Read. Mr. Pemberton Spake to me as went by the foreseat in the morning. I Spake against it as I could so on a sudden surprise, mention'd the Exception, or provision be made. Mr. Sewall pray'd as formerly. Mr. Pemberton ask'd if I had read it, I said yes: Said he should have seen it! At Noon I carried it to him borrowed of Mr. Newton: He had it of Mr. Cambbell before, was reading it; Said he was amaz'd I should speak as I did; twas as far from it as East from West: New-England, he fear'd, would pay dear for being Fond of Government. I say'd unless he knew those that were Fond of Government he did ill so to Censure. Said I came only to give him a sight of the Proclamation, he might use his Freedom. He thank'd me and I went away.

P. m. Mr. Pemberton acquainted the Congregation that he had received an Order for a Fast from Civil Authority, he had it not with him, Spake of reading it next Lord's Day. He never said a word that I know of, though the President and Three other of the Council were of his Church, and before him: he saw not fit to advise with them. Pray'd for those that were or might be called to the Government. A little before night Mr. Paul Dudley, and Mr. Wm Dumer come to my house; call to Speak with me. Mr. Dudley acquaints me that the Govr intended to be here in Town about Eleven a-clock to publish the proclamation, that I might be there; said would goe to every one of the Council. I said, but is this sufficient, meaning the Copy. His eyes Sparkled, Said he had no orders to dispute, there had been great Friendship between him and me. I said I had done nothing to forfeit it. As was going out said his Father would come to Town with two Troops of Horse.

Monday, March, 21. Govr comes to Town with Four Troops in stead of two. Twelve of the Council were there at the proclamation. I was not there, I used to be with Mr. Addington; and was griev'd at the forbidding to read the Fast; *i. e.* Mr. P. Dudley writ to the Ministers to pray for his father, and not to read the Order for the Fast. I knew nothing of the Fast, till Mr. Pemberton declin'd reading it. Dr. Mather,

Mr. Bridge, Mr. Webb read it; Mr. Pemberton and Colman did not. Dr. C. Mather said it was sign'd by the hon'ble Wait Winthrop esqr. the president of the Council and 17. more of the council, and Countersign'd &c.

Friday, March, 25. Mr. B. Lynde and I take the Hackney coach and wait on the Govr. I wish his Excellency good success in his Return to the exercise of his Government; ask'd if had any Service to Plimouth; entertain'd us very pleasantly, came with us to the Gate.

April, 21. News comes that Col. Burgess is to be our Governour. Arriv'd just before Lecture, which is Mr. J. Sewall's. Sarah Cumins was Married this day; This News will damp my daughter of Brooklin her Triumph.

July, 6. This day it is Fifty four years Since I first was brought ashoar to Boston near where Scarlet's wharf now is, July, 6, 1661, Lord's Day. The Lord help me to Redeem the Time which passes so swiftly. I was then a poor little Schoolboy of Nine years and ¼ old.

Monday, Augt. 8. Set out at 11. at night on Horseback with Tho. Wallis to inspect the order of the Town.

Constable Eady, Mr. Allen, Salter, Herishor Simson, Howel, Mr. John Marion. Dissipated the players at Nine Pins at Mount-Whoredom.

Benjamin Davis, Chairmaker, and Jacob Hasy were two of them. Reproved Thomas Messenger for entertaining them.

As came home between 2 and three took up Peter Griffis the notorious Burglarer, and comitted him to Prison. Generally, the Town was peaceable and in good order.

Lord's Day, Jany 15, 171⅚. An Extraordinary Cold Storm of Wind and Snow. Blows much worse as coming home at Noon, and so holds on. Bread was frozen at the Lord's Table: Mr. Pemberton administered. Came not out to the Afternoon Exercise. Though twas so Cold, yet John Tuckerman was baptised. At six a-clock my ink freezes so that

I can hardly write by a good fire in my Wive's Chamber. Yet was very Comfortable at Meeting. *Laus Deo.*

Second day, Jany. 16. About Noon my Wife is taken Extream ill, Overcome I supose with the Cold. Vomits, shakes; so that I fear'd a Fever. She was aprehensive of Death; had a very bad night. This was very distressing to me.

17. p. m. Joseph prays with her Excellently. Has a much better night. Though the Emetick Physick was very tedious in the Operation; yet I hope it had a good Effect. *Laus Deo.* Had both Mr. Oakes and Cutler with her. David Sinclar's Wife Nurses her, Watches [Watchers], Lydia Avery, Mrs. —— Kay.

Febr. 15. Visit daughter Hirst, tell her her Mother has enter'd the 59th year of her Age; gave each of the children 2^{s} each and to my daughter an Angel, her Salary as Treasurer. Went thence to the Burying of David Sinclar's daughter; Mr. Wadsworth and I went together. To the Meeting at Thornton's.

June, 20. I went over to Charlestown in the morn, and drave a Pin in Charlestown Meetinghouse, in the Corner-post next Mr. Bradstreet's; gave an Angel. I sat in the nearest Shop, and saw them raise the 3^{d} post towards the Ferry from the Corner-post. Gave me a Cool Tankard. Gave Mr. Graves one of my Son's Books. Got to the Council Chamber before Ten.

I essay'd June, 22, to prevent Indians and Negros being Rated with Horses and Hogs; but could not prevail. Col. Thaxter brought it back, and gave as a reason of the Nonagreement, They were just going to make a New Valuation.

June, 30. 1716. Visited my Daughter Hirst when I came home; I fear her stay with us is very short: the Good Lord undertake for her and us!

July, 10. Son Sewall prays in the Counting Room. Afterwards Mr. Colman prays there. Then I go to Mr. Pemberton to ask his Prayers. My wife goes home in the Coach after

Nine; was willing that I should stay all night. When I went into my daughter's Chamber, she lay upon her Left side next the Pallat Bed, I went to her there. She complain'd of Cold, and call'd for a Gown to be laid on her, and warm Linen Cloaths to her Hands. I went to the other side again. Not long after she desired to be turn'd on her right Side. I ask'd her whether her pain took her Right Arm that Caus'd her to turn: She said No, all was quiet; but she was weary with lying on that Side. The Watcher, Mrs. Welsteed, and the Nurse had much adoe to turn her; at last my daughter was satisfied: but begun to be uneasy; yet call'd for something to drink; which she had much adoe to take though given her in a Spoon. I said, when my flesh and my heart faileth me, God is the strength of my heart and my portion for ever. Said, I am just a-going, Call Mr. Hirst. She Moan'd lower and lower till she dyed, about Midnight.

I lay in Mr. Hirst's Bed, that I might not disturb my family at home. Thus have I parted with a very desirable Child not full Thirty five years old. She liv'd desir'd and died Lamented. The Lord fit me to follow, and help me to prepare my wife and Children for a dying hour.

Octr. 16. p. m. Went a foot to Roxbury. Govr Dudley was gon to his Mill. Staid till he came home. I acquainted him what my Business was; He and Madam Dudley both, reckon'd up the Offenses of my Son; and He the Vertues of his Daughter. And alone, mention'd to me the hainous faults of my wife, who the very first word ask'd my daughter why she married my Son except she lov'd him? I saw no possibility of my Son's return; and therefore asked, that he would make some Proposals, and so left it. Madam Dudley had given me Beer as I chose; G: Dudley would have me drink a Glass of very good Wine; and made a faint of having the Horses put in, to draw me; but with all said how many hundred times he had walked over the Neck. I told him I should have a pleasant journey; and so it prov'd; for coming over with Mrs.

Pierpoint, whose maiden name was Gore, had diverting discourse all the way. Met Mr. Walter in his Calash with his wife returning home, were very glad to see one another, he stopping his Calash. 'Twas quite night before we got to our house.

Decr. 20. Mr. Pemberton preaches Excellently from Psal. 24. 7. Lift up. 93^{d} Psalm sung: was but a thin Meeting by reason of the Snow: was pity. Dine with Mr. Stoddard, Govr, Lt Govr., Mr. Acmooty, Mr. Gray, Mr. Anthony Stoddard, Mr. David Stoddard, Mr. Legg there. Mr. Cooper was Chaplain. Mr. Acmooty read a Letter to him Bantering Matrimony; mention'd the inconvenience that the body might not be uncircumscrib'd; I disliking the Theam, said did you read uncircumscrib'd or uncircumcis'd. He said uncircumscrib'd. I think this a little check'd the Career of his Eleuthera. From thence went to the Funeral of Mrs. Katherine Mather, a vertuous, pious Gentlewoman. Was a great Funeral notwithstanding the Snow under foot, and keen Aer. When came home was told that Mrs. Sewall of Brooklin was brought to bed of a Son last night.

July, 3. 1717. Last night my wife was taken very sick, This extraordinary Pain and Fainting was of long Continuance, whereby I was oblig'd to abide at home and not go to the Commencement. This is the Second year of my Absence from that Solemnity. Great Plenty of Rain quickly after the Fast which was July 11th. Mr. Mayhew preaches at Roxbury.

29. 5. Mr. Colman preaches Excellently from 119. 32. Son, the Minister, dines with us, his Wife being at Brooklin. Mr. Sheaf and I follow'd next after the Relations of Joshua Cornish to his Funeral. Note, As I came out of the Meeting-house, Mr. Eliot's youth told me Govr Dudley would speak with me at Mr. Attorney's: I said, I think it will be best after Dinner; and went accordingly, after a little Waiting on some Probat business, which I thought not of Govr Dudley mention'd Christ's pardoning Mary Magdalen; and God hates put-

ting away; but did not insert *sine causa,* as Pareus notes. I said my Son had all along insisted that Caution should be given, that the infant lately born should not be chargeable to his Estate. Govr Dudley no ways came into it; but said 'twas best as 'twas, No body knew whose twas. I said I hoped to speak with Mr. P. Dudley in the Circuit. As Govr Dudley went along, took little Hanah into his Chariot, and carried her home without any fore-warning.

8^{r}. 15. My Wife got some Relapse by a new Cold and grew very bad; Sent for Mr. Oakes, and he sat up with me all night.

16. The Distemper increases; yet my Wife speaks to me to goe to Bed.

17. Thursday, I asked my wife whether twere best for me to go to Lecture: She said, I can't tell; so I staid at home. put up a Note. It being my Son's Lecture, and I absent, twas taken much notice of. Major Genl Winthrop and his Lady visit us. I thank her that she would visit my poor Wife.

Friday, 8^{r}. 18. My wife grows worse and exceedingly Restless. Pray'd God to look upon her. Ask'd not after my going to bed. Had the advice of Mr. Williams and Dr. Cutler.

7th day, 8^{r}. 19. Call'd Dr. C. Mather to pray, which he did excellently in the Dining Room, having Suggested good Thoughts to my wife before he went down. After, Mr. Wadsworth pray'd in the Chamber when 'twas supos'd my wife took little notice. About a quarter of an hour past four, my dear Wife expired in the Afternoon, whereby the Chamber was fill'd with a Flood of Tears. God is teaching me a new Lesson; to live a Widower's Life. Lord help me to Learn; and be a Sun and Shield to me, now so much of my Comfort and Defense are taken away.

8^{r}. 20. I goe to the publick Worship forenoon and Afternoon. My Son has much adoe to read the Note I put up, being overwhelm'd with tears.

8^r. 21. Monday, My dear wife is embowelled and put in a Cere-Cloth, the Weather being more than ordinarily hot.

Midweek, 8^r. 23. My dear Wife is inter'd. Bearers, Lt Govr Dumer, Maj^r. Genl Winthrop; Col. Elisha Hutchinson, Col. Townsend; Andrew Belcher esqr and Simeon Stoddard esqr. I intended Col. Taylor for a Bearer, but he was from home. Had very Comfortable weather. Bro^r Gerrish pray'd with us when return'd from the Tomb; I went into it. Govr had a Scarf and Ring, and the Bearers, Govr Dudley, Brother Sewall, Hirst, Gerrish. Was very destitute for want of the help of Son Hirst, and Cousin Jane Green. This was the first day of the Genl Court. Gave the Deputies Books. Allen's Alarm. They sent Mr. Isa. Tay and Capt. Wadsworth to me to Thank me.

Novr. 7. 5. Last night died the Excellent Waitstill [Wait Still] Winthrop esqr., for Parentage, Piety, Prudence, Philosophy, Love to New England Ways and people very Eminent. His Son not come, though sent for. Dr. Cutler, a very useful physician, dyes now, and my amiable Tenant Deacon Thomas Hubbart; Help Lord!

Decr. 1. Madam Winthrop comes not to Meeting in the Afternoon. I enquire of Mr. Winthrop. He saith She was not well at Noon: but was better.

Decr. 2. Serene and Cold. Dr. Cotton Mather dines with us. I visit Madam Winthrop at her own House; Tell her of my sending Hanah to Salem tomorrow; ask her Advice as to selling Mr. Hirst's Goods: She advises to sell all but plate and Linen. I ask her to give and take Condolence. She thanks me for my Kindness; I tell her she is before-hand with me. When I came away I pray'd God to dwell with her, Counsel and Comfort her. She desired my Prayers. Goe to Mr. Hirst's and there meet with Mr. Oliver.

Tuesday, Decr. 3. Serene pleasant Wether. I goe and hasten Nathan^l Green away with Hannah Hirst in the Coach about 10. m. Visit Mr. Secretary Willard, who came to Town last night from Cape-Anne, where he arriv'd on the Lord's Day, 7. Weeks from the Downs. Go to Mrs. Turin's; only her daughter at home, I speak to her earnestly, to warn her Mother and Aunts, that of necessity they must now take up their Mortgage: She promis'd to do it, and shew'd her Inclination. P. m. I go to the Funeral of Mr. Saml Bridge. Col. Townsend was one of the Bearers: Six Councillors follow'd the Relations, Sewall, E^{m} Hutchinson; Bromfield, Cooke; Tho. Hutchinson, Col. Winthrop. The Aer was grown very Cold, and snow'd before we got to the Grave. As came back, visited Mr. J. Sewall, Mr. Abiel Walley was with him, with whom he had much pleasant Discourse. Then went up to my daughter, and gave her my Wive's Wedding Ring, saying I hoped she would wear it with the same Nobility as she did who was the first owner of it. While her Husband and I were fitting part of his Sermon for the Press, she came in and gave us excellent Sack-posset. I told her, the Ring I had given her was her Mother's Wedding Ring; and this entertainment Savour'd of a Wedding; Went home in the Rain.

Monday, Xr. 9th Do a great Mornings work in the office of Probate. Am much refreshed with Mr. Sol. Stoddard's Letter of Condolence, which is excellent. I soked it in Tears at reading. Sent to enquire of Col. Hutchinson, who grows worse. Hear of Mr. Watt's death at Arrowsick, a great Loss to that Infant Plantation. I take Mr. Stoddard's Letter to be an Answer to my Prayer for God's gracious looking upon me. *Laus Deo.*

January 1, 17$\frac{17}{18}$. Wednesday. Privat Meeting at our House: read Mr. Scudder's Sermon about Hearing the Rod. Sung Clauses out of the 143 Psalm. Joseph Pray'd last. Had with Joseph read this Sermon before in the Castle Chamber, Decr. 30. The widow Tilly was not here, but sent to invite the Meeting.

Febr. 3. 2. I sent Madam Winthrop, Smoking Flax Inflamed, the Jewish Children of Berlin, and my small vial of Tears, by Mr. Gerrish with my Service: She thanks me, and returns her Service to me.

Feb^{r}. 6. This morning wandering in my mind whether to live a Single or a Married Life; I had a sweet and very affectionat Meditation Concerning the Lord Jesus; Nothing was to be objected against his Person, Parentage, Relations, Estate, House, Home! Why did I not resolutely, presently close with Him! And I cry'd mightily to God that He would help me so to doe!

Feb. 19. Midweek, Mr. Boydell comes to me, and says the Govr would speak with me at 11.; would send his Chariot; which was done, and I went. His Excellency shew'd me Capt. Arthur Savage's Petition to stop the Bills of Cost. I pray'd Mr. Boydell might write me a copy; spoke once or twice: but his Excel'y declin'd it, and would give me the Petition itself. I said I was to Tax the Bills in Course, it being the Judgment of the Court. Govr sent his Chariot with me home agen. Went after and paid Mr. Willoughby £50. Mrs. Willoughby seem'd to hint persons had need be ware how they married again. I said, (to humour it), They that had been at Sea should be carefull how they put to Sea again, especially in winter time; Meaning of Old Age. Rains, I think, all day long.

Tuesday, Feb. 25. Went to Roxbury to speak to Mr. Walter about my eldest Son. He advises to his going home to his wife. Went first to Jno Ruggles, lyeing Sick; and took his Oath to Jno Gore's Acquittance; had not time to visit the widow Ruggles, it being near night. Mr. Walter says she is a very good woman. Says Madam Winthrop gave him Mr. Eyre's Suit of black Cloth which fitted him well; now wore the silver Shoe-buckles, Govr Dudley had laid her out for me: Or they had laid one out for me: and Govr Dudley told him 'twas Madam Winthrop. I told him had been there but thrice, and twice upon Business: He said,

Cave Tertium. When came home gave Mrs. Hornbuckle Dr. Mather's four Sermons, one about believers being Married to Christ. Her Son and daughter were gon; but I gave her the Sermons for her Son, having written his Name in the book. Her Maiden Name was Thorowgood.

Feb. 27. I told Mr. White Next Sabbath was in a Spring Moneth, he must then set the Tune. I set now Litchfield Tune to a good Key.

Feb. 28. I told Mr. Nathan Williams My voice was much Enfeebled; He said twas apparently so. I bid him tell Mr. White of it. p. m. My Son Sam Sewall and his Wife Sign and Seal the Writings in order to my Son's going home. Govr Dudley and I Witnesses, Mr. Sam. Lynde took the Acknowledgment. I drank to my Daughter in a Glass of Canary. Govr Dudley took me into the Old Hall and gave me £100. in Three-pound Bills of Credit, new ones, for my Son; told me on Monday, he would perform all that he had promised to Mr. Walter. Sam agreed to go home next Monday, his wife sending the Horse for him. Joseph pray'd with his Bro^{r} and me. Note. This was my Wedding Day. The Lord succeed and turn to good what we have been doing.

March, 10. In the afternoon, though 'twas a very cold day, I carried Madam Usher her Letter, delivered it to her with my own hand. I was held below Stairs where a Fire was made. In Madam Usher's absence Madam Henchman took occasion highly to comend Madam Winthrop, the Major General's Widow.

March, 14. Deacon Marion comes to me, sits with me a great while in the evening; after a great deal of Discourse about his Courtship—He told [me] the Olivers said they wish'd I would Court their Aunt. I said little, but said twas not five Moneths since I buried my dear Wife. Had said before 'twas hard to know whether best to marry again or no; whom to marry. Gave him a book of the Berlin Jewish Converts.

March, 17. Do much business. Prove 4. Wills, Grant Administration on Col. Hutchinson's Estate. Dr. Mather sends me his Marah in a Letter in which is this expression, "But your Honor will allow me now at length, to offer you my Opinion, that all the Regards are not yet paid, which you owe unto the *Widow,* and which are expected from you."

March, 19. Mr. Leverett, when he and I alone, told me his wife and he had laid out Madam Brown for me, and yet took occasion to say that Madam Winthrop had done very generously by the Major General's family in giving up her Dower. I said, if Madam Brown should leave her fair Accomodations at Salem, she might be apt to repent it.

Second-day, April, 7th I prove Mr. William Denison's Will. Her brother Edmund [Weld] brought the widow to Town, and gave me notice before hand. I ask'd her how old Mr. Denison was, She told me he was born in September; was 53. years old last September. I gave her 10s to give her sister Weld for her Indian Bible. Ask'd me whether 'twas necessary to bring in an Inventory. Inclin'd to think she ought; but I would speak with her again. Mr. Dorr took occasion in her absence to say she was one of the most dutifull Wives in the world. Her Cousin, the Widow Hayden, accidentally came in with her.

April, 8. Mr. Boydell when I was at his office, and sign'd the Papers, smiling said Mr. Denison's Will look'd as if it was written by me. I told him yes, but there was not a tittle of it mine but the form. Writ to Mr. Mayhew per Mr. Jno Allen.

April, 25. Friday, Col. Quinsey comes to Town, and Col. Townsend and Mr. Bromfield by vertue of a Dedimus from the Govr, administer the Oaths to him and me; and Congratulat us in our Offices. In the evening Sister Northend comes in, brought by her son John, which is a Refreshment to us. The Lord help me, that as He is anointing me with fresh oyls, as to my office; so He would graciously pardon my Sin, and furnish me with Renewed and augmented Ability for the rightful discharge of the Trust reposed in me!

June 3. Go to Roxbury in my Son's Calash and with him Visit Govr Dudley,—Mr. Walter, Talk with him about Mrs. D——n [Denison]. He advises me not to see her then, lest should surprise her undress'd. Told him I came on purpose; yet finally submitted to his Advice. he spake of her Coming to Town on Thorsday.

June, 9. Mr. Corwin dies about 9. m. Col. Brown sent me word of it by Chapman. Note. Mrs. D——n came in the morning about 9 aclock, and I took her up into my Chamber and discoursed thorowly with her; She desired me to provide another and better Nurse. I gave her the two last News-Letters—told her I intended to visit her at her own house next Lecture-day. She said, 'twould be talked of. I answer'd, In such Cases, persons must run the Gantlet. Gave her Mr. Whiting's Oration for Abijah Walter, who brought her on horseback to Town. I think little or no Notice was taken of it.

June, 17. Went to Roxbury Lecture, visited Mr. Walter. Mr. Webb preach'd. Visited Govr Dudley, Mrs. Denison, gave her Dr. Mather's Sermons very well bound; told her we were in it invited to a Wedding. She gave me very good Curds.

July, 7. 2. I give Mrs. Denison her Oath to the Inventory; gave her a Catalogue superscrib'd to her. Her Bro^{r} brought her. Mr. Shelden of North-Hampton dines with me. At night, when all were gone to bed; Cousin Moodey went with me into the new Hall, read the history of Rebekah's Courtship, and pray'd with me respecting my Widowed Condition.

16. 4. Went to Woodell's and rode in his Coach to Meers's, from thence went and visited Mrs. Denison; Gave her K. George's Effigies in Coper; and an Engl. Crown of K.

Charles 2^d 1677. Eat Curds with her; I craved a Blessing, and Returned Thanks; came home after it.

Aug^t, 1. 6. Court rises, gave Mr. Apleton 20^s, who had pray'd 4 times. This was the longest Court that I remember at Cambridge. Rode home round with Stedmand, visit Mrs. Denison. Madam Rogers and Leverett much congratulated me upon my Courting her.

Augt 6. 4. Visited Mrs. Denison, Carried her, her Sister Weld, the Widow, and Mrs. Weld to her Bro^r Mr. Samuel Weld, where we were Courteously entertained. Brought Mr. Edmund Weld's wife home with me in the Coach; she is in much darkness. Gave Mrs. Denison a Psalm-Book neatly bound in England with Turkey-Leather.

15. I, with my Son and daughter, J. Sewall, dine at Govr Dudley's, Mr. Walter and his wife and Son, Son and daughter Sewall of Brooklin and their Daughter there, and Col. Dudley: Mrs. Denison I supose was the principal Guest, I waited on her home.

22. 6. I take my daughter Judith, and Cousin Green with me in the Coach and sup with Mrs. Denison.

27. 4. I ride and visit Mrs. Denison, leave my Horse at the Gray-Hound. She mentions her discouragements by reason of Discourses she heard: I pray'd God to direct her and me.

Octr. 11th. Visit Mrs. Denison, Bring Dr. Cotton Mather's youngest Daughter home with me in the Coach, at Mr. Walter's desire.

Wednesday, Octr. 15. Visit Mrs. Denison on Horseback; present her with a pair of Shoe-buckles, cost 5^s 3^d. Went and gave my Condolence to Madam Walter on account of the death of her Son Increase at Jamaica, which she took well. Hold the Privat Meeting at my house.

Friday, 8^r 24. Brother Sewall visits me. While he was here, Mrs. Elizabeth Byles, Dr. Mather's daughter, Tells me of Col. Thomas's Death, whereby he is freed from his solicitude as to a Judge of the Super^{r} Court at Salem next 9^{r}. Mr. Dwight of Woodstock dines with us. Visit Mrs. Denison.

The privat Meeting was at her house, which I was not aware of. I went to Mr. Walter's to Condole him; and knocking at the door was called to, and told they were all gon to the Meeting. I ask'd where? they said at Mrs. Denison's. I went thither where I found Mr. Walter at prayer. Mr. Thomas Walter made a very good Sermon from John, 13. 7. Shewing the Duty of Submitting to God's Soveraignty, the great Sin of doing contrarily. Pray'd. Sung part of the 145. Psal. which he set to Low Dutch very well. Pray'd.

The room was full; Govr Dudley and his Lady, widow Ruggles, &c. there. Rain'd hard. I sup'd with Mrs. Denison, got home about 8. at night. *Laus Deo*. Noyes, March here.

7th day, 9^{r} 1. His Excellency comes not into Council. My Son from Brooklin being here I took his Horse, and visited Mrs. Denison. Sat in the Chamber next Maj^{r} Bowls. I told her 'twas time now to finish our Business: Ask'd her what I should allow her; she not speaking; I told her I was willing to give her Two [Hundred?] and Fifty pounds per anum during her life, if it should please God to take me out of the world before her. She answer'd she had better keep as she was, than give a Certainty for an uncertainty; She should pay dear for dwelling at Boston. I desired her to make proposals, but she made none. I had Thoughts of Publishment next Thorsday the 6th. But I now seem to be far from it. May God, who has the pity of a Father, Direct and help me!

Friday, 9^{r} 28. 1718. Having consulted with Mr. Walter after Lecture, he advised me to goe and speak with Mrs. Denison. I went this day in the Coach; had a fire made in the Chamber where I spake with her before, 9^{r} the first: I enquired how she had done these 3 or 4 weeks; Afterwards I told her our Conversation had been such when I was with her last, that it seem'd to be a direction in Providence, not to proceed any further; She said, It must be what I pleas'd, or to that purpose. Afterward she seem'd to blame that I had not told her so 9r 1. Because the man had been there several times to take the Living, and she knew not what Answer to give. I said I knew not but that intended to Let the Living although she lived single. I repeated her words of 9r 1. She seem'd at first to start at the words of her paying dear, as if she had not spoken them. But she said she thought twas Hard to part with *All,* and have nothing to bestow on her Kindred. I said, I did not intend anything of the Movables, I intended all the personal Estate to be to her. She said I seem'd to be in a hurry on Saturady, 9r 1., which was the reason she gave me no proposals. Whereas I had ask'd her long before to give me proposals in Writing; and she upbraided me, That I who had never written her a Letter, should ask her to write. She asked me if I would drink, I told her Yes. She gave me Cider, Aples and a Glass of Wine: gathered together the little things I had given her, and offer'd them to me; but I would take none of them. Told her I wish'd her well, should be glad to hear of her welfare. She seem'd to say she should not again take in hand a thing of this nature. Thank'd me for what I had given her and Desired my Prayers. I gave Abijah Weld an Angel. Mr. Stoddard and his wife came in their Coach to see their Sister which broke off my Visit. Upon their asking me, I dismiss'd my Coach, and went with them to see Mr. Danforth, and came home by Moon-shine. Got home about 9. at night. *Laus Deo.*

My bowels yern towards Mrs. Denison; but I think God directs me in his Providence to desist. The first time that I mention'd making an Agreement, She said if we could not agree we must break off. When I came home, Mr. Mayhew told me the Deputies had Negatived Mr. Belcher's Memorial about reimbursing £500. Sterling for what he had laid out in England. I do not know I heard any thing of it before; that any such Motion was made this Court. Note. Mrs. Denison told me she came afoot to Lecture; but I saw her not, nor knew anything of it till she told me.

Novr 30. Lord's-day. In the evening I sung the 120. Psalm in the family. About 7 a-clock Mrs. Dorothy Denison comes in, her Cousin Weld coming first, saying she desired to speak with me in privat. I had a fire in the new Hall, and was at prayer; was very much startled that she should come so far a-foot in that exceeding Cold Season; She enter'd into discourse of what pass'd between us at Roxbury last Friday; I seem'd to be alter'd in my affection; ask'd pardon if she had affronted me. Seem'd to incline the Match should not break off, since I had kept her company so long. Said Mr. Denison spake to her after his Signing the Will, that he would not make her put all out of her Hand and power, but reserve somwhat to bestow on his Friends that might want. I told her She might keep all. She excus'd, and said 'twas not such an all. I Comended the estate. I could not observe that she made me any offer of any part all this while. She mention'd two Glass Bottles she had. I told her they were hers, and the other small things I had given her, only now that they had not the same signification as before. I was much concern'd for her being in the Cold, would fetch her in a plate of somthing warm: (for I had not sup'd), she refus'd. However I Fetched a Tankard of Cider and drank to her. She desired that no body might know of her being here. I told her they should not. Sam. Hirst went to the door, who knew not her Cousin Weld; and not so much as he might stay in the room while we talked together. She went away in the bitter Cold, no moon being up, to my great pain. I Saluted her at parting.

2^d day, Decr 1. Had much probat Business. Mr. Mayhew tells me he preach'd at Needham yesterday: they had no Minister there. Preach'd a Lecture to day at Natick at Jno Nesnumun's house. He is not well. Dr. Clark says the Small pocks is in Town. Capt Sargent of Newbury, his daughter, has it in Charter-street. The Lord be Mercifull to Boston!

Monday, Dec[r] 22. Mrs. Dorothy Denison brings an additional Inventory. I gave her the Oath; ask'd her Bro[r] Brewer and her to dine with me: She said she needed not to eat; Caus'd her to sit by the fire, and went with her to the door, at her going away. She said nothing to me, nor her Bro[r] Brewer.

19. 5. After the Comissioners Meeting I visited Mr. Foxcroft and his new-married Wife. They entertain'd me courteously, and the father and Mother. Mr. Prince came to my house, just sat down with me, and desired to be excused, went through the Kitchen to Lydia Kay's Chamber, (Sam Hirst shewing him the way,) was knocking and pleading a long time at the door before they would let him in; Judith trembled much, and is more and more alienated from him by his rough upbraiding Carriage towards her. The Lord be mercifull to her and me, pardon our Sins, and guide us!

April, 1, 1719. Midweek. Col. Townsend and Mr. Wood dine with me. In the morning I dehorted Sam. Hirst and Grindal Rawson from playing Idle Tricks because 'twas first of April; They were the greatest fools that did so. N. E. Men came hither to avoid anniversary days, the keeping of them, such as the 25th of Dec[r]. How displeasing must it be to God, the giver of our Time, to keep aniversary days to play the fool with ourselves and others. p. m. John Arcus brings me a superscribed paper, wherein were a pair of very good white Kid's Leather Gloves, and a Gold Ring with four peny weight wanting 3 Grains, with this Motto, *Lex et Libertas*. A. T. I have received 4. Presents lately; 4 Oranges, 2 Pieces of Salmon, Madam Foxcroft's Wedding Cake; and this which is a very fair Present indeed. I have hardly any to compare with it. The good Lord help me to serve faithfully the Supream Donor!

29. 7. I visit Mrs. Tilly the 2[d] time; it seems she was

born in Elisabeth's Town in the Jerseys. In her 20th year when she married Mr. Woodmansey.

Septr 2. Visit Mrs. Tilly, and speak with her in her Chamber; ask her to come and dwell at my house. She expresses her Unworthiness of such a thing with much Respect. I tell her of my going to Bristol. I would have her consider of: she answered she would have me consider of it.

7^{r} 16. After the Meeting I visited Mrs. Tilly.

7^{r} 18. ditto.

7^{r} 21. I gave Mrs. Tilly a little booke entitled *Ornaments for the daughters of Sion.* I gave it to my dear wife Augt 28. 1702.

23^{d} 24th eat Almonds and Reasons with Mrs. Tilly and Mrs. Armitage; Discoursed with Mrs. Armitage, who spake very agreeably, and said Mrs. Tilly had been a great Blessing to them, and hop'd God would make her so to me and my family. At my coming home am told that Col. Wm Dudley had call'd and said that Judith was sick of the Fever and Ague at the Lt Gov^{rs}

7^{r} 25. Visited Madam Pemberton to enquire after Judith: She aplauded my Courting Mrs. Tilley: I thank'd her for her Favour in maintaining what I did. Met with the Lt Govr there beyond expectation: Thank'd him for his Kindness to my daughter: He received me very courteously. Discours'd with my Son the Minister about this, and Hanah's Motion to have Ministers pray with her. Discours'd with Mr. Cutler, president [of Yale College]. Son and Daughter visit us from Brooklin and dine with us. Visited Mrs. Sewall and enquired of her Sick Son. Visited Mrs. Tilly. When came home they told me Mr. Stoddard had invited me to eat Salt-Fish with him.

7^{r} 26. Col. Wm Dudley calls, and after other discourse, ask'd me [leave?] to wait on my daughter Judith home, when 'twas fit for her to come; I answered, It was reported he had aplyed to her and he said nothing to me, when rode with me to Dedham. As came back, I call'd at his house, as I had said, and he was not at home. His waiting on her might give some Umbrage: I would Speak with her first. Spoke to him about Newman's Execution. Delay was Disobedience to the Precept. He said 'twas attach'd; I told him it was not yet Newman's Money.

8 9th 6. Waited on Mrs. Tilley and Armitage, and visited Mr. Prince and Mrs. Deborah Deny, at Mr. D. Olivers.

8^r 12. Monday, write to my daughter Judith, inclosing it to Bro^r Northend by the Post: Would have her advise with her unkle Moodey as her father.

Octob^r 13. Tuesday p. m. Govr Dudley visits me in his Chariot; speaks to me in behalf of Col. Wm Dudley, that I would give him leave that he might visit my daughter Judith. I said 'twas a weighty matter. I would consider of it &c.

8^r 14th. I went to James William's, and left a Note with his wife and 1^s for my Publishm'^t. Meeting is at Sister Emons's. By the way as I went, visited Col. Checkley who is very sick, says he is this day 66. years old; takes my visit very kindly and desires Prayers. Mr. Belcher, Dedham, visited Mrs. Tilley this day.

8^r 15. I am Publish'd the first time. Govr Phillips sits above our Governour all Lecture-time, although Govr Shute put him upon it 2 or 3 times to go into the Seat first, which he would not doe, Whether through real, or feigned mistake, I say not. Mr. Colman preach'd from Mal. 1. 14. For I am a great King, saith the Lord of Hosts. The first five verses of the 99th Psalm sung.

26. or 27. I visited Dr. I. Mather, designing to ask him to Marry me. I ask'd him whether it was convenient to marry on the evening after the Thanksgiving; he made me no answer. I ask'd agen. He said Mr. Prince had been with him to marry him; but he told him he could not go abroad in the evening. Then I thought twas in vain to proceed any further: for Mrs. Tilley's preparations were such that I could

not defer it any longer; and could not be Married sooner, because I was Out-published on the Thanks-giving Day, and not before.

Octob^{r} 28. 4. I went to Mr. Prince and ask'd him to be at my Wedding, and Mrs. Deny, which he readily agreed to. I ask'd him to make the 2^{d} Prayer. In the evening Bro^{r} Moodey brings home Mary Hirst. I sent to each of the Doctors [Mather] an Angel as I us'd to do, and invited them to Dinner on Friday and their Wives.

Octob^{r} 29. Thanks-giving-day: between 6 and 7. Brother Moodey and I went to Mrs. Tilley's; and about 7, or 8, were married by Mr. J. Sewall, in the best room below stairs. Mr. Prince pray'd the 2^{d} time. Mr. Adams the Minister of Newington was there, Mr. Oliver and Mr. Tim^{o} Clark Justices, and many more. Sung the 12, 13, 14, 15, and 16. verses of the 90th Psalm. Cous. S. Sewall set Low-dutch Tune in a very good Key, which made the Singing with a good number of Voices very agreeable. Distributed Cake. Mrs. Armitage introduced me into my Bride's Chamber after she was a-bed. I thank'd her that she had left her room in that Chamber to make way for me, and pray'd God to provide for her a better Lodging: So none saw us after I went to bed. Quickly after our being a-bed my Bride grew so very bad she was fain to sit up in her bed; I rose to get her Petit Coats about her. I was excedingly amaz'd, fearing lest she should have dy'd. Through the favour of God she recover'd in some considerable time of her Fit of the Tissick, spitting, partly blood. She herself was under great Consternation.

Friday, 8^{r} 30. Govr Shute, Govr Dudley and his Lady, Councillors and Ministers in Town with their Wives dined with us, except Dr. Incr. Mather and Mr. Belcher. Had a very good diner, at Four Tables, Two in the best Room. Many Coaches there. In the evening Mr. Oliver invited me and my Bride to Mr. Prince's Wedding. We went half way up the Hill, and my Bride could go no further; but was fain to return back by reason of her great Cold and Shortness of breath. Then I went, and saw Mr. Sewall Marry Mr. Prince and Mrs. Deborah Denny at Mr. Oliver's. Mr. Oliver, Dr. Noyes, Mr. Anth° Stoddard, and their Wives present. Had a good Super and Cake. Sung about two Staves in the 4th part of the 73. Psalm. I set the Tune. Mr. Oliver in the name of the Overseers [of the Meeting house] invites my Wife to sit in the Fore-Seat. I thought no other but to have brought her into my Pue, and sat with her there a day or two, and so I told Mr. Oliver: but he insisted. I thank'd him and the Overseers.

29. 3. My wife had a very bad night, thought she should have died, had such a shaking Ague-Fit. But through Mercy, all went over well.

Govr Saltonstall visits us, wishes my wife Joy.

30. 4. Great Storm of Snow.

Lord's Day, March 20, 1719-20. Madam Winthrop comes to Meeting, p. m. puts up a Note of Thanks-giving to God. Capt. Tim Clark, and Dr. Noyes were with us all day. Ebenezer baptised.

March, 25. Friday, I visited Govr Dudley, Sat a-while with Madam Dudley, who excus'd my not being asked to go up, from the very great Weakness of Govr Dudley, and the want of the Exercise of his Understanding. He is lifted to and fro like a child. Drank a Glass of Mead. Mr. Foxcroft and his Wife visit us.

Feria sexta, April, 8. Govr Dudley is buried in his father Govr Dudley's Tomb at Roxbury. Boston and Roxbury Regiments were under Arms, and 2 or 3 Troops: Bearers, His Excellency Governour Shute, Samuel Sewall; Col. Townsend, Col. Appleton; Mr. President Leverett, Col. Samuel Brown. Scarvs, Rings, Gloves. Scutcheons. Councillours and Ministers had Scarvs, and Consulary Men. Col. Otis, Thaxter, Quincey, Dows, Norden, Judge Lynde, Col. Pain were there out of Town. Judge Dudley in a mourning Cloak led the Widow; When I took leave of her, She desired my Prayers.

Were very many people, spectators out of windows, on Fences and Trees, like Pigeons. The Bells in Boston were rung for the Funeral; which was finish'd when the Sun was near an hour high. I and my wife, and Son and daughter Sewall went and came back in the Hackney Coach very well. *Laus Deo.* The Lord grant that I may be clothed upon before uncloathed. Thursday night, the evening before the Funeral, Hanah Hirst read in Course the 19th of the Revelation.

May, 12. Mr. Sewall Preaches. Mr. Colman and he dine with the Governour; Strive to enter in— In the evening I join the Revd Mr. William Cooper, and Mrs. Judith Sewall in Marriage. I said to Mr. Simeon Stoddard and his Wife, Sir, Madam, The great Honour you have conferr'd on the Bridegroom and the Bride, by being present at this Solemnity, does very Conveniently supersede any further enquiry after your Consent. And the part I am desired to take in this Wedding, renders the way of my giving my Consent very Compendious: There's no maner of room left for that previous Question, Who giveth this Woman to be married to this Man?

Dear Child, you give me your Hand for one moment, and the Bridegroom forever. Spouse, You Accept and receive this Woman now given you &c. Mr. Sewall pray'd before the Wedding, and Mr. Colman after. Sung the 115. Psalm from the 9. verse to the end, in the New-Hall, St David's, which I set There we had our Cake, and Sack-posset.

May, 15. My wife goes not out in the morning, and I read part of Mr. Willard's Sermon out of the Fountain open'd, and prayed with her, which she took very kindly. Went out in the afternoon, and visited little Sam. Sewall, very sick. Mr. Cooper and his Bride went to our Meeting, and sat in my Pue.

May 26. Din'd with the Churches at the Dragon. Between 4 and 5. the Govr adjourned to Ten a-clock Satterday morning, and presently rose up and went away. NB. Went to Bed after Ten: about 11 or before, my dear Wife was opressed with a rising of Flegm that obstructed her Breathing. I arose and lighted a Candle, made Scipio give me a Bason of Water (he was asleep by the fire) Call'd Philadelphia, Mr. Cooper, Mayhew. About midnight my dear wife expired to our great astonishment, especially mine. May the Sovereign Lord pardon my Sin, and Sanctify to me this very Extraordinary, awfull Dispensation. Major Epes, Dr. Cotton Mather, Mr. Williams of Hatfield, of Derefield, Mr. Prince, Mr. Whiting of Concord, visit me in a very friendly and Christian manner. Before Super I sung the 130th Psalm, and a staff out of the 46. Mr. Williams of Hatfield, sympathising with me, said twas what befell the Prophet Ezekiel.

May, 29. God having in his holy Sovereignty put my Wife out of the Fore-Seat, I aprehended I had Cause to be asham'd of my Sin, and to loath my self for it; and retired into my Pue. Mr. Williams of Derefield preach'd in the morning from Rom. 5. Christ died for Siners. Mr. Sewall administered the Lords Super. I put up a Note to this purpose; Samuel Sewall, depriv'd of his dear Wife by a very sudden and awfull Stroke, desires Prayers that God would sanctify the same to himself, and Children, and family. Writ and sent three; to the South, Old and Mr. Colman's. Mr. Prince preaches p. m. Mat. 25. At midnight behold a Cry was made.

Tuesday, May, 31. Buried my dear Wife. Bearers, Col. Tailer, Bromfield, Stoddard, Davenport; Dudley, Mr. Danl Oliver. Govr and Lt Govr had Scarvs and Rings. Bro^{r} heard the Funeral was not over, by the Post, came away after 2. and was timely at the Funeral: had a Comfortable day; though threatened with Rain. *Laus Deo.* I went into the Tomb: The good Lord prepare for me a House not made with Hands, eternal in the Heavens, and the Consideration of that will make the Grave a Lightsom place. My Son prays in his Sister's Chamber very pertinently, affectionatly.

June, 1. Brother goes home; gave him a Scarf: prov'd the will of Jn° Loring of Hull. Eat a good Dish of Strawberries, part of Sister Stoddard's present.

Sept[r] 5. Mary Hirst goes to Board with Madam Oliver and her Mother Loyd. Going to Son Sewall's I there meet with Madam Winthrop, told her I was glad to meet her there, had not seen her a great while; gave her Mr. Homes's Sermon.

7[r] 30. Mr. Colman's Lecture: Daughter Sewall acquaints Madam Winthrop that if she pleas'd to be within at 3 p. m. I would wait on her. She answer'd she would be at home.

8[r] 1. Satterday, I dine at Mr. Stoddard's: from thence I went to Madam Winthrop's just at 3. Spake to her, saying, my loving wife died so soon and suddenly, 'twas hardly convenient for me to think of Marrying again; however I came to this Resolution, that I would not make my Court to any person without first Consulting with her. Had a pleasant discourse about 7 [seven] Single persons sitting in the Fore-seat 7[r] 29th, viz. Mad[m] Rebekah Dudley, Catharine Winthrop, Bridget Usher, Deliverance Legg, Rebekah Loyd, Lydia Colman, Elizabeth Bellingham. She propounded one and another for me; but none would do, said Mrs. Loyd was about her Age.

Octob[r] 3. 2. Waited on Madam Winthrop again; 'twas a little while before she came in. Her daughter Noyes being there alone with me, I said, I hoped my Waiting on her Mother would not be disagreeable to her. She answer'd she should not be against that that might be for her Comfort. I Saluted her, and told her I perceiv'd I must shortly wish her a good Time; (her mother had told me, she was with Child, and within a Moneth or two of her Time). By and by in came Mr. Airs, Chaplain of the Castle, and hang'd up his Hat, which I was a little startled at, it seeming as if he was to lodge there. At last Madam Winthrop came in too. After a considerable time, I went up to her and said, if it might not be inconvenient I desired to speak with her. She assented, and spake of going into another Room; but Mr. Airs and Mrs. Noyes presently rose up, and went out, leaving us there alone. Then I usher'd in Discourse from the names in the Fore-seat; at last I pray'd that Katharine [Mrs. Winthrop] might be the person assign'd for me. She instantly took it up in the way of Denyal, as if she had catch'd at an Opportunity to do it, saying she could not do it before she was asked. Said that was her mind unless she should Change it, which she believed she should not; could not leave her Children. I express'd my Sorrow that she should do it so Speedily, pray'd her Consideration, and ask'd her when I should wait on her agen. She setting no time, I mention'd that day Sennight. Gave her Mr. Willard's Fountain open'd with the little print and verses; saying, I hop'd if we did well read that book, we should meet together hereafter, if we did not now. She took the Book, and put it in her Pocket. Took Leave.

8^r 5. Midweek, I din'd with the Court; from thence went and visited Cousin Jonathan's wife, Lying in with her little Betty. Gave the Nurse 2^s. Although I had apointed to wait upon her, M^m Winthrop, next Monday, yet I went from my Cousin Sewall's thither about 3. p. m. The Nurse told me Madam dined abroad at her daughter Noyes's, they were to go out together. I ask'd for the Maid, who was not within. Gave Katee a peny and a Kiss, and came away. Accompanyed my Son and dâter Cooper in their Remove to their New House.

8^r 6th. A little after 6. p. m. I went to Madam Winthrop's. She was not within. I gave Sarah Chickering the Maid 2^s, Juno, who brought in wood, 1^s. Afterward the Nurse came in, I gave her 18^d, having no other small Bill. After awhile Dr. Noyes came in with his Mother; and quickly after his wife came in: They sat talking, I think, till eight a-clock. I said I fear'd I might be some Interruption to their Business: Dr. Noyes reply'd pleasantly: He fear'd they might be an Interruption to me, and went away. Madam seem'd to harp upon the same string. Must take care of her Children; could not leave that House and Neighbourhood where she had dwelt so long. I told her she might doe her children as much or more good by bestowing what she laid out in Hous-keeping, upon them. Said her Son would be of Age the 7th of August. I said it might be inconvenient for her to dwell with her Daughter-in-Law, who must be Mistress of the House. I gave her a piece of Mr. Belcher's Cake and Ginger-Bread wrapped up in a clean sheet of Paper; told her of her Father's kindness to me when Treasurer, and I Constable. My Daughter Judith was gon from me and I was more lonesom—might help to forward one another in our Journey to Canaan.—Mr. Eyre came within the door; I saluted him, ask'd how Mr. Clark did, and he went away. I took leave about 9 aclock. I told [her] I came now to refresh her Memory as to Monday-night; said she had not forgot it. In discourse with her, I ask'd leave to speak with her Sister; I meant to gain Mad^m^ Mico's favour to persuade her Sister. She seem'd surpris'd and displeas'd, and said she was in the same condition!

In the Evening I visited Madam Winthrop, who treated me with a great deal of Curtesy; Wine, Marmalade. I gave her a News-Letter about the Thanksgiving; Proposals, for sake of the verses for David Jeffries. She tells me Dr. Increase Mather visited her this day, in Mr. Hutchinson's Coach

8^r^ 11th I writ a few Lines to Madam Winthrop to this purpose: "Madam, These wait on you with Mr. Mayhew's Sermon, and Account of the state of the Indians on Martha's Vinyard. I thank you for your Unmerited Favours of yesterday; and hope to have the Hapiness of Waiting on you tomorrow before Eight a-clock after Noon. I pray God to keep you, and give you a joyfull entrance upon the Two Hundred and twenty ninth year of Christopher Columbus his Discovery; and take Leave, who am, Madam, your humble Servt

S. S.

Sent this by Deacon Green, who deliver'd it to Sarah Chickering, her Mistress not being at home.

Mrs. Anne Cotton came to door (twas before 8.) said Madam Winthrop was within, directed me into the little Room, where she was full of work behind a Stand; Mrs. Cotton came in and stood. Madam Winthrop pointed to her to set me a Chair. Madam Winthrop's Countenance was much changed from what 'twas on Monday, look'd dark and lowering. At last, the work, (black stuff or Silk) was taken away, I got my Chair in place, had some Converse, but very Cold and indifferent to what 'twas before. Ask'd her to acquit me of Rudeness if I drew off her Glove. Enquiring the reason, I told her twas great odds between handling a dead Goat, and a living Lady. Got it off. I told her I had one Petition to ask of her, that was, that she would take off the Negative she laid on me the third of October; She readily answer'd she could not, and enlarg'd upon it; She told me of it so soon as she could; could not leave her house, children, neighbours, business. I told her she might do som Good to help and suport me. Mentioning Mrs. Gookin, Nath, the widow Weld was spoken of; said I had visited Mrs. Denison. I told her Yes! Afterward I said, If after a first and second Vagary she would Accept of me returning, Her Victorious Kindness and Good Will would be very Obliging. She thank'd me for my Book, (Mr. Mayhew's Sermon), But said not a word of the Letter. When she insisted on the Negative, I pray'd there might be no more Thunder and Lightening, I should not sleep all night. I gave her Dr. Preston, The Church's Marriage and the Church's Carriage, which cost me 6[s] at the Sale. The door standing open, Mr. Airs came in, hung up his Hat, and sat down. After awhile, Madam Winthrop moving, he went out. Jn[o] Eyre look'd in, I said How do ye, or, your servant Mr. Eyre: but heard no word from him. Sarah fill'd a Glass of Wine, she drank to me, I to her, She sent Juno home with me with a good Lantern, I gave her 6[d] and bid her thank her Mistress. In some of our Discourse, I told her I had rather go to the Stone-House adjoining to her, than to come to her against her mind. Told her the reason why I came every other night was lest I should drink too deep draughts of Pleasure. She had talk'd of Canary, her Kisses were to me better than the best Canary. Explain'd the expression Concerning Columbus.

8[r] 15. I dine on Fish and Oyle at Mr. Stoddard's. Capt. Hill wish'd me Joy of my proceedings i. e. with M— Winthrop; Sister Cooper aplauded it, spake of Visiting her: I said her Complaisance of her Visit would be obliging to me.

8[r] 16. L. Day, I upbraided my self that could be so solicitous about Earthly things; and so cold and indifferent as to the Love of Christ, who is altogether Lovely.

8[r] 17. In the Evening I visited Madam Winthrop, who Treated me Courteously, but not in Clean Linen as sometimes. She said, she did not know whether I would come again, or no. I ask'd her how she could so impute inconstancy to me. (I had not visited her since Wednesday night being unable to get over the Indisposition received by the Treatment received that night, and I *must* in it seem'd to sound like a made piece of Formality.) Gave her this day's Gazett.

8[r] 18. Visited Madam Mico, who came to me in a splendid Dress. I said, It may be you have heard of my Visiting Madam Winthrop, her Sister. She answered, Her Sister had told her of it. I ask'd her good Will in the Affair. She answer'd, If her Sister were for it, she should not hinder it. I gave her Mr. Homes's Sermon. She gave me a Glass of Canary, entertain'd me with good Discourse, and a Respectfull Remembrance of my first Wife. I took Leave.

8[r] 19. Midweek, Visited Madam Winthrop; Sarah told me she was at Mr. Walley's, would not come home till late. I gave her Hanah 3 oranges with her Duty, not knowing whether I should find her or no. Was ready to go home: but said if I knew she was there, I would go thither. Sarah seem'd to speak with pretty good Courage, She would be there. I went and found her there, with Mr. Walley and his wife in the little Room below. At 7 a-clock I mentioned going home; at 8. I put on my Coat, and quickly waited on her home. She found occasion to speak loud to the servant, as if she had a mind to be known. Was Courteous to me; but took occasion to speak pretty earnestly about my keeping a Coach: I said 'twould cost £100. per anum: she said twould cost but £40. Spake much against John Winthrop, his false-heartedness. Mr. Eyre came in and sat awhile; I offer'd him Dr. Incr. Mather's Sermons, whereof Mr. Apleton's Ordination Sermon was one; said he had them already. I said I would give him another. Exit. Came away somewhat late.

8^r^ 20. At Council, Col. Townsend spake to me of my Hood: Should get a Wigg. I said twas my chief ornament: I wore it for sake of the Day. Bro^r^ Odlin, and Sam, Mary, and Jane Hirst dine with us. Promis'd to wait on the Govr about 7. Madam Winthrop not being at Lecture, I went thither first; found her very Serene with her dâter Noyes, Mrs. Dering, and the widow Shipreev sitting at a little Table, she in her arm'd Chair. She drank to me, and I to Mrs. Noyes. After awhile pray'd the favour to speak with her. She took one of the Candles, and went into the best Room, clos'd the shutters, sat down upon the Couch. She told me Madam Usher had been there, and said the Coach must be set on Wheels, and not by Rusting. She spake somthing of my needing a Wigg. Ask'd me what her Sister said to me. I told her, She said, If her Sister were for it, She would not hinder it. But I told her, she did say she would be glad to have me for her Brother. Said, I shall keep you in the Cold, and asked her if she would be within to morrow night, for we had had but a running Feat. She said she could not tell whether she should, or no. I took Leave. As were drinking at the Governour's, he said: In England the Ladies minded little more than that they might have Money, and Coaches to ride in. I said, And New-England brooks its Name. At which Mr. Dudley smiled. Govr said they were not quite so bad here.

8^{r} 21. Friday, My Son, the Minister, came to me p. m. by apointment and we pray one for another in the Old Chamber; more especially respecting my Courtship. About 6. a-clock I go to Madam Winthrop's; Sarah told me her Mistress was gon out, but did not tell me whither she went. She presently order'd me a Fire; so I went in, having Dr. Sibb's Bowels with me to read. I read the two first Sermons, still no body came in: at last about 9. a-clock Mr. Jno Eyre came in; I took the oportunity to say to him as I had done to Mrs. Noyes before, that I hoped my Visiting his Mother would not be disagreeable to him; He answered me with much Respect. When twas after 9. a-clock He of himself said he would go and call her, she was but at one of his Brothers: A while after I heard Madam Winthrop's voice, enquiring somthing about John. After a good while and Claping the Garden door twice or thrice, she came in. I mention'd somthing of the lateness; she banter'd me, and said I was later. She receiv'd me Courteously. I ask'd when our proceedings should be made publick: She said They were like to be no more publick than they were already. Offer'd me no Wine that I remember. I rose up at 11 a-clock to come away, saying I would put on my Coat. She offer'd not to help me. I pray'd her that Juno might light me home, she open'd the Shutter, and said twas pretty light abroad; Juno was weary and gon to bed. So I came hom by Star-light as well as I could. At my first coming in, I gave Sarah five Shillings. I writ Mr. Eyre his Name in his book with the date Octob^{r} 21. 1720. It cost me 8^{s}. Jehovah jireh! Madam told me she had visited M. Mico, Wendell, and Wm Clark of the South [Church].

Octob^{r} 22. Dâter Cooper visited me before my going out of Town, staid till about Sun set. I brought her going near as far as the Orange Tree. Coming back, near Leg's Corner, Little David Jeffries saw me, and looking upon me very lovingly, ask'd me if I was going to see his Grandmother? I said, Not to-night. Gave him a peny, and bid him present my Service to his Grandmother.

Octob^{r} 24. I went in the Hackny Coach through the Comon, stop'd at Madam Winthrop's (had told her I would take my departure from thence). Sarah came to the door with Katee in her Arms: but I did not think to take notice of the Child. Call'd her Mistress. I told her, being encourag'd by David Jeffries loving eyes, and sweet Words, I was come to enquire whether she could find in her heart to leave that House and Neighbourhood, and go and dwell with me at the South-end; I think she said softly, Not yet. I told her It did not ly in my Lands to keep a Coach. If I should, I should be in danger to be brought to keep company with her Neighbour Brooker, (he was a little before sent to prison for Debt). Told her I had an Antipathy against those who would pretend to give themselves; but nothing of their Estate. I would a proportion of my Estate with my self. And I supos'd she would do so. As to a Perriwig, My best and greatest Friend, I could not possibly have a greater, began to find me with Hair before I was born, and had continued to do so ever since; and I could not find in my heart to go to another. She comended the book I gave her, Dr. Preston, the Church Marriage; quoted him saying 'twas inconvenient keeping out of a Fashion comonly used. I said the Time and Tide did circumscribe my Visit. She gave me a Dram of Black-Cherry Brandy, and gave me a lump of the Sugar that was in it. She wish'd me a good Journy. I pray'd God to keep her, and came away. Had a very pleasant Journy to Salem.

8^{r} 25. Sent a Letter of it to my Son of Wakefield, who delivered it not till Wednesday; so he visited her not till Friday p. m. and then presented my Service to her.

31. 2. She proves her Husband's Will. At night I visited Madam Winthrop about 6. p. m. They told me she was gon

to Madam Mico's. I went thither and found she was gon; so return'd to her house, read the Epistles to the Galatians, Ephesians in Mr. Eyre's Latin Bible. After the Clock struck 8. I began to read the 103. Psalm. Mr. Wendell came in from his Warehouse. Ask'd me if I were alone? Spake very kindly to me, offer'd me to call Madam Winthrop. I told him, She would be angry, had been at Mrs. Mico's; he help'd me on with my Coat and I came home: left the Gazett in the Bible, which told Sarah of, bid her present my Service to Mrs. Winthrop, and tell her I had been to wait on her if she had been at home.

Novr 1. I was so taken up that I could not go if I would.

Novr 2. Midweek, went again, and found Mrs. Alden there, who quickly went out. Gave her about ½ pound of Sugar Almonds, cost 3^s^ per £. Carried them on Monday. She seem'd pleas'd with them, ask'd what they cost. Spake of giving her a Hundred pounds per añum if I dy'd before her. Ask'd her what sum she would give me, if she should dy first? Said I would give her time to Consider of it. She said she heard as if I had given all to my Children by Deeds of Gift. I told her 'twas a mistake, Point-Judith was mine &c. That in England, I own'd, my Father's desire was that it should go to my eldest Son; 'twas 20£ per añum; she thought 'twas forty. I think when I seem'd to excuse pressing this, she seem'd to think twas best to speak of it; a long winter was coming on. Gave me a Glass or two of Canary.

Novr 4th. Friday, Went again about 7. a-clock; found there Mr. John Walley and his wife: sat discoursing pleasantly. I shew'd them Isaac Moses's [an Indian] Writing. Madam W. serv'd Comfeits to us. After a-while a Table was spread, and Super was set. I urg'd Mr. Walley to Crave a Blessing; but he put it upon me. About 9. they went away. I ask'd Madam what fashioned Neck-lace I should present her with, She said, None at all. I ask'd her Whereabout we left off last time; mention'd what I had offer'd to give her;

Ask'd her what she would give me; She said she could not Change her Condition: She had said so from the beginning; could not be so far from her Children, the Lecture. Quoted the Apostle Paul affirming that a single Life was better than a Married. I answer'd That was for the present Distress. Said she had not pleasure in things of that nature as formerly: I said, you are the fitter to make me a Wife. If she held in that mind, I must go home and bewail my Rashness in making more haste than good Speed. However, considering the Super, I desired her to be within next Monday night, if we liv'd so long. Assented. She charg'd me with saying, that she must put away Juno, if she came to me: I utterly deny'd it, it never came into my heart; yet she insisted upon it; saying it came in upon Discourse about the Indian woman that obtained her Freedom this Court. About 10. I said I would not disturb the good orders of her House, and came away. She not seeming pleas'd with my Coming away. Spake to her about David Jeffries, had not seen him.

Monday, Novr 7th. My Son pray'd in the Old Chamber. Our time had been taken up by Son and Daughter Cooper's Visit; so that I only read the 130th and 143. Psalm. Twas on the Account of my Courtship. I went to Mad. Winthrop; found her rocking her little Katee in the Cradle. I excus'd my Coming so late (near Eight). She set me an arm'd Chair and Cushoon; and so the Cradle was between her arm'd Chair and mine. Gave her the remnant of my Almonds; She did not eat of them as before; but laid them away; I said I came to enquire whether she had alter'd her mind since Friday, or remained of the same mind still. She said, Thereabouts. I told her I loved her, and was so fond as to think that she loved me: She said had a great respect for me. I told her, I had made her an offer, without asking any advice; she had so many to advise with, that twas a hindrance. The Fire was come to one short Brand besides the Block, which Brand was set up in end; at last it fell to pieces, and no Recruit was made: She gave me a Glass of Wine. I think I repeated again that I would go home and bewail my Rashness in making more haste than good Speed. I would endeavour to contain myself, and not go on to sollicit her to do that which she could not Consent to. Took leave of her. As came down the steps she bid me have a Care. Treated me Courteously. Told her she had enter'd the 4th year of her Widowhood. I had given her the News-Letter before: I did not bid her draw off her glove as sometime I had done. Her Dress was not so clean as somtime it had been. Jehovah jireh!

Midweek, 9r 9th. Dine at Bror Stoddard's: were so kind as to enquire of me if they should invite M'm Winthrop; I answer'd No. Thank'd my Sister Stoddard for her Courtesie; sat down at the Table Simeon Stoddard esqr, Mad. Stoddard, Samuel Sewall, Mr. Colman, Mm Colman, Mr. Cooper, Mrs. Cooper, Mrs. Hanah Cooper, Mr. Samuel Sewall of Brooklin, Mrs. Sewall, Mr. Joseph Sewall, Mrs. Lydia Walley, Mr. William Stoddard. Had a noble Treat. At night our Meeting was at the Widow Belknap's. Gave each one of the Meeting One of Mr. Homes's Sermons, 12 in all; She sent her servant home with me with a Lantern. Madam Winthrop's Shutters were open as I pass'd by.

Novr 11th. Went not to Mm Winthrop's. This is the 2d Withdraw.

Novr 21. About the middle of Decr Madam Winthrop made a Treat for her Children; Mr. Sewall, Prince, Willoughby: I knew nothing of it; but the same day abode in the Council Chamber for fear of the Rain, and din'd alone upon Kilby's Pyes and good Beer.

Febr. 5, 1720-21. Lord's Day, Lord's Super at the South; Expostulated with my daughter Sewall for her receiving the Elements with her Gloves on; had spoken to her about it before, and she had once practic'd otherwise, and I understood she had promised, or resolved to hold on. The Lord help me to receive Christ by the naked Hand of Faith; and not rest in outward Order and Comliness.

March, 3. 6. Mr. Foxcroft preaches the Sacramental Lecture. Keep the Feast. Very good Discourse, great Auditory. I think Madam Dudley, widow, was alone in the Fore-seat.

March, 4. 7. Violent Storm of Snow; so that I go not out of doors.

March, 5. Lord's Day, Serene, and good but very cold, yet had a comfortable oportunity to celebrate the Lord's Super. Mr. Prince, p. m. preach'd a Funeral Sermon from Psal. 90. 10. Gave Capt. Hill a good character. Just as I sat down in my Seat, one of my Fore-teeth in my under Jaw came out, and I put it in my pocket. This old servant and daughter of Musick leaving me, does thereby give me warning that I must shortly resign my Head: the Lord help me to do it cheerfully!

July, 4. 1721. I carry my daughter Hannah in the Coach to Brooklin; called at Deacon Mayo's; Rebekah Morris came out to her. Then I call'd at Mrs. Ruggles's, who came out to her and Hanah thank'd her for her Kindness when she lodg'd at her House. Went on to Brooklin, and I to Cambridge. My dâter returned home very well that night, who had not been out of doors for two years and a half before. *Laus Deo.*

Satterday, July, 15. I came home round. Visited my Sons and dâters at Brooklin: Mr. Cooper preaches there to morrow. Call, and sit awhile with Madam Ruggles. She tells me, they had been up all night, her dâter, Joseph Ruggles's wife, was brought to bed of a dâter. I shew'd my Willingness to renew my old acquaintance [as a suitor]; She express'd her inability to be Servicable. Gave me Cider to drink. I came home.

Thursday, Augt 3. Went in the Coach and visited Mrs. Ruggles after Lecture. She seems resolv'd not to move out of that house. May be of some use there; None at Boston—till she be carried out; made some Difficulty to accept an

Election Sermon, lest it should be an obligation on her. The Coach staying long (going to Boston for a new Fare), I made some excuse for my stay; she said should be glad to wait on me till midnight, provided I should solicit her no more; or to that effect. I said she was willing to get rid of me. She answer'd, That was too sharp. I gave her Mr. Moodey's Election Sermon, Marbled, with her Name written in it. Visited her daughter Ruggles, wished her joy of her little daughter in her Lap; and left a 2^s Bill with Mrs. Ruggles, which she gave to Mrs. Pierpont, the present Nurse, who thank'd me heartily for it just as I came away.

This day, 7^r 16. I set up my Conecticut stone post in Elm pasture, in Remembrance of my loving Wife Mrs. Hanah Sewall.

Copy of a Letter to Mrs. Mary Gibbs, Widow, at Newtown, Jany 12th 1721-22.

Madam, your Removal out of Town, and the Severity of the Winter, are the reason of my making you this Epistolary Visit. In times past (as I remember) you were minded that I should marry you, by giving you to your desirable Bridegroom. Some sense of this intended Respect abides with me still; and puts me upon enquiring whether you be willing that I should Marry you now, by becoming your Husband; Aged, and feeble, and exhausted as I am, your favourable Answer to this Enquiry, in a few Lines, the Candor of it will much oblige, Madam, your humble $Serv^t$

MADAM GIBBS. S. S.

Friday, Jany 19, 1721-2. I rode in Blake's Coach, and visited Mrs. Mary Gibbs at Mr. Cotton's at Newton, told her that in my Judgment she writ incomparably well; ask'd her acceptance of a Quire of Paper to write upon. It was accompanied with a good Leather Inkhorn, a stick of Sealing Wax, and 200. Wafers in a little Box. Gave her little Granddaughter, Mary Cotton, a 12^{d} Bill; some of Meers's Cakes. Gave 3^{s} among the Servants. Carried 2. 6^{d} Loavs. Din'd with Mr. Cotton, Mrs. Gibbs, Mrs. Cotton, Mrs. Anne Noyes; Mrs. Cotton, Mr. Cotton's Sister. Came away about 4. p m. Had a very Comfortable Journy out, and home. Set out about ½ hour past Ten. *Laus Deo.*

Friday, Jany 26. I rode to Newtown in the Coach, and visited Mrs. Gibbs. Spake of the proposals I had intimated per Mr. H. Gibbs; for her Sons to be bound to save me harmless as to her Administration; and to pay me £100. provided their Mother died before me: I to pay her £50. per añum during her Life, if I left her a Widow. She said 'twas hard, she knew not how to have her children bound to pay that Sum; she might dye in a little time. Mr. Cotton, whom she call'd, spake to the same purpose, spake of a Joynture. I said I was peremptory as to the indemnifying Bond; Offer'd to take up with that alone, and allow her £40. per anum; Scolly's Tenement yielded but £33., and then I made no question but that there must be a Deduction for Repairs. She said she would consider of it: I said, I would also Consider. Afterward she excus'd her speaking to me. I supose she meant the word Hard. Carried her a pound of Glaz'd Almonds, and a Duz. Meers Cakes; Two bottles of Canary. Visited Mrs. Cotton, wish'd her Joy of her young daughter Elizabeth. Gave little Mary 2^{s}. Had a very good Legg of Pork, and a Turkey for Diner. Mrs. Gibbs help'd me on with my Coat at Coming away; and stood in the Front door till the Coach mov'd, then I pull'd off my Hat, and she Curtesied. I had moved to be published next Thorsday; to carry in our names to Col. Checkley.

Jany 25. When I ask'd H. Gibbs what was the effect of his proposals, He answer'd, What his Mother would have done the Children would agree to it.

Copy of a Letter to Mrs. Mary Gibbs at Newtown, Midweek,
Jan[y] 31. 1721-22.

Madam, One of the Crowns under this cover I intended for Mrs. Lane. But she not attending Madam Cotton, to Nurse her, be pleased to dispose both of them, as you think convenient. What the Gazette reports concerning France, is well worth the Reading.

I have consider'd of our discourse last Friday, and, waiting for your Answer to my Second Proposal, am Madam, your humble Servant, S. S.

Note. I inclos'd last Monday's Gazette, two fair 5[s] Bills of Credit, and India Christiana Very well Bound, gilded on the edge, inscribed to Her with my own Hand.

Jan[y] 31. Ask'd Mr. H. Gibbs whether Mrs. Gibbs were come to Town; He said he had sent to her to know when she would come. Just as I was ready to go to Dorchester, he came in, and deliver'd me his Mother's Letter of the 30th Current; and took mine lying in the Window ready Sealed up, to send to his Mother. May God provide! and Forgive, and Doe as the Matter may Require.

Feb. 2. Stormy-day; Mr. Dan[l] Oliver came to advise with me about Mr. David Jeffries Debt to Mr. Hirst's Estate.

I took the Opportunity to speak plainly to him about Mrs. Gibbs; that her Children were not so Releas'd, but must be Bound to indemnify me as to former Debts, her Administration. Told, I hoped she was not so Attach'd to her Children, but that she would carry it Tenderly to me; or else there would soon be an end of an old Man. I said, suposed they would Clothe her, Answered, no question; And would be Tender of me. Shew'd him both her Letters.

Febr. 5th. Put Mr. Hugh Adams his Letter into the Post-house with my own Hand.

Copy of a Letter to Mrs. Mary Gibbs at Newtown, Febr. 6th, 1721-22.

Madam, I Thank you for your Kind Letter of Jany 30th, which I receiv'd the next day, after Noon. I hope it is a Token for Good, that your obliging Answer harmonizeth with the Proposal mentioned in mine of January, 31, Which was seal'd up, and ready to be sent, before I received yours.

These Preliminaries being agreeably stated, I long now to see you. You told me you would come to Boston; which makes me expect you; seeing you did not acquaint me with any alteration of your mind. Your Affairs will necessarily call you to Town; and I persuade my self, my being here, will not hinder your Coming hither; Chusing your own Time for Returning. My service to Mr. Cotton and his Lady. Praying God to keep you, I am, Madam, your humble Servt.

S. S.

To Mrs. Mary Gibbs at Newtown.

Feb^{r} 10th 1721-22. Madam, These are kindly to salute you, and to say, that the Omission of Answering one or two of my Letters, and of coming to Town, makes it needful for me to enquire, what the plain meaning of your Letter of Jany 30th may be. "I do chuse to comply with your last proposal, of Releasing my children, and Accepting of the sum you proposed."

The last Proposal was, For your children, or some in their behalf, to give Bond to indemnify me from all debts contracted by you before the Marriage; and from all matters respecting the Administration. This I told you, I peremptorily insisted on. I was to secure you Forty pounds per añum during the term of your natural Life, in case of your Survival.

This proposal must be taken entirely, every part of it together. And if the words *Releasing my Children,* intend a Releasing them from this Bond, my last Proposal is not accepted by you; and my Letter of Febr. the sixth, rests upon a mistaken foundation. I would prevent Misunderstanding, and therefore I thus write; praying an Answer as soon as conveniently can be. My service to Madam Cotton. A am, Madam, your humble servant, S. S.

I sent this by Joshuah Kibbe presently after twas written. Note. I had sent this proposal by Mr. H. Gibbs before I made it my self. When I ask'd his sentiments, He said, What his Mother did, he should Consent to it.

Febr. 12. Mrs. Gibbs Came to Town; which her Son Henry told me of.

14th return'd. I went to Col. Checkly, and enter'd our Names. Went to Mr. Williams, and ask'd his License to call him Brother: Was entertain'd Courteously. Went to James, and order'd our Publishment. Visited Mr. Daniel Oliver.

Febr. 15. were publish'd the first time; were more to hear it than is usual.

To Mrs. Mary Gibbs at Newton, Feb. 16, 1721-22.

Madam, Possibly you have heard of our Publishment last Thorsday, before now. It remains, for us to join together in fervent Prayers, without ceasing, that God would graciously Crown our Espousals with his Blessing. A good Wife, and a good Husband too, are from the Lord. I am bound as far as Deacon Brewer's to-day. The Council sits in the Afternoon next Monday. And I am to wait on the Committee of the Overseers of the College next Tuesday the 20th Inst. Please to accept of Mr. Mitchel's Sermons of Glory, which is inclosed. With my Service to Madam Cotton, I take leave, who am, Madam, your humble Serv[t]. S. S.

To ditto Feb. 19, 1721-22 inclosing the Gazett, congratulating Madam Cotton as having accomplished the time of her Lying in. Desiring she would intimat a day when it would be convenient for me to wait on her to bring her to Town.

Febr. 22. Thorsday, were publish'd the 2[d] time. Mr. Vivien and Lydia Kay the first. Dr. Cotton Mather said aloud, The Voice of the Lord Thundereth; the voice of the Lord parts the Flames of Fire: and then read his Text, Ezek. 15. 7. They shall go out of one Fire, and another Fire shall devour them.

Friday, Febr. 23. Having received no Letter, I went in the Coach to Newton, with Mrs. Henry Gibbs and Mrs. Mary Williams. Dined there, and came away late; Ways very heavy, and pretty much Rain. Met Mr. Cotton about the middle of the way, which much refresh'd me, to think that his wife would have his Company, now her Mother was come away. 'Twas near Ten a-clock before got home. *Laus Deo.*

Feb. 24. Very pleasant day, Din'd with Mr. Stoddard on Fish and Oyle. Visited daughter Cooper. Mr. Cooper mention'd Dr. I. Mather's preface to Mr. Belcher's Sermon; and his passing over to the Great Grandfather. Visited Mrs. Gibbs, gave her an Orange.

March, 29th. Samuel Sewall, and Mrs. Mary Gibbs were joined together in Marriage by the Rev[d] Mr. William Cooper, Mr. Sewall pray'd once. Mr. Jn[o] Cotton was at Sandwich, sent for by Madam Cotton after her Husband's death.

Lord's day, April, 1. Sat with my wife in her Pue.

April, 2. Brought her home to my House.

April, 8. introduc'd her into my Pue, and sat with her there.

Tuesday, Nov[r] 27. I view the Eclipse in Scipio's Garret, till the Eclipse it self was eclipsed by the Clouds. Afterward saw the ending of it below stairs.

Friday, Aug[t] 23, 1723. Dr. Increase Mather [dies], just at Noon, after long and grievous Sickness. Mention is made of it by Mr. Thacher at the Sacramental Lecture held this day.

Lord's Day, April, 5th, 1724. The Ways are dry, and the Weather moderat, so that I comfortably goe to the solemn Assembly Forenoon and Afternoon: Hear my Son preaching from the first Commandment; and Mr. Prince from Prov. 8. 17., both exhorting to the Love of God; may I be enabled to hear through the Long-Suffering and Goodness of God! Ana an Infant was baptised. My wife wore her new Gown of Sprig'd Persian.

Sept[r] 14th. Last night died my good old Christian Neighbour and Friend, Mr. Elisha Odlin, Sensible and Calm to the very last. He was born July 1. 1640, upon the same Lot in Newbury Street where he all along Liv'd, and now dyed in the 85th year of his Age.

June, 15, 1725. I accompanied my Son to Mad. Winthrop's. She was a-bed about 10. *mane.* I told her I found my Son coming to her and took the Oportunity to come with him. She thank'd me kindly, enquired how Madam Sewall did. Ask'd my Son to go to Prayer. Present Mr. John Eyre, Mrs. Noyes, Mrs. Walley and David Jeffries. At coming I said, I kiss your hand Madame (her hand felt very dry). She desired me to pray that God would lift up upon her the Light of his Countenance.

Monday, Aug[t] 2. Mrs. Katherine Winthrop, Relict of the honble. Waitstill Winthrop esqr., died, *Aetatis* 61. She was born in September 1664. The Escutcheons on the Hearse bore the Arms of Winthrop and Brattle, The Lion Sable.

Augt 5. 1725. Bearers, His Hon^{r} Lt Govr Dummer, Saml Sewall; Col. Byfield, Edw. Bromfield esqr; Simeon Stoddard esqr., Adam Winthrop esqr. Was buried in the South-burying place, in a Tomb near the North-east Corner. Will be much miss'd.

Fifth-day, April, 21, 1726. The swallows unanimously and cheerfully proclaim the Spring. They have been discouraged and made much to abscond for about a Week, by reason of the Constantly N. E. Wind and Rain.

Satterday, April 15, 1727. Last night three musicians serenaded me under my Chamber Window once or twice; but being very early, I was so fast asleep, I scarce heard any thing of it: Several of the family heard it.

Septr 10th 1728. Last night I dreamed that a little boy had got away my watch, I found him on the Comon, and by giving him another Watch persuaded him to give me that round which was engraven

Auris, mens, oculus, manus, os, pes; munere fungi
Dum pergunt, præstat discere velle mori.

When I awaked I was much startled at it. The Lord help me to watch and pray that I may not enter into Temptation.

October, 19. 1728. Seeing this to be the same day of the week and Moneth that the Wife of my youth expired Eleven years agoe, it much affected me. I writ to my dear Son Mr. Joseph Sewall of it, desiring him to come and dine with me: or however that he would call some time to join my Condolence. He came about Noon and made an excellent Prayer in the East Chamber. *Laus Deo.*

Ditto, *die, feria Septima.* I gave my dear Wife a Book of 7 Sermons, which had been my Daughter Hanah's, for whom she had laboured beyond measur.

Feria Secunda, Octob^{r} 13, 1729. Judge Davenport comes to me between 10 and 11 a-clock in the morning and speaks to me on behalf of Mr. Addington Davenport, his eldest Son, that he might have Liberty to Wait upon Jane Hirst now at my House in way of Courtship. He told me he would deal by him as his eldest Son, and more than so. Inten'd to build a House where his uncle Addington dwelt for him; and that he should have his Pue in the Old Meetinghouse. I gave him my Hand at his going away and acknowledegd his Respect to me and granted his desire. He said Madam Addington would wait upon me.

His Honour the Lieut Governour visited me quickly after, and acquainted me that he design'd for Newbury in a day or two, to stay for a week or fortnight.

I inform'd his Honor of what Mr. Davenport had been about; His Honor approved it much, Comended the young Man and reckon'd it a very good Match.

THE END